GRIT AND
GOOSE FEATHERS

GRIT AND GOOSE FEATHERS

Chasing Medals and Finding Me.
My Olympic Journey Uncovered.

GAIL EMMS
MBE

pitch

First published by Pitch Publishing, 2025
1

Pitch Publishing
9 Donnington Park,
85 Birdham Road,
Chichester, West Sussex,
PO20 7AJ

www.pitchpublishing.co.uk
info@pitchpublishing.co.uk

A CIP catalogue record is available for this book
from the British Library.

ISBN 978 1 83680 216 7

Typesetting and origination by Pitch Publishing

MIX
Paper | Supporting
responsible forestry
FSC™ C016779

Printed and bound on FSC® certified paper in line with our continuing commitment to ethical business practices, sustainability and the environment.

Printed and bound in India by Replika Press Pvt. Ltd.

CONTENTS

'I knew she was a good badminton player, but I never thought she'd actually make it.'

Jan Emms, mother of Gail Emms, in an interview post the 2004 Athens Olympic Games, for *BBC Look East*

INTRODUCTION

IF THE girls of the TV show *Friends* had a love child after a Peroni-fuelled night out, that chaotic hybrid would be me.

Imagine Monica without the OCD, Rachel with the fashion sense but more emotional drama, and Phoebe … well, keep all of Phoebe – the randomness, the weird charm, the occasional bursts of comedy genius. Now throw in a ray of sunshine, a love of dirty burgers and a tendency to cry a lot, and *voilà* – me. Gail Emms.

I like to think I'm tough. I give off big Scrappy-Doo energy – plenty of bark, absolutely no bite. Or one of those sharks that look really scary but don't bite. That big lion that roars loudly, but was reared by humans, and comes over for a tickle. A T. Rex. Well, a vertically challenged one. Strong legs but no strength in the arms whatsoever. I couldn't punch my way out of a paper bag. The only fight I have been in … well, it didn't even end up as a fight. It was in a nightclub in Bedford and a girl jumped the cloakroom queue. I shouted in my 'God, I am so hard' voice: 'Oi, there's a queue – get to the back!' I probably should've looked at the size of the girl before I shouted that out. As she turned round, she was on the 'powerful' side and she looked me up and down and said, rather menacingly, 'I'll see *you* outside.' I was all like, 'Fine!' I picked up my coat, strutted out eyeballing her, and then broke the world record sprint in stilettos back to my flat, a mile away. There were sparks as I sprinted across the pavement, passing every kebab shop, and even KFC. I love KFC too.

Welcome to my chaos. Let's begin.

'One person's craziness is another person's reality.'

Tim Burton

DECEMBER 2024

I HAD just landed in St Lucia; those who have been there before will know it is a Caribbean paradise, all turquoise seas and lush rainforest. It was meant to be my first proper holiday with the man I'd been seeing for six months. Instead, I'd arrived at London Gatwick alone.

Classic Gail moment: my suitcase was a few kilos over the baggage allowance (standard), and the British Airways check-in staff flagged it. When she politely informed me there'd be a charge, I shot back with my usual dry wit, 'Well, I've just been dumped, so that's 85kg not travelling with me.' She gave me a nervous laugh … and still charged me the £50, damn it.

I headed to the airport lounge and made a beeline for the Bloody Marys on offer at breakfast, and I didn't stop drinking for the entire flight. I stared at the empty seat beside me and cried. It was meant to be filled by someone who'd now made me believe the break-up was *my* fault. According to him, my 'behaviours' had caused a breakdown in trust. I hadn't done anything wrong. I *knew* that. But still, some part of me felt like the villain, like I needed to apologise for something I didn't do. I felt the need to chase, to fix, to win him back. I felt like a failure. Again.

The St Lucian resort, Stolen Time, was the kind of place built for loved-up couples; it was all candlelit dinners, spa treatments by the sea, romance woven into every palm leaf. Meanwhile, I spent the first week hoping he'd show up, apologising in some grand, Hollywood-style moment. That fantasy slowly twisted into something darker. The daydreams turned to nightmares. I'd wake up drenched in sweat, haunted by his face, that cold stare he gave me as he scrolled through my phone. 'I *had* to do it,' he'd said, accusing me of cheating. I hadn't. Not even close. But to him, 'You women are all the same.'

Somehow, I got through that first week. Likely helped along by a heroic number of bottles of wine. But something shifted when I checked my emails and saw a message from David Hurren, a client-turned-friend, who said he'd met a life coach called Stephanie Burge. He thought we'd get on. She worked with athletes navigating the difficult transition out of elite sport, albeit something I didn't even realise might apply to me as I had been retired for a long time. I was sceptical, honestly (you'll gather from this book that I don't sugar-coat much), but I called Steph anyway – from a sun lounger, glass of rosé in hand.

We chatted. And in the middle of explaining my recent break-up, I started talking about my retirement from badminton back in 2008, all on *my* terms, or so I thought. And that's when it hit me: I hadn't actually processed any of it. Not really. I still had dreams that I was on the court. I still defined myself by those career highs. My identity was wrapped up in a version of me that no longer existed. I hadn't moved on. I had just buried it all.

Sixteen and a half years after I last stepped on to the court as a pro, I arrived at Steph's house, in January 2025, and spent three days with her. We unravelled my story, every twist and trauma. She's the first and only person who knows *everything* about me. And by the end of it, I felt like I could breathe again. The weight had finally lifted.

I felt free.

WEDNESDAY, 22 JANUARY 2025

DRIVING DOWN the M1 from Leicestershire to Milton Keynes, the late afternoon winter sun was breaking through the clouds, casting a soft glow on the side of my face. There was a warmth to it … not just from the sun, but from somewhere deeper. A comforting calm settled over me. I was riding a high I hadn't felt in a long time.

I cued up one of my all-time favourite tracks – 'Opus' by Eric Prydz – and within seconds, my fingers were instinctively tapping along to the rhythm. Each melodic note felt like it was playing through me. As the track built, I turned the volume up. My hand floated above the steering wheel, tracing the music in the air as the tempo quickened. The beat began to rise … slow, pulsing, hypnotic. I felt myself lift with it. That unmistakable build-up. That euphoric anticipation. And then …

Boom.

The drop hit. One of the best in progressive house. A rush of emotion surged through me: elation, release, joy. I burst into tears, not from sadness, but from something bigger. Something beautiful. I glanced to my right, and a van full of lads was smiling and raving along with me. To my left, another car, more strangers, waving their hands to the beat, too. We were all in it together, all united by a track, a moment. It was pure freedom. That, right there, is what I live for. Connection. Joy. Presence. That *spark.*

Now, for a bit of context, I don't typically cruise up and down the motorway trying to start spontaneous car raves. I'm fairly certain I'd be sectioned or banned from driving if that were the case, but I had just finished day two of a three-day intense life-coaching and mentoring session with Steph, a trauma survivor herself, and someone I've been working closely with whilst writing this story. Steph had made it clear it was my decision to condense what many clients do over many months into three days of conversations; but you know me, once I'm in, there's no half measures. We started talking, the flood gates opened, and I just couldn't stop.

Thank goodness Steph agreed I could record our conversations, and I have included snapshots of our discussions throughout this book with her permission.

And let me be clear, if I'd tried to write this book five years ago, two years ago, even six months ago, it would have been an entirely different story.

For the first time, I had someone to help me unpack the *why* and *how* behind who I am. And honestly, it's one of the most adult, sensible, and life-changing decisions I've ever made. Which, if you know me, you'll know that adult and sensible are not words often associated with Gail Emms.

But maybe … they are now.

Enjoy.

EXIT WOMB, ENTER DRAMA

I WAS born Gail Elizabeth Emms, in Hitchin on 23 July 1977. 'Elizabeth' because it was Queen Elizabeth's Silver Jubilee year. As for 'Gail', well … no one knows. When I asked my parents why they chose it, they genuinely couldn't remember. There were no famous Gails at the time, no gales blowing outside, no long-lost relatives with the name. My best guess? They forgot to stick 'Abi' in front, and I've been stuck with a name more fitting for a middle-aged woman ever since.

I arrived in the world weighing a hefty 9lb 2oz. Considering my mum is only 5ft tall, it's fair to say I didn't exactly glide into existence. There was some birth trauma, and I was rushed straight to the ICU. My parents still laugh, telling the story of how I filled the entire incubator, while all the other babies around me were tiny 3lb or 4lb preemies. Apparently, they were a bit embarrassed to point me out. 'That's ours,' they'd say, as their newborn linebacker took up most of the crib.

Interestingly, I was almost born in Rhodesia, now Zimbabwe. My parents had the papers and plane tickets to start a new life there, but, with my mum pregnant, she had a change of heart at the last moment. So instead of the wild beauty of Africa, they settled in … Stotfold, Bedfordshire. Practically the same, right?

My mum, Janice Barton, was born in north London in 1951, deep in Arsenal territory. Her dad, my grandad, was a diehard Gooner, as were her older brothers Peter and Ray. Naturally, Mum decided to support Tottenham Hotspur, just to wind them all up. That act of rebellion sparked a lifelong love of football.

Mum grew up during a time when girls weren't allowed to play football. They were banned by the FA in 1921 as they declared it 'unsuitable' for them. But my mum didn't care. She played anyway, kicking a ball around with Ray, her boy cousins, and the local lads. When her family moved from London to Biggleswade, Bedfordshire, she finally saw green fields and threw herself into playing properly. She idolised Spurs striker Jimmy Greaves and spent hours practising her dribbling, pretending to be him. My grandad, despite his allegiances, even took her to watch Spurs games, albeit reluctantly. When she got older, she went by herself, often dressing as a boy to blend in with the crowd.

After England's 1966 World Cup win, there was a spark of interest in women's football again, despite the FA ban still being in place. A few clubs began to form, and one stood out to Mum: Chiltern Valley Ladies in Luton, run by Harry and June Batt. She wrote them a letter, asked for a trial, and was soon banging in goals as their star centre-forward.

(There's a lot more about Mum's incredible football story later in the book in a chapter called 'The Lost Lionesses', but you'll have to keep reading to get there, I'm afraid.)

One of my earliest memories is watching Mum play football. I must have been about four. We were in some fields in Stopsley, Luton. My sister was in a pushchair, my nan and grandad were cheering her on, shouting, 'Go on, Janice!' It felt completely normal to me that Mum played football. But my dad was moaning and grumbling about being 'left with the kids', not exactly thrilled with his wife running around on a football pitch. And shortly after that, Mum gave it up. It just wasn't the 'done thing' in the early '80s, and Dad said it was not the image of a good housewife and mother. Dad expected her at home, not on the scoresheet.

Growing up, I never kicked a ball with Mum. She didn't want me to play football at all. Not because she didn't love the game anymore, but because of the abuse she endured. 'Get back in the kitchen!' was a regular chant from the sidelines for her, and, at the time, when I was a little girl, there were no pathways in football for girls. No teams. No leagues. So, in my mum's eyes, what was the point of me playing?

She still has a scrapbook filled with clippings and photos from her footballing days, and when she talks about Chiltern Valley Ladies, she lights up. Every Wednesday, my nan and grandad would come over, and I'd sit with them, flicking through the pages as they told stories about the trophies in their house. Visitors would always assume they belonged to the boys. 'Oh no,' my nan would say proudly. 'They're my daughter Janice's.' I *loved* that. I didn't see Mum play again until years later, when my younger brother Adam came along. Then suddenly, she was in the garden, kicking a ball about with him.

My dad, on the other hand, was born on 16 August 1941, in the brilliantly named village of Little Snoring, Norfolk. Incredibly ironic, because he was the loudest snorer known to mankind. It honestly could've been used to calibrate the Richter scale. He only found salvation late in life with a sleep apnoea machine, which probably could have saved a few relationships (and eardrums).

He was born on a farm as an only child. His mum passed away when he was still young, and my dad left school at 14 to start work. He helped out on the farm and then trained as a carpenter. He was brilliant at it ... truly. Ask him for a table, and he'd build you a piece of furniture that transformed into a cupboard, a ladder and a bloody spaceship. Any scrap bit of wood lying around, and dad would look at it and say, 'I can make something out of that.' His shed was always full of randomly collected pieces of wood.

Eventually, he set up his own carpentry business, which evolved into a shopfitting and building company. But his true passions were food, drink, and entertaining. He was a fantastic cook, and most of my best memories with him revolve around the kitchen or the barbecue. Meat, more meat and a side of meat. His roast dinners were legendary. Honestly, no one's matched them since. He struggled with his weight, though. He was around 5ft 10 but ballooned to nearly 26st at one point. He'd yo-yo diet, lose loads, then gain it back. One year, he dropped to 13st by taking up running, including marathons, but it didn't last. Most of his life, he hovered around the 20st mark.

My parents met in the most '70s way imaginable. Mum was working as a petrol station attendant (yep, that used to be a job), and Dad kept 'running out of petrol' just to see her. Apparently, she was completely oblivious. I'll let your imagination fill in the rest … petrol, pumps, refuelling … this was 1970s romance, after all. I now feel a bit queasy.

Mum was ten years younger than Dad, so my nan and grandad were wary, but, eventually, they saw he could provide for her. In hindsight, maybe their concerns about his love of partying and drinking weren't so far off the mark, but Mum and Dad married in 1975 and soon after moved from Stotfold to Bedford, a town full of promise.

My sister Lisa was born three years after me, and Adam three years after her. I'll talk more about them later, but let's just say I fully leaned into my role as the bossy eldest sibling, until they got big enough to fight back.

Despite Mum's football past, it was Dad who introduced me to the game. My first match was Norwich vs Liverpool on 25 August 1984. I was seven, and Dad took me to the season opener. It ended in a 3–3 draw, and all I remember is the noise. It physically hurt my ears. Full-grown men shouting, singing, swearing – it was chaos. And the journey to the ground was pure torture. Back then, the road from Bedford to Norwich was a single carriageway, and I counted something like 37 tractors.

When we finally got home, Mum took one look at my face and pulled me aside. 'It's okay,' she whispered, like she was sharing a secret. 'Come to Spurs.' It felt like a blessing. A calling. A light. And so began my lifelong sentence of supporting Tottenham, a legacy of heartbreak, hope, and an eternal stream of cocky Arsenal fans.

From Rattle to Racket

My family lived around the corner from Bedford and County Tennis and Badminton Club. It was a nice part of Bedford, popular with families and it wasn't too far outside the town centre. Bedford Rugby Club was also nearby, but my parents became members of the tennis and badminton club, rather than the rugby one. Both were keen at racket sports, my mum especially.

My childhood was spent at the club – 'Bradgate Road' as we affectionately called it, as it was on, yes, you've guessed it, Bradgate Road. I have the fondest memories of being a ball girl on the many grass tennis courts in the summer, and then watching my parents play with friends on club evenings.

The three badminton courts were in a 'tin hut' by the side of the tennis courts (it's a corrugated iron building where grain was stored in World War II and was turned into a community badminton hall after the war). There were 12 grass courts, and four red clay courts alongside the tin hut, and there was also a bar and viewing gallery for the members. I loved it there. I loved the smell of the tennis balls and putting them in the tin boxes, all labelled one to 12 for the courts, and then handing them out to the players as they went to their assigned court. There was a sense of fun, a sense of community. Even if they were not playing that day or evening, members would be there, being social, having a drink, supporting others. The tennis courts and the clubhouse are now gone. Turned into a housing estate. The land was too valuable as it was so close to Bedford town centre. The tin hut is still there, as it is a listed building. It pains me every time I go back to Bedford and see my childhood playground, which is now a residential area.

I remember holding a cut-down badminton racket in my right hand and a plastic shuttlecock in the other. I held the shuttle out in front of me, and I dropped it, expecting it to bounce, just like a tennis ball does. I must have been three or four years old at the time. As I dropped it, of course, the shuttle just landed right at my feet. Margaret Smith, a formidable lady in her 40s, with a huge bosom, who ran the whole club, was standing by my side as this happened. She looked at me, and said, 'Well, of course it doesn't bounce, dear, it's a shuttlecock,' as if I was supposed to know this, even though I had never seen a shuttlecock before in my life.

Eventually, I hit that bloody plastic thing and took every opportunity I could to play badminton with one of the other members.

That's what I love about sport … the first time trying a skill, you fail, but with practice, you start to see the results. You get better. Your confidence soars, and you want more. You want to keep improving.

There were other kids who loved running around the club too, and eventually, I was allowed to join the junior badminton club, when I was about six years old. I used to look forward to Friday evenings and, Sunday mornings, as those times were junior club times, and I was allowed to play. Even thinking about it now, it makes me smile. As the club was only a few minutes' walk from our house, I used to just get my racket and walk there by myself, usually the first one there, waiting for the door to be opened, as I was so eager.

I wore my favourite tracksuit every time – a bright pink number from the C&A in Bedford town. I wore it all the time. I really was a vision from the 1980s, with my blonde bowl haircut, though this did progress to a bob. God, I was trendy. In between practice, my friends and I would walk through the club room, sneak behind the bar and pretend we were serving drinks, then play hide and seek. The changing rooms were always so cold, a little bit creepy even. There was a musty, damp smell, and there were black and white photographs of original members all over the walls. We would listen for the rats scurrying under the floorboards and marvel at the huge spider webs in the corners of the roof, wondering why no one ever cleaned the place.

The advantage badminton has over tennis is that you can play all year round. Damn those rainy days and winter months; if it wasn't for them, I would have been a champion tennis player, she says … The reality was that I just remember playing badminton more. I was also small for my age, and tennis suits the taller ones. Bigger court and all that.

Gail: I always played better mixed doubles. The badminton club had hardly any girls, so I always had to play against boys. I really loved playing against boys.

Steph: Maybe it was a way of showing off for you?

Gail: I think you're beginning to understand me, Steph.

Small, Shouty and Already Competitive

Mum was a good badminton player. In fact, by 1980, she'd already claimed her place on the club championship winners' board as the Ladies Singles champion, while pregnant with my sister – just to rub it in a little more. That cheeky win gave me someone close to look up to and learn from when I discovered my own love for badminton.

I don't remember playing much with Dad, but Mum was always up for a game. She was good enough to try out for the Bedfordshire County team, which was a big deal at the time. I was around seven years old when she turned to me and said, 'Fancy a game?' I was thrilled. I imagined an exciting match, maybe even scoring a few points, but Mum had other ideas, and absolutely destroyed me, 11-0. Shuttles zipped past me with no mercy. That was her coaching style – she never gave me a point. I had to earn it. She was *so* competitive, but I loved it. It became a personal mission: I HAD to win a point against Mum.

I was obsessed. Anyone who visited our house was roped into garden matches so I could practise. I stayed late at the junior club, always looking for extra games. All in the hope that next time I played against Mum, I might win a point.

People often ask if my parents pushed me into sports. The honest answer is no. It came entirely from me. My parents never forced me to practise, never told me to go to the club practice sessions; I chose to every time. They were there in support.

What also helped me thrive were the grassroots volunteers who made the sport accessible; those unsung heroes who gave up their evenings to run junior clubs, mediate shuttlecock-related squabbles and offer a safe place to compete. To the likes of Margaret Smith, Mike Hardy and Brigitte Crossman, thank you. You helped spark my passion.

That competitive fire first truly ignited when I saw a notice at the junior club: 'Bedfordshire Schools U11 Tournament – Entries Now Open.' I begged to enter. Some people were concerned I was too young at the age of just seven, but Dad said, 'Why not?' And off we went.

I vividly remember stepping into Stopsley Leisure Centre in Luton in my pink tracksuit. Everyone else looked so tall, and most were aged ten or 11. I was the tiny one, and they all went, 'Awwww, isn't she cute?' They were right, I was cute – until we got on court. Then I beat them. Word spread, and people started coming over to watch me play. I reached the final and walked away with the girls' singles runner-up trophy. My first one. I was hooked.

I was selected for the Bedfordshire County team and regularly played U11 and U12 matches. At 12, I was even playing for the U16s. I'd grown out of my pink C&A tracksuit by then and upgraded to a blue shell suit with pink balloons on it, with matching scrunchies, of course. Oh, and I fell in love too, I fell in love with my mixed doubles partner, Simon Blundell. Sadly, the feeling wasn't mutual. I suspect the balloon pattern might've had something to do with it. I really wasn't cool enough for him.

But through all the county matches and tournaments, my personal Everest remained: beating Mum. It took five long years. Then, on 26 August 1989, at the grand old age of 12, it finally happened. I'd been creeping up with the scores, pushing her harder and getting closer to the win. That day, the stars aligned. I had match point. Mum looked flustered. I served. We rallied. She lifted the shuttle short, I pounced and smashed it. Winner. Game over.

I did what any 12-year-old would do – I celebrated like I'd just won Olympic gold. I sprinted around the hall yelling, '*Yeeeesssssss*!!!' Five years of effort exploded in that moment. Mum, however, was *not* pleased. She threw her racket and stormed to the corner of the tin hut. I, ever the humble champion, strolled over grinning and casually said, 'Wanna play again?'

Her response? 'No. I'm not playing you anymore.'

What? Was she joking?! After all those years of losing, this was *my* time to dominate! But Mum looked at me and explained, 'You're too good for me now. If you keep playing me, you won't get better. You need stronger opponents.'

Looking back, it was very Jedi Master and Padawan, with Yoda passing the lightsaber to young Skywalker. Except we had badminton rackets, not lightsabers. (And no, I'm *not* calling my mum old, small and green.)

It wasn't the response I expected, but it stuck with me. People assume elite athletes are born to win everything. That's not true. I *lost* far more matches than I ever won, especially early on. After Mum retired from our duels, she set me up with tougher opponents. I got battered. Regularly. And still, she'd whisper to them, 'Don't go easy on her.'

I hated losing. I'd sulk, maybe cry, get it out. But then I'd regroup and start asking, 'How can I win next time? What do I need to do differently?' Losing turned into learning.

That was Mum's parting gift as my badminton partner. By stepping aside, she taught me something far bigger than how to hit a shuttle. She taught me that failure isn't the end, it's just a step toward improvement. These days, they call it 'resilience'.

I just called it 'finally beating Mum at badminton'.

Steph: There aren't many kids who would have been prepared to let their mum beat them time and time again. Most would be utterly demoralised. There was some innate determination that just kept you going.

Gail: I've had a lot of therapy.

I started to play a few national tournaments at this stage too. This was the chance I got to understand the motorway system in the United Kingdom. I had one of those large AA map books on my lap, and it was my job to navigate Dad to the destination sports hall. To this day, I really don't know how we managed to find our way across the country. We often stopped at petrol stations or asked people on the street for directions, but I do think I did a good job overall for someone so young.

Gail: You feel the need to fit in in life. Then there was this wonderful place known as sport, where I could actually be myself. That feeling of being able to be free. Freedom, a clear mind and nothing mattered except for the result. I was able to be in the present. Just be in the moment. My team-mates need me. I want to win this point.

Steph: It sounds like it was really a form of escapism for you?

Gail: It was a lot better than the real world.

Slammed Doors and Silent Treatment

Gail: I remember I used to check my dad's wardrobe. See if his clothes were still hanging in there.
Steph: Children are very intuitive. You knew something was wrong, and it must have made you anxious. I'm curious to know if you remember having the feeling that you wanted to protect your mum?

Gail: I felt I had to support her and my brother, and my sister.

Steph: You were only ten years old, so looking at it through a child's eyes now, particularly now you have kids yourself, maybe you can appreciate that was really tough?

Gail: I just kept hoping the clothes would still be there, and it would all be fine. And then it wasn't fine. One day, they had gone. It was a strange feeling, just seeing the emptiness staring back at me. I had known it was coming. I closed the door on the wardrobe and went to school as normal.

I remember the shouting in the house, and I didn't like it. We were living in a house on Kimbolton Avenue, still near the badminton club, and in this house, the stairs split into two halfway up. One way was the 'children's area', the other was the 'grown-ups'. There was a square landing bit, before it split off, and I used to sit on that square, and listen to my parents screaming at each other. My brother and sister were usually asleep, but the shouting used to wake me up. Sometimes, stuff, a cup, a plate, was thrown, and I would hear the smash on the floor of broken crockery. The words were muffled behind the closed door, but I could make a lot out about what was happening. There had been an affair on my dad's part.

No one divorced back then … one had heard of these 'split families', but not in our circle, or in our neighbourhood. Definitely not at my fee-paying school either. Dad's building company had been flourishing with big-money contracts coming in; however, he was loving the flashy lifestyle that came with it, and entertaining clients became dad's favourite hobby. We had a nice five-bedroom house, two new cars on the drive, all reflecting the income coming in. Often, Dad would leave the house on a Friday night and not come home until Monday morning. I remember opening the door to leave for school one morning, and he was there, on the doorstep, in person but not in spirit. He was a mess. Still drunk. Vomit spilled down his shirt, and he had urinated all over himself. It was such a gluttonous sight, taking everything to excess. I ran and hid in the downstairs toilet, spraying perfume that I found in there, Anais Anais, I remember, to get rid of the mix of smells of him, and waited for him to get into the house so I could leave without seeing him again. I hate the smell of that perfume now.

Dad had built an office in our back garden, and I used to love going in and seeing all the architectural drawings. I could visualise the houses, the different rooms, the kitchen designs, all by just looking at the 2D drawings. The interior designers had a board with their vision and all the colour palettes and designs. I loved being in that environment. Sometimes, Dad would take me out on site, especially if it was a house he was building for us to live in, and we would walk around the foundations and he would talk to me about where everything was going, so I could visualise it.

My dad recognised what we would now call 'stereotypical male characteristics' in me, and if I had been born a boy, he would have taught me everything he knew. Yet he held back – I know he did – as I was a girl. Girls didn't build, in his eyes. He wanted me to be ambitious, no doubt about that, but not in the building trade. He knew I was interested in what he did, but he kept me away, too. It was an incredibly male chauvinistic environment back then. The men wolf-whistling to any female that went past, the Page 3 girls calendar on the walls, the secretaries with the tight skirts and big boobs spilling out of their blouses knowing they weren't hired for their shorthand or typing expertise.

Prime Minister Margaret Thatcher's reign in the 1980s hit my dad hard with the recession that came about. My dad was a stubborn git and thought he could push through when many sold out. He had good deals, he was confident, and the business did the work. There was even a contract to build the holiday chalets at Butlin's, Minehead, but some people couldn't pay after the work had been done. Dad was losing money badly. This had an effect on Mum and Dad's relationship and, in another overheard argument, it was revealed that my dad had remortgaged the house without telling my mum. She was absolutely livid, and rightly so, but Dad kept reassuring her, 'It will be okay. I promise.'

The business was also fitting out Chinese restaurants. Dad was obsessed with Hong Kong after a visit there, and he lent some money (around £250k) to a Chinese businessman for investing. Cue Chinese man disappearing and, later that year, Dad found out he was wanted by the FBI for fraud. There were contacts of his in London, so Dad used to take me to Chinatown, usually on a Friday night before a badminton tournament. We would sit in a random Chinese restaurant waiting for his associates to meet us, and a brown envelope of cash would be passed over the table, between the egg fried rice and Peking duck, as my dad desperately tried to claw back some of his money. I realise now, I was there to make sure there was no trouble, or any fights breaking out. Thanks, Dad. Luckily, there were no unpleasant situations, but eventually the trips stopped as Dad admitted defeat.

Dad moved out of the family home for a while. It was strange to adjust to this new way of life. Even though they were split, there was still arguing, pleading and screaming. It was tense. It all got too much for Mum, and she asked Lisa, Adam and myself if we wanted Dad to come back home. We all said yes, as good children would. Truthfully, we said yes because we had no idea what the hell was going on, and I was sick of all the noise and Mum's friends giving advice.

Dad coming home meant 'a new start', which in our family meant 'a new house', and we moved into a renovation at 177 Kimbolton Road, Bedford. This house, oh my gosh, it was amazing. Originally, it was a Victorian detached house, with four bedrooms and a good-sized garden (sounding like an estate agent here), but Dad put everything he had into transforming this house and got all his staff working on it, to make it the dream home for us kids and my mum. By the time he had finished, he had put side, loft and back extensions on the house: the back extension had an indoor swimming pool, sauna, steam room, Jacuzzi, gym, huge breakfast room area overlooking the pool, and a massive kitchen. Mum was, and still is, rubbish at cooking, so ironically the kitchen was for Dad really – if he was ever home, that is.

I got to design my bedroom exactly how I wanted. The new cars on the driveway were a Jaguar and a convertible Escort. Yet, for some reason, it never felt like home. It felt cold … too big for us. We used the swimming pool lots at the start, then the appeal wore off, and it was hard to maintain.

Gail: Dad was always building houses, and we'd move every year.

Steph: So you've had quite a transient life.

Gail: My dad was always saying, 'We're going to build this house. Then we're going to build this house!' We were always living on a building site.

Steph: It's interesting that the big house never felt like home. It didn't give you any street cred for having a house with a swimming pool?

Gail: No, I didn't have many mates, to be honest.

The strain of the bigger bills and the impending money problems the business was facing didn't help Mum and Dad's fragile relationship, and the inevitable happened. After a year in that house, they sat us down in the 'posh living room' and told us they were splitting up again. All three of us went, 'Oh, okay.' Then my parents said they would have to sell the house. That's when we cried. Another upheaval, and we knew there was more shouting and screaming coming.

I was 13 years old by now, and it was time to admit to school that my parents were one of just three families in the whole year group that would be split. The divorce word was whispered around.

Dad moved out, the furniture was sold, all to try and keep our heads above water. The house was put up for sale, but the recession had hit house prices hard and 177 Kimbolton Road was going to be sold for way less than it was worth. It broke my dad. I know that his behaviour wasn't the best, but to see all that hard work, the painstaking effort, the design, his dream home being sold for a fraction of what it was worth – let's just say Margaret Thatcher's name was never to be mentioned ever again.

Lisa, Adam and I made the most of the playroom being empty and created weird games. We taped big bean bags to each other and ran into each other with the lights out. To this day, I have no idea how or why we came up with that game, but it seemed to make us laugh and take our minds away from it all.

The stress of the split started to take its toll on Mum. Dad would not be allowed up to the house at this point, and I would have to go to the end of the drive to meet him if he was taking me to a badminton tournament. He moved into a house in Northampton with his new girlfriend, Rachel (who I got on very well with), but Mum couldn't handle him moving on, and there was a lot of resentment. I can see it from her side; she let my dad back in and believed his promises, but he let her down, over and over again. I used to like going away for the weekend for badminton tournaments with Dad – it was like an adventure. It was exciting and I got to meet up with all my badminton friends, but I was never allowed to say that in front of Mum, as she would get angry and upset, so I kept it all to myself.

Lisa, Adam and I saw Dad a hell of a lot more after he and Mum split, because Dad had to put the effort in, though it was hard to entertain three kids of seven, ten and 13. I did not want to go to the cinema to watch kids' films or go ten-pin bowling, but my brother and sister loved that. I got to see Dad at badminton tournaments anyway, so most of the time I left them to it.

Dignity Lost in Translation

I was reaching the quarter-finals of national badminton tournaments, results good enough to make an impact on the English junior badminton scene. As a result, I was selected to participate in an U14 international tournament in Holland. I was so excited. The minibus left England with a ten-strong squad, and off we set.

It seems that junior tournaments in Holland are run pretty much like they are in this country. There's the obligatory big tournament desk with lots of paper on it, two stressed-out adults trying to fill in results and keep everything on time, while coping with lots of teenagers hanging around.

It was time for my first match, and I was keen to make an impression. The Dutch tournament organiser announced me on to court over the PA system, and as my name was said, echoing in the six-badminton-court hall, the Dutch junior players all started laughing hysterically at me. Not quite the reaction I expected, and it caught me off guard.

Luckily, I managed to win the game, and as I came off the badminton court and back to the England players' base, a Dutch player came up to me and asked, in perfect English with a Dutch accent, 'Is your name really Gail?' and laughed again. I replied, 'Yes, it is.'

This is where I have to put in a formal complaint to my parents for not doing their research to see if their new baby daughter's name had any other meaning in a foreign language. It appears there is a Dutch word '*geil*', pronounced like 'Gail', just a bit throatier, and it means 'horny'. At my first international tournament, I was 'Horny Emms'. Still to this day, whenever I go to Holland and say my name, the Dutch have a little giggle.

Navigating Teens and Sport

Dad and I got accustomed to our weekends at badminton tournaments over the coming years. I was there, in the passenger seat, with the now-worn AA road map, the address of where to go, a packed lunch from Mum if I was lucky (cheese and pickle sandwiches which always went soggy), and there was always a fight over the radio station. BBC Radio 1, or Radio 5 on MW to listen to the football. Occasionally, Dad would put his Johnny Cash music cassette on to play, which I didn't mind, but I never admitted that to him. I drew a line at Dolly Parton, though.

The atmosphere in the car on the drive back home would be dependent on whether I had won or lost. There were many times when I had lost to someone I shouldn't have, and my dad would be fuming. 'Do you want me to say what I think?' he would say, and I'd moodily return, 'No, I don't want to know.'

To be honest, I could tell exactly what he was thinking. His driving said it all. When Dad was angry, he took it out on the speed limit. Driving at 95mph was his way of saying, 'You need to do better.' But when I won, 'Oh my goodness! You were incredible today!' The compliments would flow, and we'd happily talk about the points I had won and the great shots I had played.

It is not easy being a 'sport parent', and I had no appreciation for what my dad gave up for me at the time. There is no financial support for talented kids; there is only 'Bank of Mum and Dad', and a lot of my rackets were donated to me or second-hand. The same with my kit. I am forever thankful to my coaches – Bill Goode, especially, who knew what my dad was going through, and if he was struggling to pay for the coaching sessions, then Bill would waive the cost. My dad was a proud man, and if he had the money, he always gave Bill what he owed.

I had no idea just how much of a struggle it was, and now, being a sports parent to two boys, I realise. And it's not just the money, it was the time given up taking me to sports halls around the country, which really wasn't that exciting. Most of them were cold in temperature, with only a crappy coffee machine that would stop working by 11am. But he did it. He showed up. And I can't say 'thank you' enough. And now it's too late.

It was extremely hard for Mum to adjust to this new life; no husband, no job, three kids and limited money. And it didn't help that I was now in my teenage years – yay, go hormones – and that I am very much like my dad in personality characteristics and body shape. Every time Mum looked at me, she saw him. I am not saying

I looked like a middle-aged man when I was 13 years old, but you know what I mean.

It was so tough, as I could see the glimmer of resentment as she caught me being like my father, so I learned to zone out. She needed an outlet for her pain and frustration, and there was no one there to help or support her. I took a lot of the anger, but I also didn't help matters. I used to wind my mum up constantly with my behaviour, and the way I spoke to her was shocking. I was going to a school (they kept us on with scholarships) that promoted 'girl power', to be independent women that would rule the world, and here was my mum, left with nothing after my dad had left us. The irony of it all. It wasn't her fault, yet my selfishness decided she was the problem. In my mind, she could have studied and gotten a job to get more money for us when we were struggling. I thought it was that easy. I didn't know any better.

Gail: I was angry.

Steph: Where do you think the anger was coming from?

Gail: Because I was like my dad. It was the only way I knew to be at that point. To annoy Mum, I don't know. I just didn't understand what was going on.

Zoning out was easy for me. There were times when I could transport to another place for a few hours, and no matter what was going on around me, I could just be wherever I wanted to be. My imagination would take me to the stage in a theatre, into my favourite film or even running a business.

Sport helped me hugely; when I stepped on to that badminton court or that hockey pitch, nothing else mattered except for being present and in the moment. I had my role to play; I had my job, and that was to win. I could forget the arguments, the money problems, the shouting, the body-image crisis I was going through, because all I wanted was to be the star on that sports team. To feel wanted meant so much at that time. To be picked, to be selected because you were the best gave me such a rush. I used to feel sad when it was time to go home and back to reality, and I'd often sign up for three or four sports clubs a day, just so I could get my fix of sport and being needed.

Steph: What are the words that you would use to describe how you felt over that period?

Gail: It felt like I just didn't fit in. I was lost, I guess. At least I had sports. You're not really supposed to be sporty as a girl. You're supposed to be this princess, you know? With painted nails – all delicate and sweet. I was anything but. I was made to feel like there was something wrong with me for wanting to run fast and have all this energy and competitiveness.

Steph: Was no one fighting your corner to say you could be proud of who you were?

Gail: No, I just felt like I was the odd one out.

Steph: So you felt alone?

Gail: Yeah.

Steph: Being a hormonal teenager probably didn't help?

Gail: Teenagers can be mean – I was called chunky. The boys wanted the pretty delicate girls, not the one with the big arse from lunging in badminton.

Steph: Maybe this is what drove you even harder towards sport? Because that's where you could fit in and excel?

Gail: Exactly. I was accepted and praised. I was getting all that I wasn't getting at home. The coaches were saying, 'Oh my gosh, that was incredible!' It was acceptable to be me. There were other girls who had muscles like me!

Steph: What a contrast you're painting ... in badminton, you were Gail, and you felt like you belonged.

Gail: Yep.

The next move was to a newish estate, Amberley Gardens in Bedford, and even though my mum's and my relationship was very fragile, I do have some of the best memories from this time. Next door to our house lived a girl called Rosie Garner, who went to my school too, but she was in the school year below. She was also a member of the 'divorced family' club, so we instantly knew the s**t that came with it.

Rosie and I started to hang out together, and generally just be stupid, bringing along a boy named Mat Aram. Mat (one t, not two) lived around the corner. They were my best mates, and I absolutely adored Mat. I was completely in love with him, but I was too shy to say anything. Every time I had the opportunity to do so, I bottled it. Mat and Rosie were boyfriend and girlfriend for a while, and it broke my heart.

I always struggled to fit in with the other girls. I didn't quite know how to be the kind of girl I was apparently supposed to be. I was sporty, strong, stocky and muscular, and that meant I didn't match the typical 'girly girl' mould. I wasn't petite or dainty. My legs, especially, stood out. I had calves like a powerlifter and thighs that belonged on a shot-putter. Thanks, Dad.

I had puppy fat clinging to me, and although I loved fashion and wanted to go out with boys like everyone else, I also loved living in tracksuits and trainers. I was stuck in the middle, constantly conflicted. I wasn't one thing or the other.

I loved chatting with everyone, regardless of whether they were cool, nerdy, goth or somewhere in between. But with girls, it didn't work like that. You had to pick a clique and stay in it. That was the problem: I didn't have one. I didn't fit into any category. I tried to be cool (a disaster), dabbled with goth (blonde hair and minimal make-up didn't help), and eventually just floated around aimlessly. If I got invited somewhere, great. More often than not, I didn't.

And then I began to resent my body. I couldn't understand why I wasn't skinny like the others. Sport made me constantly hungry, but I seemed to gain weight just by *looking* at food. It became a lifelong frustration with that stubborn fat gene I inherited. No matter what

I wore or ate, I couldn't escape the fact that this was just how my body was built.

I began to feel like something was wrong with me – like I was a freak, even. Mum didn't understand either. She was small and slim, and had no idea what to say other than 'maybe stop eating so much.' What made me strong in sport – my powerful build – made me feel like an outsider in teenage life.

Fortunately, I had two things in my favour: I had boobs and waist-length blonde hair. So, I leaned in with that. Armed with a padded Topshop bra and some strategic cleavage, I created a temporary solution to help me feel like I belonged. Even if it was only skin deep.

I hope Mum didn't hate me during those times … but I felt this anger about why she had been left in this position. There were many women in those days who weren't allowed a career, or society expected that they would stay at home and look after the house and kitchen; then, when the man leaves, they are left on their own, almost helpless.

My mum would have made an awesome PE teacher, but she was left to get jobs as a dinner lady or after-school care assistant, as that was all she was qualified to do. I hated the injustice of it all, and I vowed that I would never be in her position. I would never be so dependent on a man that if he left, I would have nothing. It is important to note here that I was seeing this situation through the eyes of a schoolgirl who was excelling in sports, going to an independent school that encouraged me to be strong-willed, and listening to a *lot* of Spice Girls. I feel differently now, and I wish there had been more support and help for Mum. Mental health wasn't a thing back then, you just got on with it, but it was a 'thing', and it wasn't a great time for her.

Sport was my escape … I still didn't have many close friends, so I used to play sport every lunchtime, as at least then I didn't have to sit on my own or walk around school to see if anyone would talk with me. I used to sit in the PE changing rooms on my own lots, just because no one else would hang out with me. I wasn't a nasty person, I just didn't have the ability to connect with one person intensely like a lot of girls can do so easily. They used to pick a 'best friend' and it was like a pact for life. I was genuinely interested in everyone, but that wasn't playing by the rules.

If school sport was cancelled at lunchtime, it meant that I was on my own again, and I would have to find somewhere to be until lessons started again. I wish there had been honest conversations back then. I have the self-awareness now to understand that my personality was difficult for many of the girls to manage. They weren't nasty to my face, I wasn't bullied, but I was often left out on purpose. When it came to giving out Christmas presents or birthday gifts, it became obvious I wasn't included. It hurt, I'll admit, and I will always remember a lovely, kind girl called Marianna Stango sticking up for me and buying me a little something when the others didn't want her to.

I did the typical teenager thing, and hung out by the river in Bedford, drinking some cider, trying a cigarette, standard coming-of-age in the early 1990s, as there wasn't much else to do. The first time I got *very* drunk, and I mean *very*, was on a family holiday to the Greek island of Rhodes. Dad and his girlfriend Rachel had taken us in the school holidays, as Dad had found a new job working for a mate of his from his building days, and had saved up enough to take us away. It was a few days before my 15th birthday, and I had made some awesome friends of the same age.

One of the boys, Matt, had bought a bottle of vodka and a packet of Benson & Hedges cigarettes from the shop in the hotel. We started drinking on the beach, before finding our way to a disco nearby, where I discovered a taste for brandy and chocolate milk. I had been more used to cheap cider – Thunderbird, White Lightning – not vodka and brandy. I could usually stop drinking when I felt too drunk, but this time I went too far. The end result was me thinking I was physically dying and begging to go to the hospital in Rhodes to get my stomach pumped. I was throwing up so much, retching bile, horrible to think about it now.

Dad was fuming, so I acted all innocent, telling him I had never had alcohol before and I had been corrupted. My dad stormed up to Matt the next day, got him by the neck and pinned him up against the wall, telling him to stay away from me. He scared the living s**t out of him. I did apologise to Matt: it was all me, and not Matt.

Looking back, it was all a cry for help. I was looking for affection that was not attached to winning a trophy. I was looking for friendship because it was me as a person, not because I could play hockey well. I tried to make people laugh, tried to be cool, all to please everyone and make them like me. It didn't work, but I still had sport, and I was popular in this space.

Gail: I know now, weird people produce extraordinary results. You cannot be spectacular and fit in at the same time. If I could go back and tell my younger self this, I would.

Steph: 'Weird' is still how you choose to describe yourself? If you described this scenario, but it was about a good friend, I wonder how you would describe them?

Gail: I would probably focus on the spectacular bit.

Born to Annoy and Occasionally Adore

Lisa

Lisa is the middle child … and I could leave it there, because we all know the stereotypes. But let's give her the credit she deserves.

Lisa, my lovely little sister, is everything I'm not. She's gentle, kind and naturally nurturing. As a child, she adored playing with dolls, looked perfectly at home in pastel colours and always had a close-knit circle of friends. Physically, she's tall and slim with soft, natural curls in her light brown hair, a sprinkle of freckles across her nose that wouldn't look out of place on a catwalk. But despite all that, Lisa has always struggled with self-confidence, and that's something that has always tugged at my heart.

From a young age, she showed a quiet determination. At primary school, she learned how to study well and apply herself, and when we moved on to the girls' school, she really began to shine in science. Sport was also on her radar – she wasn't chasing the glory like her big sister, but she was always the trusted team-mate. Often made captain,

Lisa was the steady and dependable one. Honestly, if triathlon had been more of a thing in the '90s, she would have nailed it. But with Dad busy taking me to badminton tournaments and Mum focused on football with our brother Adam, I think Lisa missed out on the chance to find her own sporting passion.

I noticed early on that Mum and Dad were gentler with her. The way they spoke about her was different. I'd often hear things like, 'Lisa needs more help,' or 'she's not like you,' and 'Lisa needs more looking after.' Meanwhile, I was mostly left to figure things out myself. I can't recall a single 'talk' with either of them about boys, sex, relationships or make-up. I had to learn as I went and then pass it all down to Lisa. Not exactly textbook parenting, but I'd like to think I did a half-decent job as a big sister.

Of course, I wasn't always the angelic older sibling. I teased her relentlessly growing up and, let's be honest, I still do. One of my favourites (which still makes me laugh) is from when she was about three and suddenly stopped breathing through her nose for no apparent reason. She'd just follow me around the house, wheezing loudly through her mouth like a tiny, wheezy Darth Vader. To make things even more surreal, she used to twist her hair into tight knots, so this matted-haired, heavy-breathing shadow would trail behind me.

And then there were the matching outfits Mum used to dress us in. Mortifying. The idea of trying that now, with our completely different body types and complexions, is enough to make anyone laugh – or cry. We looked nothing like each other, and our personalities couldn't have been more different. The family used to joke that Lisa had been left under a bush and we were just waiting for her real parents to show up.

But perhaps the quirkiest thing about Lisa, and she will *hate* that I'm telling you this, is her absolute phobia of holes in clothes. Yes, holes. That tiny tear in your favourite jumper that you barely notice? For Lisa, it was full-blown horror. This irrational fear brought me years of entertainment. I'd chase her around the house with a sock that had the smallest hole in it while she screamed, cried and, once, even threw up. Did I stop? Of course not! That's what big sisters are for. To this day, she still has that phobia. And while I no longer throw holey socks at her (public disclaimer: I do not condone this behaviour), it remains one of the many wonderfully bonkers things about my brilliant, beautiful, sensitive sister. I wouldn't change her for the world.

Adam

Finally … a boy for Dad! I still remember the celebrations like they were yesterday. The day my brother was born felt like a national holiday in our house. Apparently, having four daughters (counting my two half-sisters in this) wasn't quite enough and, *finally*, the Emms name had an heir. Classic Dad: no half measures, especially when it came to celebrating. The party lasted for days. Always nice to hear when you're one of the daughters …

Adam and I share a lot in common, especially our fiery competitiveness as kids. From the moment he could walk, Mum had him out in the garden kicking a football. He was constantly in a football kit, usually the latest England strip. Mum tried her best to nudge him toward supporting Spurs, while Dad quietly pitched the virtues of Norwich City. In the end, Adam went rogue and chose Liverpool. Cue the bedroom walls plastered with posters, and two very disappointed parents.

When Adam was still small for his age but full of skill, he was offered a trial at Luton Town. It was a big moment; unfortunately, the reality of playing against much bigger, more physical boys hit hard, literally and figuratively. To their credit, Luton were honest with him: come back when you've grown a bit. But as life would have it, by the time Adam grew into his frame he'd also discovered the joys of drinking and smoking, as many teens do. Let's just say that the return trial never quite happened.

Despite that, Adam's talents shine in so many ways. He's one of those people I don't need to see or speak to regularly, but we can be in the same room for hours, barely say a word, and still have a great time. He's incredibly gifted musically, having taught himself guitar purely by ear, just by listening to songs on the radio. His artwork is genuinely impressive, he's sharp as anything (straight As at A level), and he's got the biggest heart – he works for a charity in Bedford, giving so much of himself to help others.

He's also in a band, and I absolutely love watching him perform. I always think I should make more time to go and see him. If there's anyone who deserves a bit more luck in this world, it's Adam.

Surviving School

I was clever. I like to think I still am clever, but I was a very bright child. Mum was adamant that her children would get a good education, as she had failed her 11+ exam, and always regretted not trying harder. Dad left school at 14 and went straight to work, so private schooling was what they wanted for us.

It was clear from the start that I found lessons easy. I would finish the school exercises set on the board and ask for extra ones. Yes, I was that show-off. When I was younger, I never understood why people took so long to do what I thought were simple maths problems. Being good was normal for me. School was the perfect fit for me to shout, 'Look at me, look at me!'

I attended Walmsley House, which was a private primary school in Bedford, and then I passed the entrance exam at seven years old to go to Dame Alice Harpur School for Girls. I remember the uniform. I had a bowler hat.

I set out my intentions as soon as I arrived. I wanted to be the best. I would come home from the Dame Alice preparatory (or prep) department with a 95 per cent score on a test, glowing with pride, but, often, Mum and Dad would say, 'Why did you not get 96 or 97 per cent?' Being in that environment of competitive girls just made me more ambitious than ever.

There was money everywhere – most of the mothers didn't work. The cars parked in the school car park were all high-end. The mothers would dress smartly to pick the children up. Some girls had nannies to pick them up. At the weekends, most of my classmates would be at ballet recitals, or gymkhanas with their ponies. I wasn't allowed a tutu. Mum said ballet wasn't a sport, and I didn't really want to go on a horse, as everyone at one point seemed to fall off them and break a bone.

'Show and Tell' became a battleground for medals and rosettes. The girls were constantly eyeing each other to see who was the 'best'. I loved 'Show and Tell' and bringing anything and everything I won at badminton into class.

I did feel that living in the 1980s was all about the 'show', all about the money, and living that yuppie lifestyle. *Dynasty* or *Dallas* were the TV programmes that influenced women's fashion and introduced shoulder pads in blouses.

One's children doing well in private education and sport was an extension of gloating and having one-up on your friends. 'Our Gail has achieved this', 'Gail has got into *all* the sports teams', 'Gail achieved distinction'; I heard all of this said to other adults around. My 'golden child' achievements were a perfect accompaniment to Dad's rising status in the building world.

I am not going to lie; I relished it all. I knew my role – to achieve greatness – but it started, inevitably, to become a vicious cycle. I soon only got praise when I achieved something: a medal, a top test result or a distinction, and so this fuelled my need to be competitive. EVERYTHING became a competition. Even at an early age, I had associated praise with coming only when I won.

The teachers at school were also part of that competitive spirit. All our results were compared against the three other private schools in Bedford. Almost all of the teachers at my school were female and incredibly passionate about girls' education. After schooling, they wanted us to go out in the world and create more opportunities in the workplace that had not been available for women not that long ago. There was a sense of 'women taking over the world', and one headmistress even had the motto for us 'Busy girls are happy girls, and happy girls are busy girls!'

Gail: Even my exams were a way of showing off. Everything was a competition

Steph: I think that is absolutely fascinating, that it is a natural part of you, that you're such a highly competitive spirit underneath it all.

Gail: Even getting changed for PE. I had to be first. No one else was in this competition. It was just me thinking, 'I could be first here.' French vocabulary tests were a great example. I was always finished first in them. I used to look around all smug, seeing everyone else still working. Same for the dinner queue. Had to be first.

Steph: (Laughing) Maybe you were just hungry?

Jolly Hockey Sticks

Along came school sport – hockey, netball, rounders, athletics, cross country, swimming – you name it, I was in the team. Badminton wasn't played much at the school; for Dame Alice Harpur School, it was all about hockey. I did love hockey, and I was pretty good at it. I had a good hit on me, surprisingly. Probably a bit too good, as I walloped Angela Sampson's nose one time, and I can still hear the bone crunch as my stick connected with her face. Angela has since told me that she had to have four operations to fix it. Sorry, Angela.

I preferred indoor hockey; it was faster. And indoors. I wasn't a fan of playing sports in British weather. Though if you think it is any safer playing indoor hockey than outdoor hockey, my team-mate Megan Parkhouse went in for a tackle on me, just as I went to flick the ball for the goal. The ball connected with her forehead. Ten stitches were needed. There was so much blood. It took days to clean the sports hall floor as Megan's blood had soaked into the fibres. I was traumatised, but not as traumatised as Megan, obviously.

Megan was our hockey captain. A great hockey player and feisty as hell. I remember her on the coach home from a big tournament that we had just won. Tina Turner was blaring out on the speakers, and we were all singing 'Simply the Best' as loudly as we could. Another team-mate, Hazel Knight, was going up and down the aisle with Megan, both doing their best Tina impressions. 'I call ya when I need ya, my heart's on fire …' It was the best time and a moment I will remember forever. The camaraderie, the team spirit; you can't beat school sport memories.

I had been doing well in badminton tournaments at this point in my life, and hockey and badminton were on a level par in terms of what I was achieving. I knew that if I wanted to excel at hockey, I would have to go and join a club and get coaching. The good thing with the sport of badminton was the fact that I knew exactly where I ranked. That's the beauty of an individual sport; if you play against somebody and beat them, you know you are better than them. I had trouble understanding where I ranked in a team sport. How did I know I was better than another player who played in my position? It is a subjective opinion, a manager's or coach's decision. In hockey, I was one of a squad of many, and one of 11 on the pitch.

As we were singing and dancing, Megan stopped the music on the tape player, looked us all in the eye, and she screamed, 'I LOVE YOU GUYS! I WOULD DIE FOR YOU!' It was at this point that I realised I was a badminton player. Don't get me wrong, I liked the other girls on the coach, but I wasn't sure I'd die for them.

I told this story to legendary England rugby player and World Cup-winning captain Martin Johnson when explaining why I chose badminton and not hockey. He looked at me in utter disgust.

Gail: I like showing off, and I like the attention, and I didn't get that with hockey. I didn't get the gratification or the validation in hockey. It wasn't all about me.

Steph: Bearing in mind that you found social situations and making friends quite difficult, maybe you couldn't cope with all the issues around the team dynamics, particularly the politics of who was being picked. You picked the safe option for you. The one you could control.

I decided to concentrate on badminton from that point on. It was the summer of 1992, and the Barcelona Olympic Games had started. Badminton was in the Olympics for the first time, as a test event. Everyone was excited that our sport could be integrated into the Olympic programme.

Despite that, it was another sport that had a huge impact on me that year. Growing up, I don't remember seeing many sportswomen on TV. Athletics and tennis were the only sports I could think of that would have had female representation. The Barcelona Olympic Games in 1992 came at the perfect time for me. For the first time in my life, I saw that there were people like me. Girls and women who had muscles, females who loved winning medals, females being celebrated for being strong and fast, rather than teased or mocked.

On 6 August 1992, Sally Gunnell, representing Team GB in the 400m hurdles, won the gold medal. I had never done 400m hurdles in my life, but it didn't matter. I screamed at that TV, willing her to run so fast. I loved how she looked so powerful, so determined, and cheered loudly when she crossed that line first. And as Sally stood on the podium, the Olympic gold medal around her neck, with the British national anthem playing, I cried along with many other people watching. Sally Gunnell was my new hero. I wanted to be Sally. I wanted to be an Olympian.

It was as if a lightbulb had switched on in my head. Everything I did, from that moment on, was all about the Olympic Games. I walked into school and told the teachers, 'I'm going to be an Olympian,' and they just laughed. 'Don't be silly, dear, you can't do sport as a career. You can only be a professional sports*man*, with cricket, football and rugby. You can't be a professional sports*woman*.' Annoyingly, they were about right. In 1992, there was no such thing as a professional sportswoman – with the only exception probably being tennis; I would have to see my Olympic badminton journey as a 'hobby'.

I always say that something needs to 'click' with girls and sport. This was my 'click'. Badminton was an Olympic sport; it passed the test. I could make my mark. This dream fuelled me. I trained harder.

INTRODUCING ... NATHAN ROBERTSON

MY FRIEND Rob Mauchlen suggested the title of this book should be 'Thank God for Nathan', and though we had a good old laugh, he's not far off. The Gail Emms and Nathan Robertson partnership started in September 1992. We were both 15 years old and were in what would be considered the England B team. The Nottinghamshire U16 tournament at Chilwell Sports Centre was coming up and I needed a mixed doubles partner. My dad said, 'Why don't you ask Nathan? I don't think he has a partner.'

Now, there was a bit of an issue here, as Nathan was cool and very good-looking. If you looked at the rest of us junior badminton players, it was clear why he stood out. He was already 6ft tall, had chiselled cheekbones, wore earrings (hoops with a cross on, I remember), had long dark hair covering an in-fashion undercut, and was James Dean moody.

I thought he was very fanciable, but also a bit of a knobhead, quite frankly, and there was no way in hell, as a very uncool 15-year-old girl, I was going to go up to 'Mr Cool Nathan Robertson' and ask him to play the Nottinghamshire U16 mixed doubles. However, my dad was being stubborn and doing some 'parenting', so I had no choice but to give it a try.

I went over ... trying to be calm, suddenly aware of my walk, and now my walk felt stupid. I think I had upgraded my blue balloon shell suit to a more 'casual' look of sweatpants and baggy hoodie jumper, paired with the classic Hi-Tec indoor squash trainers.

I was shaking. This was up there as one of the most nerve-wracking situations I'd ever been in, up there with trying to ask someone to slow dance with me at the school disco. I took a deep breath in, willed myself not to blush, and I turned to Nathan and said, 'So ... wanna play ... er Notts mixed?' What came out of my mouth didn't even really make sense, but I had done it. I had got words out without turning the colour of beetroot.

Nathan looked down at me. I think I had reached my height of 5ft 3 by this stage. There was a horrible pause, probably only about five or six seconds, but it felt like an hour in my head. It was painful. He looked like he was thinking about it, and then replied, 'Yeah, alright then.' And that was it. I walked off, told my dad, and that was how the Emms/Robertson partnership started.

Stealing the Show

As I mentioned before, Nathan and I were England B level, so we were not expected to win the Notts U16 tournament. I think we were seeded to reach the quarter-finals, and there we faced the number-one seeded pair. We didn't speak to each other one bit. The most we could muster up was a grunt. I wasn't too worried; it just seemed to be our way of communicating, and I wasn't bothered if Nathan didn't like me. I chucked him the shuttle when it was his serve and just got on with the job at hand. That was what I was there to do.

I still remember, to this day, there being a feeling of magic on that court. I remember thinking that I knew exactly where Nathan was without having to look behind me. No matter where I was, I knew he was covering the space and vice versa. It felt as though the stars had aligned and everything felt in sync. There was a telepathy, a chemistry. We beat the No.1 seeds in the quarter-finals, won the semi-finals and then we were victorious in the final. We were champions on our first outing as a pair.

After the final, the coaches came over to see Nathan and me, and they just looked quizzical. They looked at each other, and then at us. My dad and Nathan's dad, John, walked over to us, smiling, and the coaches said, 'We would never have put you two together.

What the hell just happened there?' As Nathan and I clutched our trophies, we didn't know either, or care, frankly, but we both knew it was the start of something. And our gut feeling was right. Nathan and I barely lost a match for the next three years.

It was at this time in my life in badminton that I decided to give up playing in the singles discipline. It made sense, as I had a 6ft 3-tall man running around, playing most of the shots in the rallies, and I was getting success and a lot of glory with that. Playing singles on my own, I looked like a headless chicken scrapping around, hustling and not winning as much. See? Genius me. And I loved the speed and power element that doubles badminton produces; it was much more my style.

By the time Nathan and I had reached the U18 England team, we had a great group of talented players all coming through to challenge the best nations in Europe as well as Asia: Mark Constable, Michael Edge, Angela Goodhall, Ella Miles, Donna Kellogg, Joanne Wright, Natalie Munt, Allan Cottell, Ian Sullivan, Anthony Clark. The future was looking good for English badminton and I had found my tribe. It was my happy place.

Creepy Coach

The relationship between a coach and a sportsperson is something very special, but there are times, sadly, when the adult coach, the one who's in power, abuses this. There is a line that *must not* be crossed. In many sports, time and time again, there have been cases of abuse.

The only time that anything untoward happened to me was at one U16 England squad training camp at the National Badminton Centre in Milton Keynes. The coach at the time, a male in his 30s, called each player in, one by one, to talk about what the plans were for them. For example, the doubles players would be told who they would be playing in a partnership with, and for the singles players, he would decide which tournaments they would be entering. This coach decided to have these conversations in private, in his bedroom. The room was tiny; let's say it was the size of a box room typically found in a house. There were two beds (I have no idea how they got those beds in there), but there was hardly any room between them.

It was my turn to be called up. As a reminder, I was 15 years old at the time. The coach in question sat on one bed and I sat opposite. He then told me who I would be playing ladies' doubles with, that person being Ella Miles. And then the mixed doubles with Nathan Robertson. All very simple, and no real surprises, it was what I expected. I thought that was it, and I got up to leave ... but then he came out with a question.

'So, Gail, who do you fancy in badminton then?' I remember being shocked by this question and thinking, 'Well, it's none of your business.' But I didn't want to be rude, so I said, 'Oh, no one.' He said, 'Oh, come on, there must be someone. I'm sure it's Nathan. All the girls fancy Nathan.' And I said, 'No. I don't fancy anyone.'

He then replied, 'Do you want to know who I fancy?' I said, 'No, not really.' But he said, 'Well, I'll tell you anyway. It's you. But don't tell anyone, will you?'

I immediately looked at the door. I wanted to be anywhere but in this room at that moment. I quickly got up and reached for the door handle. I felt suffocated, and I didn't want to be near him. Luckily, he didn't try to stop me from leaving. I will stress that he didn't try and touch me, but, still, what he said was wrong and I knew it. I went down the stairs and into the badminton hall, still shocked and processing what had happened. I remember some girls in the squad coming over to me to ask what had been said, and I just blurted out, 'Oh, he just told me he fancied me.'

I am so lucky I am who I am, and I said that out loud straight away. I'm not sure some girls believed me, but that doesn't matter. What was important was that I managed to tell someone, anyone, it didn't matter. The secret he wanted me to keep was out in the open. Many young athletes don't have the confidence or don't feel that they have a voice that will be heard. I did.

I *never* told my dad, though, as I know my dad would have killed him. He would have punched him so hard in the face, and more. What is worse is that it makes me think back to the multiple times when this coach offered for me to stay at his house when my family was struggling with finances, to enable me to go to certain holiday badminton camps. It makes me think I should have reported him. I am not sure who I could have told, as 'safeguarding' wasn't a thing then, but this person should have been 'flagged' for his behaviour. Nothing more happened with this coach, although he did approach me a few weeks later and accused me of telling people. I said, 'Yeah, I did.' He never approached me again.

Eventually, this coach was caught behaving inappropriately and reprimanded. He got caught being more forward with another young badminton girl. Years later, and I mean many, many years later, just as historical abuse in sport was being reported on in the press, I was surprised when Adrian Christy, the then chief executive of Badminton England, asked me about my 'altercation' with this man, and whether I would say anything to the media if they found out. My dad had passed away at this stage, so I said, 'I'm not going to lie to hide anything. If I am asked if this person said anything inappropriate to me, I will say yes, and I will explain. And I will say that this man did not touch me.'

England Calling

Let's get back to the badminton.

The England senior selectors started to notice Nathan's and my results. People were talking about us. 'Have you heard about Nathan Robertson and Gail Emms?' We were on the watch list.

I got my first England senior cap in 1995. I got the call that I had been selected to represent England Seniors, *the* England team. I was playing in the mixed doubles with Nathan Robertson against China in Boston, Lincolnshire. I was 18 years old. My family made that trip up the A1 to come and watch. They were so proud. We were the first match out of the five disciplines, got a great start, kept up the pressure, and we won!

I will never forget that moment. Playing for your country at a senior level is an honour, and I treasure all of the 68 times I represented my country. It was also right to get my first cap with

Nathan. Like many doubles specialists, there were many matches where I played the ladies' doubles as well as the mixed doubles event in the tie, but only received one 'cap' for both games. Sometimes I think that was unfair, and my 68 would have been more like 100 caps if both events had been counted. Nathan did reach the 100 mark and thoroughly deserved it.

In badminton, there was no actual cap given to us like footballers receive. There was no money awarded for representing England either – something I do believe should continue. No athlete should be paid to play for their country. The honour and privilege should be enough.

Deselected but Not Defeated

The National Lottery was introduced at this time, and this meant there was funding for athletes to be professional sportsmen or women in an Olympic sport. Each sport created 'performance pathways' for the athletes with the potential to make it to the top of the world, and in badminton the selection of players for those pathways was down to the performance director, Stephen Baddeley. Over a few meetings, I was eventually told, 'We don't think you are good enough to be on the performance pathway. We don't think you will make it to the Olympic Games or World Championships. You will be an okay senior player, but the talent is all with Nathan. We, the selectors, want to see him play with other partners, the senior women.'

I was a few months in as a fresher at university, and my fate in badminton had been decided. I was to be cast aside, and Nathan would be on the performance programme to play with other women. I'm not going to lie, it was a huge blow to my ego, and it was horrendous watching Nathan play tournaments with other female players. It was like being dumped and watching your ex upgrade from you.

I had those words from Stephen in my head for many years. A lot of people have asked me if I have gone back to him, dangled my medals in his face, and said, 'Well, you were wrong!' The honest answer is that Stephen was 100 per cent right at that time to analyse my performance the way he did. I was not the most naturally talented, nor was I the most skilful badminton player, so if you were to ask the senior players and the coaches from the late 1990s, all of them would say they didn't think I was good enough to achieve what I have gone on to achieve. Some of those players still make snide comments on social media about me, which makes me laugh – they still can't accept that I have done okay. However, if I were to see Stephen now, I would happily thank him and shake his hand; there is no animosity from me whatsoever. He was right with his decision then. I had to step up and change if I was going to have any chance of making it in senior elite sport.

Gail: The selectors put Nathan with older more experienced women for partners. I was left without. Panic set in. I needed another partner to prove everyone wrong. I started ringing round people because I didn't want to be left with no partner. My first instinct was: 'Fine, I'll find someone else.'

Steph: So, no tears and no suggestion in your mind that you might want to give up?

Gail: Maybe it was more saving face. I didn't want to be embarrassed. Nathan's dad wrote me a nice letter, and I cried at that. I remember watching him play a tournament with someone else, and I heard other players saying stuff.

Steph: Who did you talk to?

Gail: No one, I just felt embarrassed.

Steph: Incredible, that in a moment when you most needed support, you chose not to tell anyone. That's tough; it just shows you what an island you were.

Gail: My family put me on a pedestal.

Steph: Are you telling me you didn't want to let them down?

Gail: One hundred per cent. I was totally embarrassed. My ego was destroyed and I didn't want them to see it. I knew how devastated they would be, and I just couldn't deal with it. I wanted to tell them all it was fine. I'll find a way around it, and I'll get back eventually.

Steph: I hope you don't mind me sharing that this makes me feel very sad; that at that point, there was nobody to scoop you up. When my own daughter got dropped from her international sports career, she really needed us to cry her angry and distraught tears with.

Gail: I'm not gonna lie; I feel jealous about that. Looking back, I can understand why I had no option but to soldier on. I just threw myself into university life cause the alternative was that I had nothing.

Steph: So, uni gave you some credibility, and an acceptable way forward in your mum and dad's eyes?

Gail: I have to admit that was probably my motivation – to do right by them, but it was also a bit of escapism, too. Family life was tough, and I got away from it. It was a huge relief to go, but I still feel guilty about it. I felt like I abandoned them.

BROADENING HORIZONS

Beers, Biomechanics and Bad Decisions

University didn't help at all with the progression of my badminton. I turned up at Kingston University with all the hope of a fresher who had an England cap in her sport, and I came out after three years of sports science with a 2:1 degree with honours, and a lot of life experience. I mean, I had the *best* time. There was Stella Artois lager at £1 a pint, there were boys, there was sport and there were pubs. I loved the freedom of uni. And being around more normal people who were a bit older and more mature, I even managed to make friends. I was on a sports science course with a majority of boys, a stark contrast from my all-girl schooling, but I preferred being in a mixed-gender environment.

There was a nightclub called Volts that hosted a student night every Wednesday after university sports. I bloody loved it.

Steph: It must have felt so weird to be living without elite sport in your life.

Gail: Yeah, it was weird because I had friends.

Steph: Did you drop badminton completely?

Gail: I didn't drop it. I kept a little bit going ...

Steph: So, you wanted to keep the door open, but you had a good excuse if you didn't perform well?

Gail: Of course. Then if I lost, it's alright, because I'm at university, not 'taking it seriously'.

Steph: So, where did you get your adrenaline from during that time?

Gail: Partying.

The first person I met in Kingston was a girl on my course called Lucy Crickmore. We nervously said 'hi' to each other and started to talk. She was from Colchester, and she had a look about her that meant she knew her s**t. I instantly liked her. It worked out that we had been destined to meet as we were both down to do another course at another university, but neither got the grades, so we ended up at Kingston. It was fate.

I'm still good friends with Lucy to this day, and joke that she was always going to be in my life, and tell her how lucky she is. Lucy may disagree on this, but she has looked after me a lot in my life, and she is a brilliant mate. Nowadays, it's less about cheap student beer and more about skiing together. Lucy is an expert at reading maps and navigating ski slopes. I, however, am very likely to fall off a cliff or end up in another country, so I follow Lucy around the French Alps, and this relationship works out very nicely. Lucy reads maps well, and I stay alive.

I do make her come out of her comfort zone, though. I don't think Lucy has forgiven me for a very drunken night in Chamonix when she wanted to go to bed at 10pm and I made her go 'out-out' and we rolled into bed at 4am. Riding the ski lifts the next morning was not a pleasant experience. She also lives in a place outside Colchester, called Fingringhoe, which is featured in the top-ten rudest names in the UK. Bloody brilliant. I tell people all the time when we are out together.

Kingston-upon-Thames became my home for three years. I do wish I had done a bit of research before I selected that university, in the sense that I should have looked up an A-Z of the streets of the town. This may seem a very odd thing to say, but as a group of us were walking into the town centre one evening, to go to a pub, of course, we went past an alleyway. Some observant bugger looked at the name of this alleyway, and saw the sign proudly displaying, 'Emms Passage'. The boys on my course thought this was gold dust, and every time we passed said alleyway, there were shouts of: 'Who's been down Emms Passage? Wahey!'

Why Kingston, why? Of all the names out there, you had to go for 'Emms'. Just call it 'The Passage'. Does an alleyway really need a name? Three, yes *three,* years of comments. I hear 'Emms Passage' is still going strong, thank you very much. I am sure it has had many visitors, be that in groups, or solo, regular visitors and lots of newcomers. I'll get the jokes out for you. You're welcome.

My dad told me that he was renting out my room in his flat, so I stayed at university at the weekends and during some of the holidays. I made the most of my time, and I worked in a local pub when I could, to get some extra cash. My budget of £20 a week was worked out as best as possible. I would always have £5 for Wednesday night, to go 'out-out'. That was all I needed: 50p for the bus to the student bar, £3 for three £1-a-pint Stella Artois, 50p bus ride back, and £1 for a bag of chips at the Chinese takeaway. Those were the days. The sports science gang of Ben, Lordy, Crabby, Rich, Russell, Stuart, Nash, Gareth, Duffy, Lorna, Lucy and I somehow navigated our way together for three years and all came out with degrees, amazingly, as most of the time we were drunk.

I did play a bit of badminton while I was studying. I went to training at a performance centre in High Wycombe when I could afford petrol. I wasn't allowed to train at the National Badminton Centre in Milton Keynes, as I wasn't on the elite performance pathway, but I was supported to go to a few European tournaments throughout the year. I have no idea how or why I was picked; maybe there was funding for the B level of badminton players (as I would categorise myself as B level). However, there was a slight problem that these tournaments ran from Friday to Sunday on a weekend and were held in various places like Lisbon, Budapest, Oslo and so on. That meant travelling on the Thursday. This may not seem like an obvious problem, but I was at university, and on Wednesday it was the sports matches, followed by student night, which inevitably meant a visit to Volts nightclub in Kingston. I have a serious case of FOMO (fear of missing out, for those not in the know with that acronym).

The sensible thing would have been not to go out the night before a travel day to a European badminton tournament, especially when the meeting times were about 8am at Heathrow Airport. However, I certainly wasn't sensible at university, and was very susceptible to bad decision-making.

There may have been a few times when I hadn't packed my kit bag, awoke after two hours of sleep, still drunk, and I somehow managed to get the bus from Kingston to Heathrow and arrive on time. I did, on those occasions, get questionable looks from the coach who was taking the group, and all I can say is thank you for allowing me to still be part of the squad and not sending me back home. I just had to go out and win the tournament in question to make up for it. I often did, thank goodness.

Steph: At the time, you would have said getting dropped from playing with Nathan was the worst thing that could have happened for your sporting career. But imagine how different your life would have been if you'd stayed in Bedford, if you hadn't got away? You were gifted an opportunity to grow up independently and with freedom of thought, without the stress and anxiety of your home environment.

Gail: I still feel a bit of a failure for a number of things – not smashing my A levels like I should have, losing Nathan as a partner and not getting on the performance programme. But you're right. It was a blessing.

China: Shuttlecocks and Culture Shocks

When I was playing junior badminton, there was often talk about a tour of China that some players were selected to go on. These tours were infamous. We heard that the three-week tour was designed to break you, to see if you would cope with the demands of playing in that country. I was selected to play in two of these tours: one during my university years and one straight after. I learned a *lot* about myself and a *lot* about China.

I had my 21st birthday on one of the tours. I remember looking out of the airplane window and seeing lightning outside. The plane was rocking everywhere with turbulence. The China airlines plane we were on looked like it had been bought on eBay as a vintage 1970s model, and even though there was a typhoon happening, they thought, 'No problem!' and decided to go ahead with the flight. I prayed the whole flight. I really thought I was going to die in a crash; it was that bad.

The hotels we stayed in on the tour were basic. And basic in China in 1998 meant basic as basic can be. In some hotels, there were cockroaches on the walls and rats outside. We would stay in cities that had never seen Westerners before. One day, I was walking down the street to go to a local shop to get water, and a lot of Chinese people passed me on their bicycles, then stopped, turned around and just stared at me, as they had never seen blonde hair before. On many occasions, they would still be staring as they went past, which meant there were a lot of crashes, and I remember one man still staring up at me from the floor while entangled in his bike from the crash he had just had. Still staring at me while his leg was bleeding from the fall.

The humidity was what hit me hardest. Summer in south-east China is about 30 degrees in temperature, but with 90 per cent humidity. Walking into the sports hall was like walking into a steam room. That was bad enough, let alone exercising in it. Instantly, it was a struggle to breathe … the body panics, trying to get as much oxygen into the lungs as possible, but there is a risk of hyperventilating. The only way to cope is to relax as much as possible, to focus on the breath out rather than the breath in. It was often too much to take. I was craving cool air, but there was no air conditioning – only a desk or ceiling fan that was circulating hot, humid air. It made you feel sick.

It would be humiliating, too. The Chinese players, the regional teams that we were scheduled to play against, would look at us strangely, not understanding why we were struggling to breathe. We tried to explain, but they just thought we were unfit Westerners. They did have a point, to be fair. After a few days, and not soon enough, the body adapts and climatises. It is the best feeling … a huge relief. It was time to play some matches and show that we *can* play badminton.

In China, 100 million people play badminton. There's a nice stat for you. Therefore, to make it into the top squad, you have to be exceptional. Even the players in the regional teams that we were playing were exceptional. Just not as exceptional as the top players. It was relentless. Match after match, we lost. Especially in the ladies' doubles. The Chinese girls were crazily good, and the matches wouldn't last that long. They used to put us out of our misery quickly, thank goodness. I did better in mixed doubles; the traditional, European way of playing mixed doubles with the front and back format meant that we could give them a good game at least.

After one team match, we finished about 6pm, and we were stretching to get ready for the bus back to the hotel. One of the players on the tour, David Lindley, was laughing about how many shirts he had to change throughout his match, as he was renowned for sweating a *lot*. I think he had to change four shirts during play, and, after the match, he took his trainers off and poured the sweat out into a cup. He was always drinking water to keep hydrated, but on this evening, after a hot and humid day in the Chinese sports hall, David got a cramp in his calf. He started trying to stretch it out, but those of you who get cramps, you know how painful it can be. As he was stretching it out, a cramp got into his hamstring of the same leg. Double cramp, double agony. Then the quad went. His whole right leg was now cramping violently.

We were all trying to stretch and relax the muscles the best we could … and then it started in the left leg. It was like a scene from the film *Alien* when the creature was inside Sigourney Weaver, except this cramp stayed inside and continued to torture the body. Nothing we were doing was helping. Dave was now screaming, and then it hit his entire body. His upper body was now convulsing, and he was struggling to breathe, as the lungs couldn't inflate or deflate with the intercostal muscles spasming as they were. An ambulance was called, and Dave spent the night on a drip to replace all the electrolytes and fluid lost. Thankfully, he made a speedy recovery. It was a shock for all of us to see, but a lesson to respect the conditions and listen to our bodies.

We were fed basic rations of rice, eggs and watermelon. That was it. With the humidity, heat and the intensity of the matches, it was now down to us to see who could cope and who would crack under the pressure. On these tours, I have seen adult men curled up in the foetal position on the floor of hotels or sports halls, rocking and wanting to quit, saying that they had had enough. They were over it. The relentlessness, the food, the cockroaches. It got to everyone at one stage. You just didn't want to be the first.

The English players would struggle through, each of us counting down the days until the flight home. Sometimes, the Chinese hosts would invite us to a 'special dinner' to celebrate our visit to the region. For those of you who have never been to China, but like a little cheeky Chinese takeaway now and again, with a chicken chow mein, some sesame prawn toast and sweet and sour pork, I can tell you now, that Chinese food in China is *not* the same as your local Wok and Go. It is *very* different indeed. I like a bit of Peking duck with pancakes, love beef in black bean sauce, but, in China, you're more likely to get fish brains. Stewed.

One lunchtime, we went to a seafood buffet, where you picked your raw seafood from the selection laid out and then took it to your table, where there was a pot of boiling water in the middle. The idea was that you popped your raw seafood selection into the water, waited until it was cooked, then ate it. Happy it wasn't rice and watermelon, we all eagerly went to the buffet, yet the only thing I recognised was prawn. My *Mastermind* subject wouldn't be 'creatures of the sea', I get that, I'm no fisherman, but there was nothing else lying out in front of me that I had ever seen before. I went safe, I picked prawns.

Colin Haughton, a Manchester lad and our men's singles specialist, however, was a bit braver than I and went for a thing that was a cross between a prawn, a centipede and a lobster. It was weird looking. We were all marvelling at how brave Colin was at picking this thing to eat, *when it started moving and walked off his plate*! All ten of us, men included, screamed our heads off at this thing that was crawling on its legs and pincers on the table, all of us freaking out, when this Chinese waitress walked up, got two chopsticks, picked the thing up and plopped it into the boiling water, as casual as anything. Two minutes later, she picked it out of the pot and gave it to Colin to eat. Funnily enough, none of us were hungry after that.

There was one more food incident that will haunt me forever. It was an evening banquet, and we were all invited to attend to celebrate our visit. There is a custom in China that it is rude not to try the food you are given. I, and the rest of the squad, didn't know this at the time. We also didn't know that asking for rice at a formal banquet is a sign of rudeness, as it is considered 'peasant food'. These two facts would have been handy to have known before this special occasion, as events unfolded.

We arrived at the banquet room and were shown to our tables. We were tired from training and really didn't want to be there. All I wanted was some plain chicken and rice, then to leave and go back to the hotel. We had a translator on the tour; I think his name was 'Nigel'. It is normal for Chinese people to have a 'Western' name, and they just pick one out of a name book that they like the look of. So, Nigel, the Chinese translator, was next to me, and the speeches commenced. After what seemed like endless thank yous, it was time for the first course to be brought in. I looked at Nigel, who was in his early 20s and keen to impress his Chinese bosses, as translating on this tour was considered a very good job, and he didn't want to lose it. I said, 'So, Nigel, what's this then?'

He replied excitedly, 'Ah, first course is one of the region's specialities … pig's trotter!' And on cue, a fried pig's trotter was placed in front of me, a few hairs poking through the batter, and the fat seeping out. You could see it was still perfectly formed, just deep-fried. 'You know what, Nigel, I'm going to pass on this, thank you.' And I pushed the plate away, holding back the vomit I could feel at the back of my throat.

Nigel panicked at this point. 'No! No! No! You *must* try!! You *have* to!!' he said assertively under his breath to me. I replied, 'You can jog on if you think that is going near my mouth.' The stubbornness was now kicking in, and I wasn't in the mood to be told what to do by Nigel. 'Please!! I *beg* you, you *must eat*!' Nigel was nearly crying at this point, and it was at this point that it dawned on me there may be something more going on than Nigel being concerned for my eating. We didn't think we were in a James Bond film about to get poisoned by the pig's trotters, but Nigel, through his tears, explained the custom, and we all, in unison, smiled through gritted teeth, picked up the trotter and nibbled. Dear God, of all the parts of a pig, why the bloody trotter?

The plates were cleared, and Nigel had relaxed a little by this point. I said 'a little': he was still shaking with nerves. He was always sweating from being at the mercy of his employers. It seems they liked having authority over him, so much so that they didn't tell him how long he would be needed to work for, so poor Nigel didn't bring any spare clothes. Every night, he had to wash his clothes if he could, but we were five days into the tour, and he had given up washing in the sink, and the smell was beginning to be noticeable. We lent him clothes. He thought it was because we liked him, but really it was for our own benefit.

I reassured Nigel we would try to eat the next courses, but we were so hungry, I asked, 'Would it be possible to have some rice to keep us going and to refuel us for tomorrow's training, please Nigel?' Nigel turned white. He wasn't the most tanned anyway, but now he was almost transparent. 'What?!! No! No! No! No! No, you can't have rice!!' He was hyperventilating now, and any reassurance from me was not getting through to him. As Nigel was being useless for the task at hand, I looked at a waitress, and asked her for '*mi fan*' ('rice' in Mandarin), only to watch this young girl go white, panic and hyperventilate. I got the hint then. Rice was not going to be available.

The next course was being served. We had moved on from pig's trotter, and we were now served snake. My favourite. Especially deep-fried in batter with tonnes of garlic, which was how it was served on my plate. It was all curled up, and I was trying to guess what snake it was, but then I realised I didn't know many snakes other than python and boa constrictor, which seemed a bit weird if I was eating one of them. But then why would it be weird? I was in China. 'If it moves, it can be eaten' seems to be the motto out there. I nibbled at my portion of python, or whatever snake it was, and put it down straight after that. Nigel was back in the room.

Next up was a soup, chicken soup, we were told. This was a result. I like soup and I like chicken, so what could be the problem here? It seems the Chinese way of making chicken soup is to chop up a chicken and plonk it in a bowl of hot water. A waiter came over with a ladle to serve the portions out. All was going fine, until one of our team's portions on the ladle had the chicken head, all complete with beak, eyes and everything, pop up and stare at us. F**k's sake … the Chinese all cheered – apparently that's the best bit, so you can suck the brains out. I was under the impression that chickens weren't the smartest of birds, so I'm not sure if sucking the brains out of a chicken would achieve much or not. I got one of the chicken's feet. Thanks.

At this point, I was losing the will to live and signing up to the RSPCA. I was starving hungry yet traumatised about the food being served. I love meat, but I was on the edge of becoming a vegetarian, when a situation happened next that still blows my mind and, again, I will never forget. There was a big intro (in Mandarin), and then two waiters walked into the room, carrying a very large, silver platter adorned with food. *Everyone* in the room (apart from the English, as we had no idea what was going on), stood up and started to clap and cheer. The platter was placed in the middle of the room, and then there was even more cheering.

Nigel was looking very happy. I had to do it. I had to ask questions. 'Nigel, what is that, please? What is going on?' Nigel replied. 'Oh, this is very exciting! A happy day! We are going to eat tiger!' I honestly didn't think that banquet could get any worse than it was, but it just had. I stared at Nigel, stared at the platter, and instantly felt sick. 'Nigel, tigers are *an endangered species*!' I was trying to remain calm, but I was fuming inside. Nigel turned to me, looked me straight in the eyes, and said, 'Yes, that is why we eat now! Because soon … none left!' I walked out. F**k custom.

The last day of the tour was in Beijing and, as a treat we would go to TGIs or Planet Hollywood, and order as much Western food as possible. Burgers, chips and pasta dishes filled the tables in a pure, gluttonous heaven. We drank beer after beer, anything to forget the last three weeks of pain. Most of us were so tired and broken, and the last night was in a good hotel, so we were all looking forward to a good night's sleep, finally.

The next morning, we had to meet downstairs to get to the airport by 9am. We were all desperate to get home, so all of us were there on time, with our bags packed, but there was one missing person … the coach. This person also had our airport tax money, flight tickets, and all our important documents. By 9.15am, we rang the room, and still no answer; 9.30am, and one of the girls, Jill, went to knock on his hotel door. There was no answer. At this point, we were scared and getting nervous. We got the hotel staff to open the door, and there was the coach, stark bollock naked on the bed, passed out, with nothing packed, he was stinking of alcohol, vomit and piss. Somehow, he was woken up and his kit packed. I refused to look at him. The airport money had been gambled away at the casino, and we had to ask our Chinese chaperone to pay. It was so embarrassing. We got him on the flight home, where he proceeded to carry on drinking.

I am telling this story because, no matter how disgusted I was, and never wanted him as a coach on one of my trips again, coaches are people and are often forgotten about. The players are the talent, yes, but the coaches get a rough deal and can't always manage the stress. This coach had many personal issues, that was obvious, but to do what he did was unprofessional, and he was rightly sacked. He went to rehab and got himself out of badminton coaching and started a career. Then, when he was back healthy again, he got back into coaching. Unfortunately, he died in 2019.

Sofa to Savage: Missing Sydney and Unleashing the Beast

The Sydney Olympic Games in 2000 were two years away after I graduated from university. I thought, 'If I train three times a day, six days a week, I can give myself a good chance to get there.' So that is what I did. I trained three times a day, six days a week. The goal Australia – but I had to find a partner.

Gail: OMG – the politics of choosing a doubles partner! I would be at a tournament, and it was like a parade of who was playing well, to select your partner.

Steph: It's like you were back at the school disco.

Gail: Ha ha, yes! You want to get a good first choice, but don't want to get in there too early because someone else might become available that you might prefer. And then how many losses do you take? It's like being a manager in the Premier League. When do you dump them and go for someone else?

Steph: So, you might give them a couple of dances, but then move on to someone who you think has better moves?

Gail: Exactly.

I played with a guy called Ian Sullivan. We didn't have a connection like Nathan and me, but it was good enough for me to think we had a chance to get to Sydney. We knew we had to be in the top 16 of the world rankings. I worked part-time. I did bar work and waitressing on Bedford High Street in the evening to get extra cash for rent and food. If you were ever in The Litten Tree from 1998 to 2000, on a Friday or Saturday night, I probably served you.

When the final results came in, Ian and I finished 17th in the world rankings. The selectors drew a line through the ranking list to show who qualified and who didn't. It was a horrible feeling. Everyone got on the plane, and I stayed home. I watched the Sydney Olympic Games from my flat in Bedford, and it was like being punched in the stomach over and over again.

Steph: Not everyone will understand the brutality of that scenario, the Olympics being every four years. If someone has failed at a driving test or they've failed at an exam, they have a chance to retake it, maybe next month, next year.

Gail: My immediate thought was, 'What is the point of it all? Go and get a proper job.'

Steph: Most people, Gail, would have stopped at this point, but you are not most people.

I had two paths open to me at this stage. One of those paths being: 'Oh unlucky, Gail, you gave it a good go, but now it's time to do something else, because it is clear that something's not working for you in badminton.'

Well, if you are still reading this book, you'd be disappointed if that were the case. And most of you will know that this wasn't the end of my badminton. And this is me. I don't do 'giving up'. So, I went for option number two. I went into what can only be described as 'Beast Mode'. I became some sort of animal. It took watching the Sydney Olympics from my flat in Bedford for me to say to myself, 'F**k this. I'm going to push myself more, every single day from now on. I *will* go to the Olympic Games.'

I could feel it. It was so powerful. I can still feel it today. There was anger in there. There was ego. There was injustice. I knew I should've been at the Sydney Games. I knew I could still get better. By the time the Team GB badminton squad came back to the UK, I was a stone lighter, I was stronger and I was moving around the court like I was possessed. The selectors saw my improvements and said, 'We're going to put you with Simon Archer now.' Simon had just won the bronze medal at the Sydney Games with Jo Goode. Jo had announced she was pregnant and all the girls were trying to get the vacant spot. I was chosen.

I had to break the news to Ian that he was dumped; from now on, I'd be playing with Simon. I'd been selected to step in for Jo, and after the distractions of university life and the crushing disappointment of missing out on Sydney, this felt like my chance: an opportunity to finally make an impact in badminton.

Simon Archer and I began training together. Jo's shoes weren't easy ones to fill – she was one of England's greatest mixed doubles players. A two-time All England champion and an Olympic bronze medallist. She had pedigree, presence and a partnership with Simon built on years of success. Naturally, Simon wanted someone just like her. But that's where it started to get difficult … because I wasn't Jo.

In sport, I always say the worst thing you can do to an athlete is compare them to someone else or call them 'the next so-and-so'. It's impossible. Every athlete is different. We all have unique strengths and weaknesses, and no two players are ever the same.

Simon was dealing with injuries at the time, and he needed a strong, physical partner to carry him through tournaments, like Jo had. I was smaller, not as powerful from the back of the court, and my style suited a fully fit, in-form Simon. The pressure started building.

Simon, to his credit, was the kind of competitor you always wanted on your team – fiercely stubborn, wildly determined. Even with a knee that barely held together and a shoulder threatening to give out, he'd still believe he could beat the world number ones. But, for me, the chemistry just wasn't there. I craved connection, flow, rhythm … and it was missing.

Steph: It was courageous of you to articulate that, really it's all about the chemistry. Other people would have considered this partnership a gift and would have made it work.

Gail: For me, it's a feeling. It's a relationship.

Steph: Simon was the 'Prom King' because he was this established player, and you were picked to be 'Prom Queen'. For many, this would have been the dream.

Gail: I should have felt honoured, but, inside, I felt like I didn't want to be with this one. It was always Nathan, in my mind.

One day, I sat down with Finn Traerup-Hansen, our performance director at the time, and the words came out before I could stop them: 'I can't play with Simon anymore.' He looked at me like I was mad, throwing away a golden chance to partner England's top mixed doubles player. 'So, Gail, who would you like to play with, if not Simon?' he asked in his thick Danish accent. I didn't hesitate. 'Nathan. It's always been Nathan. I want to play with Nathan again.'

Finn didn't say much. Just looked at me, and I left his office. I felt lighter for having said it, but it was one of the most selfish decisions I ever had to make in my career. Now I was on my own. His silence said it all. This was mine to figure out.

That afternoon, Nathan and I were scheduled to play a training match. He'd been focusing on men's doubles but was keen to add mixed back into his schedule. We hadn't played together since 1995. But when we stepped on to the court, it was like no time had passed. We clicked instantly. We won comfortably. No one got close. I turned to him and said, 'This is a sign, you know that, right?'

We both knew a decision had to be made. With three years until the Athens 2004 Olympics, the qualification journey ahead would be long, demanding and strategic. We decided to team up. It wasn't a 'nice' decision. It hurt people. I let Simon down at a time when he needed someone in his corner. And Donna Kellogg, who had hoped to partner with Nathan, was left out, too. It was awful. And I hated how it all unfolded. But sometimes, in sport, you have to make the hard calls for your own path. It doesn't make me proud. It's the business end of sport, and it's not attractive.

After missing out on Sydney by a single place, I could finally see a clear shot at Athens, and I knew Nathan was the right partner to take that journey with me.

Steph: So, this time round, did you and Nathan talk to each other?

Gail: No, don't be silly. Only if we needed to.

Steph: I think I knew the answer to that question.

WELCOME TO MIXED TROUBLES

AS YOU may now have realised, I was most successful in the mixed doubles discipline in badminton. For those of you not in the know, this event is a specialist event. There are a lot of tactics involved, and it's not as simple as just putting a male and female on the court together. Oh no no no no no. Mixed doubles badminton is the most unpolitically correct event in sport. Hands down. To start with, you have a man and a woman on court together, which causes enough problems as it is, let alone playing against another man and woman. I mean, what could possibly go wrong? Let me enlighten you.

Mixed doubles badminton is the beautiful chaos where egos go to clash, feathers fly (literally), and gender politics are played out via smashes and passive-aggressive net shots. It's part Olympic discipline, part relationship therapy; a Netflix series waiting to happen.

First, let's talk *dynamics* on the court. You've got a male ego and a female ego, *and* two more of each standing on the other side of the net. That's four egos, one shuttlecock, and a whole lot of emotional tension disguised as tactical gameplay.

Now, in this weird but glorious world, the man gets to feel like 'The *Man*'. He's taller (maybe), stronger (hopefully), and gets to roam the back of the court, which is basically the badminton version of being handed Excalibur and told, 'Go. Smash stuff.' Because he's got the height, the reach and the delusional belief he's God's gift to sport. Let him have it.

The woman is at the net. Smaller, quicker, deadlier. Think ninja with a ponytail. This is where we stalk like cats, pounce like panthers, and maintain eye contact like we're in the final round of *RuPaul's Drag Race*. It's a game of psychological warfare in sports kit. Because at the net, only *one* woman gets to be queen. The other? Might as well jog on, love.

The tactics are simple. Man hits hard and with control. Woman stares down the guy across the net like he just tried to mansplain the offside rule. He smashes. She returns it with a flick of the wrist and a smirk that says, 'Is that all you got, big boy?'

Meanwhile, if your male partner (your so-called 'protector') dares to lift the shuttle cross-court to *their* guy, he'd better start apologising before the rally ends. Because you, the woman, now have to absorb a 400km/h meteor with your face while still looking classy. If that doesn't deserve a round of applause and a prosecco, I don't know what does.

Sometimes the men get so carried away with smashing each other (in a *badminton* sense, please) that they forget women are even on the court. All testosterone. It feels like they are comparing shuttle speed like it's a penis-measuring contest. Smash after smash, sweat flying everywhere, grunting like bulls about to charge. Meanwhile, the women are up at the net, giving each other the look: 'Shall we just pop to the bar while they finish this?'

But hey, we all have our moments. Sometimes I've tried to out-bitch a girl across the net, gone full 'Netzilla', only to end up looking like someone's overenthusiastic aunt playing at a wedding. Or I've been stuck at the back of the court like a lost child at IKEA.

In all seriousness, mixed doubles is an art form. A glorious, dysfunctional partnership where he smashes, I seduce, and we both try not to kill each other before the match ends. And the best bit? He does most of the running … and I still get a medal, half the prize money and all the media coverage

Now that's what I call a *win-win*.

Secret Racket Spank Code

Talk to each other? No, no, no. No, it is all in that 'spanking' of the racket on the arse in mixed doubles.

For those blissfully unaware of the fine art of being whacked with a badminton racket post-rally, allow me to introduce you to the Official Ranking System of the Racket Spank, a deeply complex language of frustration, encouragement, and mild-to-moderate assault.

Level 1: The 'Oops, My Bad' Tap

A hesitant, barely there tap that says, *'I think I meant to hit you, but now I'm questioning my life choices.'* Almost always accidental. Used when deciding between encouraging your partner and knowing you have to do something.

Level 2: The 'Eh, That Wasn't *Terrible*' Slap

A light flick of the wrist with a tinge of disappointment. This one is ambiguous. It could mean *'Nice try, unlucky'* or *'Do better, please'*. The verbal response that follows will determine whether you get a pat on the back or an upgrade to Level 3.

Level 3: The 'Listen, Mate ...' Thwack

Oh, now we're getting somewhere. This hit comes with a side of passive-aggression and regret. The message? *'Sort your s**t out, we are not here for cardio.'* This is an amber warning ... you are now on thin ice, and the ice is cracking.

Level 4: The 'Adrenaline-Fuelled Battle Cry' Smash

A highly flexible spank, deployed in both *'HELL YEAH'* and *'ABSOLUTELY NOT'* situations. You may receive this hit after scoring a sensational winner *or* after missing an absolute sitter. Either way, it's delivered with gusto and may leave a lingering sting (both emotionally and physically).

Level 5: The 'You Absolute Clown' Wallop

Reserved for the darkest moments of despair. This is a full-force, *'For f**k's sake, why are we even here?!'* slap of fury. The nuclear option. The *'I should've partnered with literally anyone else'* spank. Essentially, the badminton equivalent of a jockey frantically whipping a horse in the final stretch of the Grand National.

If you find yourself consistently at Level 5, congratulations – you are in a toxic badminton relationship. If you haven't reached Level 3 yet, you're either a badminton prodigy or haven't played mixed doubles long enough. Either way, may your racket spanks be firm, your patience be stronger and your apologies be swift.

Mr & Mrs

Everyone seemed to think Nathan and I were this perfectly synced, dreamy little badminton duo; easy-going, always in harmony, probably secretly dating, possibly telepathic. You know, the whole 'will they, won't they?' thing, like we were starring in the slowest romcom ever set in a sports hall.

Steph: Were you the Jayne Torvill and Christopher Dean of badminton? Did you really love him, but couldn't live with him?

Gail: No! He annoyed the hell out of me.

I get it. Mixed doubles *has* that energy – a man and a woman battling another man and woman with all the sweaty intimacy of a *Strictly Come Dancing* routine … only with more lunges and fewer sequins. We weren't dancers, *per se*, but we *did* spend a lot of time rhythmically flinging ourselves around each other. Celebrating wins, surviving losses, and navigating each other's quirks like an old married couple trying to build flatpack furniture.

But here's the truth: we were in sync *on* court – yes. Off court? We were chalk and cheese. Fire and ice. Caffeine and camomile. I'm intense, feisty, allergic to nonsense and emotionally invested in everything. Nathan is … not. He's laid-back to the point of horizontal. A man so allergic to the gym, I was amazed if I ever saw him in there. I lived for the circuit training; he lived for extra reps on the court. If there was a match happening, he was glued to it. Me? If I wasn't playing, I was out of the hall faster than a teenager escaping a family reunion.

We were complete opposites. But somehow, people found it fascinating. The BBC even did a *Mr & Mrs* style quiz with us before the Athens 2004 Olympics, clearly assuming we'd read each other's minds and finish each other's sentences like we were in a Richard Curtis film.

They asked us five questions about each other. You know, classic stuff like:

'When's Gail's/Nathan's birthday?'

'What's Gail's/Nathan's favourite film?'

'What's Gail's/Nathan's favourite food?'

I got five out of five. Smashed it. Gold medal in basic knowledge about my partner.

Nathan? He looked like someone had handed him a GCSE exam paper written in ancient Greek.

His answers, and I quote:

'I dunno.'

'Why would I know that?'

'Can I go now?'

It was like watching a bad date on national television. And yes, before you ask, he still doesn't know my birthday. (It's 23 July, Nathan. Yours is 30 May. You're welcome.) So, no, we weren't a couple. But we were a partnership. A messy, maddening, feisty, foot-stomping, medal-and-match-winning partnership. And I wouldn't have wanted to partner with anyone else.

Steph: Do you honestly think you could have succeeded without him?

Gail: No.

Steph: So, you had pinned your belief about your future success on him?

Gail: Yes, but I don't think I realised that at the time.

Steph: But he could not have won without you either.

Gail: Might just message him that.

We Need a Coach

As Nathan and I were total opposites, we needed a coach. Desperately. Think of our partnership like an electrical circuit: the spark was essential to make the magic happen. But with too much spark? Boom – meltdown. Not enough? Just a dull flicker. What we needed was someone to keep the voltage just right. Enter Mr Andy Wood. He was our official earthing wire. I'd rant at him with my frustrations about Nathan, and he'd calmly take it. Nathan would grumble about me, and Andy would absorb it like a badminton Buddha. He kept the emotional power grid stable, so we didn't short-circuit mid-match.

Andy Wood (Coach/Therapist)

I remember the first time I met Andy Wood. And to be totally honest ... I wasn't convinced straight away. I'd heard of him, of course – he'd coached players like Donna Kellogg, Simon Archer and Jo Goode – and when I stepped into their world, replacing Jo during her pregnancy after Sydney, Andy naturally became my coach too.

I wasn't the only one unsure. Andy often jokes that his first impression of me wasn't great either. It was mutual ambivalence that blossomed into something far more profound.

Andy didn't look or act like your traditional elite coach. He wore tennis gear, had long sun-kissed hair tied back with an Alice band, and a relaxed presence that made him look more at home at Wimbledon than at Milton Keynes. He resembled Richard Branson more than any hard-nosed badminton figure I'd encountered. He wasn't a shouty alpha. He wasn't Korean. He wasn't barking orders. And he hadn't stood on Olympic podiums like some of the other coaches around. He was, instead, from Derby. (Which, I'll admit, has produced its fair share of champions. Love you, Donna.)

I was suspicious. Who was this guy, asking me how I *felt* rather than telling me what I'd done wrong? Coaches weren't supposed to care like that, were they?

But that was Andy. He didn't need to impress you with credentials; he built his authority quietly through observation, patience and emotional intelligence. And, most crucially, he made me feel something that's almost taboo in elite sport: joy.

From the very beginning, Andy designed sessions around making me feel strong. Every day started with something I loved, something I was good at. Net multi-feeds. Hundreds of shuttles. Me … at the front of the court, dominating, crushing, queen of the net. That's how I began my sessions: confident, elevated, alive. And then, after my chest was out and my chin was up, he'd turn to me and ask, 'What would you like to work on now?'

I was floored when Andy first asked me this. Did he mean it? Was this a trap? Would someone jump out with a clipboard and shout, 'Wrong answer, Emms, back to the bench.' But no. Whatever I chose, be it footwork, defence, backhand clears, Andy would quietly and efficiently set the court up for it.

And here's the brilliance in that simplicity: by allowing me to begin in a place of confidence, Andy helped me approach my weaknesses without fear. I *wanted* to improve, not out of punishment, but because I felt capable. And when I felt capable, I became powerful. It took me years to realise what he was really doing. He was building a mindset. One I could carry long after he'd stepped away.

One of the most moving things I learned after retiring was this: Andy used to arrive at the training hall ten minutes before me, coffee in hand, and just … watch. Not in a weird or creepy way, though I did look at him quizzically when he told me this. He watched because he cared. He studied my posture, the manner in which I put my bag down, how I tied my shoes and whether I said hello to others. He could read my emotional state just by the way I walked in. And he adjusted everything accordingly. That's the kind of coach he was.

Andy was also fascinated by momentum in sport. Not just the physical flow, but the emotional and psychological shifts that define matches. He studied it, researched it and, along with co-author Alistair Higham, eventually wrote about it. *The Winning Edge in Badminton: Momentum, Match Flow and the Art of Competing* is a fantastic insight. I cannot recommend this book enough if you're a coach or someone who wants to understand how sport *works* beneath the surface.

But, most of all, Andy understood that athletes are, in many ways, just big kids. In the high-pressure world of elite performance, the parent-child dynamic is hardwired. We all just want to be the golden child. To be seen, valued and praised. I sought approval the only way I knew how: by trying to win, by proving people wrong, by fighting harder. That's how I earned love as a kid, and that's how I chased it in sport.

Andy helped me step out of that cycle. He treated me like an adult. He helped me become one. And when I eventually started to believe in myself, *really* believe, it wasn't because someone shouted at me to toughen up. It was because someone trusted me to take ownership.

Andy once said, 'My job is to make myself redundant.' And in many ways, he did. He helped me out of the worst of my impostor syndrome. The voices of former players, coaches, managers, critics, the ones who whispered, 'She's not that good' – they didn't go away completely, but they got quieter.

Andy's voice, his belief in me, got louder. He didn't just help me win matches. He helped me win *myself*. He simplified my chaos.

Gail. I hold the racket 'wrong', you know.

Steph: It's not wrong for you, Gail. Otherwise, you wouldn't be a champion.

Gail: That is a very good point, Steph. I guess it was the coach's opinion. That had an impact on me.

Steph: I think you have internalised a lot of this narrative: 'I don't know how I did it' and 'I'm not good enough'.

Gail: Yeah, but it sounds good for my talks, doesn't it? Because isn't that what everyone likes to hear?

Steph: Is it? Maybe that's what you want to hear? You've talked yourself into saying, 'I'm not naturally talented, I'm the wrong body shape, I am fat.' What else have you talked yourself into?

Gail: That Nathan has all the skill, and I just bring the feistiness.

Steph: But your reactions are amazing. The way you see the game is amazing. Your power is amazing.

Gail: I've been so compared to Nathan that I've accepted 'I'm not talented or skilful', because I'm not Nathan.

Steph: It's time for you to rewrite some of that narrative. You say you're not naturally talented. I would say, 'You have your own unique skill set, which is exceptional.' How do you feel about that?

Gail: I can see it now, but all the coaches I worked with (apart from Andy) only ever focused on what I was lacking in.

Steph: Do you need a tissue?

TRAINING

'I train not because I like training. I train because I like winning.'

US Olympic swimmer Nathan Adrian

Congratulations! You're Fat

Apparently, for a female athlete, the *ideal* body fat percentage is somewhere between 20 and 25 per cent. Sounds pretty reasonable, right? Nice and scientific. Except when your nutrition plan was designed in the 1990s by a bloke who probably thought carbs were the only energy source in food, and forgot that women have, you know … boobs. Hormones. Bodies that *aren't* carbon copies of their male team-mates.

This is where 'sports science' failed, for me.

I've got what we like to call 'The Emms Fat Gene'. Cheers, Dad. Sturdy, reliable, calorie-clinging stock. We are not a family built for sleek, effortless leanness. As I mentioned earlier, my poor dad battled with his weight most of his life, and I never had a hope of being described as 'skinny'. I was born big – 9lb 2oz of chunky baby fury. At 5ft 3 and a half (yes, the half matters), I am built solid. 'Well put together.' My calves could be mistaken for a rugby forward's. They've frightened small children.

When I was competing, I hovered around 64 to 65kg. Fit, powerful, fast. But then came the dreaded fat tests. Ah yes, the fat callipers. Every few months, we'd go through performance testing. Bleep test? Smashed it. Vertical jump test? Off the charts. Sprinting?

Strong. Power output? Great. But then … (cue ominous music), the skinfold test. This little torture ritual involved a sports scientist (usually male) grabbing folds of your skin and pinching them with a set of callipers. Triceps. Thighs. Stomach. Basically, anywhere you never want someone inspecting with measuring instruments unless you're dead and being embalmed.

Every time, without fail, I came back at around 26 or 27 per cent. Every. Single. Time. And every time, the message was the same: 'Gail, you're too fat. You need to be under 25 per cent. You're too heavy.'

Not once, *not once*, did anyone ask me about my genetics. My family history. The fact that weight struggles and eating disorders ran through my upbringing like some dark, dysfunctional family tradition. I'd been called fat my whole life, by people around me, by family, by coaches. And now, as a top-level elite athlete, I was being told the exact same thing by people with clipboards and degrees.

One coach, originally from Korea, very well respected and a very successful former player, once made me stand on some scales in front of the whole badminton squad, both the men's and women's players, and, as he looked at what my weight was, made a disgusted and disappointed face, saying, 'No, Gail. Too heavy! Too fat!' I was shamed in front of my peers. I was mortified, and, in my opinion, and hopefully the opinion of many others, this was *not* the way to encourage someone to lose weight. I will never forget the shame and embarrassment I felt.

One time, during a tournament stint in Malaysia, I became very unwell. Possibly food poisoning, maybe a tropical disease. I don't know. Whatever it was, I was *violently* ill. I managed to get myself to Korea (don't ask me how), to try and play the next tournament, only to end up in the hospital. They wanted to test me for viral meningitis with a needle in my spine. I screamed. Refused. All I wanted to do, was to go home.

All I could manage back in England was two weeks in bed. I barely ate. I managed water, I sweated a lot, and I was in misery. I finally staggered back to training, and guess what day it was? Yes, you've guessed it, 'Fat Test Day'. For the first time in my entire career, the callipers read 24.8 per cent. Cue the sports scientist beaming at me like I'd won the star prize. 'Gail! Congratulations! You did it. You're under 25 per cent! This is brilliant!'

I just stared at him. I was in the top five in the world rankings, fresh off a brush with death and *this* was the win he chose to celebrate? Not the medals. Not the world rankings. Not the fact that I could squat double my body weight and out-sprint half the team. No. The true achievement, apparently, was nearly starving myself into statistical acceptability.

I flipped. Fully lost it. I told him, in very clear terms, to take his callipers and shove them somewhere deeply personal. And from that moment on, I refused to be fat-tested ever again. Because here's the thing: I *was* strong; I *was* fast; I *was* a world-class athlete. But, apparently, one per cent of extra body fat was more important than all of that. That's what they chose to fixate on. Not performance. Not health. A *number*! And that's what makes me angry, still to this day. Because it's not just about me, it's about the system. The pressure. The obsession with leanness over strength. Over results. Over sanity.

Eating disorders are disproportionately prevalent among female professional athletes, with studies indicating that up to 45 per cent of elite female athletes in aesthetic or endurance sports exhibit disordered eating behaviours, especially in sports such as gymnastics, figure skating and distance running, where leanness is often equated with performance. The pressure from male coaches and athletic staff, who often emphasise weight loss or physical appearance under the guise of 'optimising performance', enhances this.

I also recall a kit sponsor giving me an outfit to wear on court that was more suited to a 12-year-old girl, so I could 'look sexy and appealing', which in turn would get me media attention. I was so conscious of my body in this outfit, I could barely play. It was horrendous.

All this so the female athletes could meet these arbitrary body fat percentages, which reinforces unhealthy standards. These dynamics, combined with the culture of perfectionism in elite sports, contribute significantly to the development and maintenance of eating disorders and *must* be handled better.

So yeah, congratulations, I was 'fat'. But I was also bloody *brilliant* and 'fat'.

Sports Psychology – What Is That?

Back in the early 2000s, sports psychology was just starting to creep its way into elite sport. And let me tell you, back then it had a reputation. 'Sports psychology? Oh, that's for the weirdos, isn't it?' The fragile ones. The headcases. The ones who couldn't handle pressure, the ones who bottled it at match point or forgot how to hit a shuttle when things got intense. That was the narrative.

Back then, going to see the sports psychologist was like walking around with a big sign on your back saying, 'I'm mentally weak.' You'd get side-eye in training. Sniggers. 'Oh, off to talk about your feelings, are you?' If you so much as mentioned the word 'psychologist', it was like announcing you were being sectioned. Banter turned into teasing. Weakness was blood in the water. So yeah, it took me years to even walk through that door.

Eventually, I met Kirsten Barnes, our assigned sports psych. A Canadian rower. Olympic gold medallist in Sydney 2000. Legit. I remember looking at her, trying to suss her out. Was she going to make me lie on a beanbag and hum my chakras into alignment?

But no, Kirsten wasn't like that. She didn't preach. She didn't come at me with breathing techniques named after forest animals. She listened. That's it. She just *listened.* And God, sometimes that was all I needed. See, I never had a problem *on* the court. You needed someone for match point? Stick me in. I thrived there. My serve was solid. My nerves were made of something between titanium and Red Bull. The chaos wasn't *on* the court; my chaos was *off* it.

Badminton was my sanctuary. My escape. My little island of order and purpose. But as soon as I stepped off that court, it was like walking straight into a soap opera I hadn't auditioned for. Family drama, friendship breakdowns, romantic disasters. The full *EastEnders* boxset. And that is what I needed the psychologist for;

not to fix my performance, but to clear the mental bin fire that came with everything outside of badminton.

To give you an example, let's go back to the Indonesian Open in 2004. I'm in the semi-finals. Big moment. I'm buzzing. I pick up the phone to call my then-boyfriend, just wanting a little love, a little 'you've got this, babe'-style motivation. What do I get? 'Yeah, babe ... this isn't working. You're away too much. I think it's over.' Cheers.

And this, *this* is the stuff nobody sees. The real life, real pain, real heartbreak that athletes are carrying under the smiley interviews and game faces. Everyone loves to judge from the sidelines: 'Oh, they're so lucky. They're living the dream.' Or even, 'They get paid loads – they should be perfect.' Let me tell you something: if an athlete's playing badly, it's very rarely just about the sport. It's usually because something else in their life is going up in flames.

Just like you at work, right? You're not smashing your spreadsheets after a break-up or giving your best sales pitch two days after a family row. But, somehow, athletes are expected to be robotic perfection 100 per cent of the time. That's why sports psychology matters. Not because we're broken. Not because we're weak. Because we're human.

Kirsten was brilliant in the lead-up to Athens 2004. And even better in the comedown after. I owe her so much. She helped me keep my head on straight when everything else was doing the conga off a cliff. And yes, for me, I think it made a difference that she was an athlete. She'd been in the arena. She'd felt the pressure. She *got it*. That doesn't mean every psychologist needs an Olympic medal to do their job, but, for me, it made all the difference.

So yeah, call us weirdos. Call us wackos. But seeing a sports psychologist might have been one of the most powerful things I ever did for my game. And for myself.

The Graft and Grind – Eat, Train, Sleep, Repeat

Let's get something straight: training to be an elite badminton player is not glamorous. It's not inspirational. It's not a bloody montage with *Rocky* soundtrack music in the background while I punch through pain barriers and then leap joyfully on to a podium. No. It's a job. A hard, repetitive, soul-sapping job that tests you to the limit.

Andy Allford, our assigned strength and conditioning coach, was the first person to make any part of training remotely fun. He got inventive – he created warm-ups with eye-tracking drills, shadow footwork that didn't feel like some medieval torture ritual. A rare sparkle in the grey.

Because the truth is training was 90 per cent of life for me back then. You don't just turn up and play five matches at a tournament and that's it. There were 12 tournaments a year, playing two events in each tournament. The training for these consisted of the 35 weeks still left, three sessions a day, five full days, one half-day, and one token 'rest day' that usually included guilt and stretches. Oh, and three or four weeks off if you were lucky enough to call lying down without seizing up 'holiday'.

I didn't hate training. But I didn't love it either. I liked the stuff I was good at, obviously: the sprints, weights and power sessions. I felt like a superhero in these sessions. But long runs and endurance work were not for me. I would have rather chewed my own racket. Still, I had to do it. No stamina meant no speed. There are no excuses.

Sports halls all seem to be painted that special institutional green, with a lovely top note smell of body odour and sweaty kit bags. The air in summer would be thick and unbreathable; you couldn't even open a door, or you'd mess with the flight of the shuttle. In winter, it would be an icebox. No heating system in the world can warm a sports hall. Welcome to elite sport!

And let's not sugarcoat it. Some days you wake up and your heels scream when they touch the floor, your ankles don't want to rotate, your back mutters, 'Not today, no way!', and your thighs have formed a resistance movement against standing. Cue the daily ritual of 'Which Body Part is Screwed Today?', a daily game show athletes know only too well. A new month would bring a new mystery pain. I'd play diclofenac roulette – how many will it take to feel human today? Two? Three? Four? Place your bets now …

Then there's the mental part. It's not just the physical burn, but the grinding, gnawing, brain-numbing monotony. You're around the same people. All. The. Time. Some of them make you laugh. Others you'd happily throw into a bin. The gossip, the passive-aggression, the politics, the fakeness. It's like *Mean Girls* in sports bras, but with shuttles flying at heads instead of insults being thrown. Shuttles slammed, drills sabotaged, eyes rolled so hard they leave orbit.

And the tears. Christ, we cried. Tears of frustration, exhaustion, anger, heartbreak, hormones, you name it. I swear the male coaches had no idea what to do. Couldn't hug, couldn't joke, couldn't do anything but stand there begging, 'Please let this end. Please don't cry on me.'

But quitting was never an option. Not a chance. I could be dying inside, legs wobbling, lungs on fire, but even if I was struggling in a circuit, I'd double down. I'm not stopping. I'm not folding. Not me. Pain was temporary; quitting is forever. Every single day, my brain whispered, 'You could give up.' And every single day, I whispered back, 'Not today.'

I possibly overtrained. It's weird to admit that. But when you're constantly panicking that someone's out there working harder than you, you do more. You push past the pain, past the logic, past the point where rest becomes recovery and turns into guilt. The voice in your head would be saying, 'She's catching you. Keep going.'

Then there's the injury guilt. Oh, the guilt. If you sit out with a niggle, you feel like a failure. But if you jump back in too early, suddenly you're faking it or attention-seeking. So, what do you do? You tape it, smile and limp in private. And crack on. Because the one thing more terrifying than pain is someone taking your place.

I lived for that end-of-the-day feeling … absolute bliss … in a masochistic, barely survived kind of way. The final shuttle strike. The last rep in the gym. The last plyometric jump. The last press-up. The final sprint that turns your lungs inside out. And then, collapse in a heap, a full-body splat on to the green rubber floor, leaving behind a very artistic, very sweaty Gail-shaped silhouette. Like a crime scene … but stickier.

Eventually, I'd peel myself off the floor, legs trembling, and start the slow stretch, half recovery, half survival, trying to coax the lactic acid to take a hike and glugging down electrolyte drinks like they were some magic elixir, praying they would undo the damage.

Then came the zombie shuffle to the physio room. If you were lucky, you'd land a massage slot. If not, it was the ice plunge pool, where your body screamed, but your brain said, 'This is recovery, apparently.'

No one sees the grind. No one sees the blood in your shoes, the silent sobs in the showers, the ache in your bones before you've even opened your eyes. They just see the medals. The podium. The polished final product.

But I see 'Day 476' of training. I see the moments I pushed beyond what I thought was possible. I see the sweat-stained mats, the broken shuttles, the scar tissue, the tears, the rage, the mental maths of how many anti-inflammatory tablets I've had today.

That's the real graft. That's what it takes.

Buxton Boot Camp

Some of the best training we ever did wasn't in a sports hall, or a gym, or under any sort of formal structure. It was in a freezing cottage in Buxton, Derbyshire, the highest, windiest, most sheep-populated place in England, where we basically tried to break ourselves *Rocky IV* style.

It was Andy Wood and Andy Allford's brainchild (because, of course it was), with Julian Robertson (a coach and former player) roped in for good measure. They decided what the Olympic squad players needed wasn't more circuits or shuttle drills, it was a 'rustic reset'. A mental bootcamp. Something to shake us out of the 'Groundhog Day' rhythm of regular training. And so, off we went to a cottage with a wood burner, no central heating, and a suspicious smell of damp and sheep poo permanently in the air.

From day one, it was crazy, in the best possible way.

The driveway alone was a beast. A vertical incline that doubled as our hill sprint track. Beyond the cottage were endless fields of sheep.

Lots of them. Which, naturally, became our first unofficial fitness test: 'Who will be first to catch a sheep?'

Spoiler alert here, but sheep are shockingly fast. You think you're fit until you're outpaced, out-dodged and outmanoeuvred by a woolly thing. After about 20 minutes of flailing arms and shouted encouragement, we downgraded the challenge to 'try to touch a sheep'. Still no luck. Final score: Sheep 1, Badminton players 0.

Next up, the quarries. We climbed boulders, chucked rocks like wannabe gladiators. We flipped massive tyres abandoned by a huge tractor in the farmer's yard and dunked ourselves in freezing brooks for recovery sessions, which mostly just meant we screamed like toddlers in a cold paddling pool.

One of my absolute favourite memories, though, was watching Nathan and Anthony Clark *really* struggle to flip this enormous tyre – both of them huffing and puffing, legs shaking, egos bruised, when Ed (my then-boyfriend, later father of my kids, who I will mention more about later) casually wandered over, nudged it with what looked like one finger and flipped it clean over. Clarky's face was pure disbelief. Iconic.

We even went cycling. It should've been a peaceful, but intense, countryside ride. It wasn't. We had clunky hire bikes, legs full of lactic acid and a gale-force headwind straight out of a nature documentary. Donna Kellogg, normally a brilliant cyclist, hit the wall so hard I thought I was going to have to carry her back. Instead, I channelled Bear Grylls, fed her wild blackberries off roadside bushes and prayed they weren't poisonous. They weren't (thank God), and she lives to tell the tale, though we did cry a bit on the return leg.

We only got to do this magical madness three times. The badminton calendar didn't leave much room for this creative training. If we were lucky, we'd squeeze in a six-week block of training in an Olympic year, like before Beijing 2008. Even then, Nathan was injured and living on some bizarre soup-only diet, walking around like a Victorian ghost with a protein deficiency.

But this was good training. The memorable stuff. The stuff that reminded us why we loved sport in the first place. Because elite training gets robotic. Clinical. All very Dolph Lundgren in his high-tech lab in *Rocky IV.* You forget sometimes that what really makes a champion isn't the heart monitor or the protein shake, it's the fire. The Sylvester Stallone stuff. Chasing sheep in freezing wind. Sled pushing through snow. Being together, moaning, laughing and crying your way through it.

We even took that energy to the indoor ski slope at Milton Keynes once. At 6.30am one morning, we were snow sprinters, all before the public came in to ski. Yes, we ran up the slope that people paid to ski down. It was brutal. The kind of cold that makes your lungs feel like they're being wrung out like a dishcloth. But it shook us awake. Got us out of the sports hall and stopped us from going completely mad.

Because sometimes it's not your legs that give out, it's your mind. You start to hate the green walls, the smell of sweat-soaked kit, the same damn rally drills. Even the lovely Teardrop Lake by the National Badminton Centre lost its sparkle when you'd run around it for the 400th time. I'd sneak off to train at a David Lloyd gym sometimes. Same exercises. Just new walls, different sweat smell. That's enough to spark the motivation again.

And that's what Buxton Bootcamp did. It reminded us we were humans first, athletes second. Gave us cold feet, bruised egos and the best laughs we'd had in months. Worth every sheep-shaped humiliation.

PRESSURE, PRIDE AND THE PODIUM

Manchester Commonwealth Games, 2002

The 2002 Manchester Commonwealth Games was my first taste of a major multi-sport event, and, oh, what a welcome it was. Held in the middle of a so-called British summer (July and August), it was cold, wet and miserable enough to make even the University of Manchester's grim grey accommodation look somehow grimmer. The Australian athletes looked around, drenched and baffled, as if to ask, 'This is your *summer*?'

I was 25 at the time, and selected to play in the team event, the mixed doubles with Nathan and the ladies' doubles with Jo Goode. The goal for me was simple. Three gold medals. That was the plan. England were favourites for the team event, and I would be No.1 seed in both the doubles events. England, and myself, were expected to clean up. I even said it out loud. Big mistake.

Lesson one: never tempt fate by announcing your greatness before it's actually achieved. The result was just one gold and one bronze, along with a giant serving of humble pie. The sting wasn't just internal. It was walking into the arena and seeing all those handmade banners of 'Go Gail!' and 'Bedford's Finest!' and knowing they wouldn't be out waving in the finals. I felt like I'd let everyone down, including myself.

Sure, two medals at a Commonwealth Games are nothing to sniff at, but when the expectation is gold across the board, a bronze feels like a consolation prize in a game you were meant to dominate. From that moment on, I vowed never again to talk about what I expect from myself. Not even to close friends. Arrogance had done me no favours.

The matches were held at Bolton Arena, which was a good 45-minute drive from our accommodation (not that anyone ever talks about the glamour of logistics). Badminton is on *every single day* at the Commonwealth Games. Five disciplines plus a team event means doubles players like me are constantly on the court. My days started at 8am and ended sometime past midnight, after returning to base, sorting laundry, trying to eat something vaguely nutritious, then getting a few precious hours of sleep.

The kit issue was almost laughable. We were given just three shirts and three skirts, and as there was no time to breathe, there was definitely not time to dry anything. Playing both mixed and ladies' doubles meant I was constantly running out of clean kit. I remember crouching over a washing machine at 2am, waiting for it to finish so I could somehow dry it with my hairdryer as I'd be wearing it again at 9am. At one point, I just cried, not from disappointment this time, but from sheer exhaustion.

And while we're on it, dear tournament schedulers, *why* put doubles players on first thing in the morning *and* last thing at night? With travel, recovery and food all somehow meant to happen in between? Where is the common sense? *Where*?!

But hey, you're not allowed to moan, right? Athletes are supposed to smile, win and move on. But the truth is that it's often a logistical and emotional assault course just to survive the day. Manchester 2002 taught me a lot. It taught me about expectation, humility, exhaustion and the unglamorous reality of elite sport.

Steph: So, how would you describe your mindset at this point in your career, training up to Athens Olympic Games 2004?

Gail: I still felt like a bit of a newbie, even though coming into the Olympic programme I was considered old, aged 27. I still felt like I had to prove myself. I never felt truly comfortable at this stage, but I was enjoying being at the top.

Steph: Had you lost those impostor feelings? Were you finally feeling confident at this point?

Gail: No, I was still feeling a bit lucky to be with Nathan. I was still carrying the weight of being in that partnership and having to prove to everyone that I was good enough to be there.

Olympic Games 2004, Athens, Greece

I was 27 years old, had been holding a badminton racket since I was four, and here I was, walking around the Olympic Village, as an Olympian. It sounds majestic, doesn't it? The culmination of years of sacrifice, training and more sacrifice. The first person I stood next to on the shuttle bus was only Australian swimming legend Ian Thorpe, all broad shoulders and quiet confidence. I remember just staring up at him, thinking, 'Yeah, this is *actually* happening. I'm really here.' I will admit, I cried big tears. I thought of all the people that had believed in me and got me to this point.

Then we got to the accommodation. Let's just say the fairy tale took a sharp turn. The apartments, which were nestled up in the mountains (lovely for keeping the 37°C Greek heat at bay), were bare. There was a bed, and that was it. No table, no chair, no duvet. I foolishly thought, 'No duvet? That's fine, it's boiling.' That night, my teeth were chattering and I was wrapped in my tracksuit and wearing every layer I'd packed. I realised my British optimism had met its match. It got very cold at night.

Thankfully, the British Olympic Association (BOA) came to the rescue with a chair, a table and the essentials: a kettle, some proper English teabags, so we could at least sit on a chair rather than a hard floor, sipping a cuppa. We pinched milk from the canteen and felt, for a moment, vaguely civilised. But the truth was: Athens had run out of money. Wires dangled from the ceiling, toilets didn't flush properly, and showers … well, let's just say they had 'character'. I'm sure people thought we were living in luxury five-star villas, but the reality was closer to student digs meets construction site.

Our flat was a lively mix, the girls on one side, the boys on the other. And joining us were Welsh weightlifter Michaela Breeze and

17-year-old boxing wonderkid Amir Khan. Amir was lovely, quiet and very much on his own. I took it upon myself to make him cups of tea whenever he looked like he needed a dose of home. The press was already swarming him, but underneath it all, he was still just a teenage lad thrown into the deep end of international sport. I felt oddly protective.

My family, Mum, Dad and my little brother Adam, made the pilgrimage out to Athens. Lisa had just joined Thames Valley Police and couldn't come, but the others made it work, somehow. The only accommodation they could find was on an island (of course), and to get to the venue, the Goudi Olympic Hall, they had to get a boat and two buses. It took them two hours *each way*. The last ferry back was at 5pm, so there was a lot of frantic dashing and even more money spent. But they weren't going to miss it. Not for anything.

Our coaching dream team of Andy Wood, the legendary Indonesian former badminton player and Olympic gold medallist Rexy Mainaky, and Julian Robertson had the team ready to go. First round, Nathan and I were drawn against Germany's Björn Siegemund and Nicol Pitro, a decent European pair, with Nicol being a crafty leftie and Björn packing a punch with his smash. A good opening match on paper. In reality, we went 0-7 down in the first game. Cue slight panic from those supporting Team GB. You could practically hear the gasps from the coaches' bench and see the silent screaming inside their heads. And yes, I've watched the replay, heard the commentary, it's not pretty. But we rallied. Won 15-12, 15-6. See? Totally under control.

On to the quarter-finals, and the part where it gets serious: bring on China. Chen Qiqiu and Zhao Tingting were our opponents, and two names you don't forget, especially when you've had to battle them on the biggest stage. Tingting was an absolute unit, her thighs looked genetically engineered to intimidate. If ever I felt bad about not fitting into skinny jeans, I thought of Tingting and found comfort. Qiqiu was left-handed, wiry, sharp and a thinker. Tingting was a destroyer. The trick with these Chinese pairs is always psychological warfare. If we could rattle Qiqiu, get Tingting nagging him mid-match (which she did with impressive volume), we'd have a chance. The male/female dynamic in mixed doubles is a thin line. We took the first game 15-8. Solid. I was in the zone. Qiqiu hadn't figured me out and Tingting hadn't fully warmed up. And then she did. She stormed the net, flipped the dynamic and suddenly Qiqiu was stepping back and Tingting was hammering Nathan. He looked rattled.

As I have mentioned before, in mixed, the job of the man is simple: make the opposing woman miserable. If she's smiling, something's gone very wrong. Tingting was grinning. I turned to Nathan and said, 'What the hell are you doing?! *Hit it on Qiqiu*!'

It was desperate. I was begging Nathan to stop playing like a gentleman. Tingting was having the time of her life, and I was over it. Angry Emms took the court, and I channelled my inner Tingting, lots of grit, grump and a better pout. My technique wasn't as good, but my attitude was unmatched. I knew I had the better man. We clawed back to 14-14 and won the second game 17-15. Game and match to us. The screams of relief. Semi-final secured. One of four pairs left battling for three medals. Take that, tree-trunk thighs.

At the press conference, the journalists, who clearly hadn't planned to cover badminton, were equal parts confused and fascinated. One asked about the shift in momentum, about me 'taking over' the match. I said, with a grin, 'Yeah, I just had to whip Nathan a bit harder in the second game.' Oops. I could see the headlines forming …

Suddenly, everyone was curious about mixed doubles. Was it like tennis mixed doubles? No. It was so much more. A partnership. A connection. A conversation played out with rackets and footwork. I loved hearing everyone in the Team GB camp talk about it. Back in the UK, people started to notice us. *The Times*, *The Telegraph*, *The Sun* and more were all reporting on this odd couple, a short blonde and a tall guy in a headband, that were storming through the rounds. 'Do Brits even play badminton?' they asked. 'Isn't that just for the Chinese? Or something you do in a village hall maybe? Or over a washing line in your back garden?' Welcome to the Olympic Games.

Semi-Finals, Mixed Doubles

We had made it exactly as far as we were expected to, into the semi-finals of the Olympic Games. Our next opponents were scheduled to be the No.1 seeds: Kim Dong Moon and Ra Kyung Min of South Korea. Let me just pause here to explain who they were. Legends. Truly. The kind of players who made the rest of us feel like we were just borrowing the court. Coming into Athens, they hadn't lost a single match in three years. Not one. They were the total package: flair, precision, calm under pressure, raw power, and the kind of synergy that made other mixed doubles pairs look like they were still on their first date. In every other badminton event in Athens, the medals felt up for grabs. But in mixed doubles? It was unanimous: Kim and Ra have got this. It wasn't even a debate.

After our quarter-final win, I walked into our Team GB block in the Olympic Village, buzzing, and popped into the HQ offices. We'd just been on the TVs, and the staff there were full of congratulations. Nathan had gone up to the flat, but I lingered to chat and bask in the moment a bit. Then I glanced up at the TV screen. Badminton was still on, and they were showing the other quarter-final, between Kim and Ra, and Denmark's Jonas Rasmussen and Rikke Olsen.

I pointed to the screen. 'Whoever wins this match, *that's* who we play,' I said. I gave the staff the full rundown on Kim and Ra, their dominance, their record, and how Nathan and I were fully expecting to be in the bronze medal match. They nodded along. It all sounded inevitable.

Then something happened. To this day, I don't know what. But sport, beautiful, ridiculous, unpredictable sport, decided to throw us a twist.

I watched Kim Dong Moon unravel, right there on screen. There's no nice way to put it, he completely lost it. The man couldn't hit a clean shot. Every error added fuel to the Danes' belief. You could see it in their eyes: 'We can actually do this!' Ra tried her best to hold them together; you could feel her willing the partnership to click, to find some magic. But it wasn't happening. The Danes stole the first game, 17-14.

The room went quiet. The same people I'd just given a rousing monologue about Korean badminton royalty were now giving me sceptical glances, like I'd made it all up. I stayed calm. 'Just wait,' I said. 'They'll bounce back. They always do.'

We waited. Watched.

And it only got worse for the South Koreans.

Kim missed an easy shuttle, just air-sliced it. Rikke Olsen, whose serve had been shaky all year and could only flick serve (everyone knew this), was bamboozling him. Kim froze. I swear, on that day, my mum could have beaten him. Ra was helpless. She did everything she could, but when your partner falls apart, there's only so much one person can do. The Danes surged ahead in the second game. Their supporters were going wild.

I messaged Nathan. 'Are you watching this?' One word reply: 'Yep.'

Jan Paterson from the BOA noticed the shift in my energy. Something had changed, and she could see it. Nathan and I had *never* lost to Jonas and Rikke. We had played them six times. Won all six. And suddenly, it wasn't Kim and Ra standing between us and the Olympic final. It was a pair we knew, a pair we knew how to beat.

I couldn't take my eyes off the screen. The Koreans' coaching bench was in meltdown. Heads in hands. The fairy tale ending to Ra's Olympic career was crumbling in front of them. The Danes closed it out, 15-8.

They had beaten the unbeatable.

Right then, I knew. *We're in the Olympic final.* I stood up slowly, walked out of the Team GB HQ, and sat on the steps outside. Jan followed me and sat beside me. We didn't speak for about 20 minutes. No words needed. She knew. I knew.

The favourites, the gold medal certainties were *out*. And instead of facing the pair we had *never* beaten, we would play the pair we had *never lost to*. The odds had flipped. The door was wide open. Destiny, as dramatic as it sounds, was in our hands. (Wow, that sounds like a *Star Wars* line.)

That night, for the first time in months, I slept okay.

Semi-final day. Time to finish the job. The Goudi Arena buzzed with tension. This was no ordinary match. You could feel the shift in pressure: the Danes hadn't expected to be here either, but now they were on a roll, full of belief after knocking out the world No.1s. They had nothing to lose, and that's dangerous.

The first game was intense, but Nathan and I stayed composed and stuck to our game plan. Our movement was sharp, communication was tight and Nathan was firing on all cylinders. We won the opener 15-6. A dream start. But in badminton, momentum is fragile.

In the second game, the Danes came out like different players, faster, braver, relentless. Rikke stepped up and Jonas was hammering his smashes. We lost our rhythm. Suddenly, we were scrambling. Everything got harder, and even the confidence in our tactics started to wobble, but we held on to win it 15-12. A series of exchanges at the net from Jonas and me, and he hit into the net. That was it. We were *Olympic finalists*! Guaranteed a medal. Guaranteed! That word was going round and round in my head. I have a medal no matter what.

The Final, Mixed Doubles, 19 August 2004

Our opponents in the Olympic final would be the formidable Chinese duo Zhang Jun and Gao Ling, the reigning Olympic champions. Their semi-final had been a demolition job. They swept aside the Danish pair Jens Eriksen and Mette Schjoldager with brutal efficiency: 15-9, 15-5. It wasn't even close. The Chinese bulldozed them.

Up to that point, Zhang and Gao had only dropped a total of 25 points across the entire tournament. Let that sink in. Across six matches, their aggregate score was 90-25. That level of dominance is almost unheard of. As the No.2 seeds, they were playing near-flawless badminton, and with the top-seeded Koreans shockingly eliminated in the quarter-finals, they were even more confident. Everything was going their way.

Meanwhile, the bronze medal match was an all-Danish affair. Eriksen and Schjoldager bounced back strongly, defeating Jonas Rasmussen and Rikke Olsen 15-5, 15-5. But spare a moment for Rikke Olsen. She was one of Europe's finest doubles players –

consistent, fierce and respected. Athens was her third Olympic Games … and her third fourth-place finish.

In Atlanta 1996, she finished fourth in women's doubles with Helene Kirkegaard.

In Sydney 2000, she finished fourth in mixed doubles with Michael Søgaard.

And in Athens 2004, her final Olympics, another fourth place, this time with Jonas Rasmussen.

Three Olympic Games. Three bronze medal matches. Three fourth-place finishes.

It was a heartbreaking end to an extraordinary career.

The match was scheduled for late afternoon, around 5pm, I think. We'd had the whole day to wait. I wandered around the Olympic Village, trying to keep my nerves at bay. At one point, I popped into the little shop that sold English newspapers. There it was. Front page of the *Daily Express*: 'Can Gail win gold for GB today?' Oh, bloody hell.

John Dennis, our physio, had been assigned to basically babysit me, mainly to keep me from having a meltdown. I must have asked him the time every five minutes. He ended up walking me around the village like a dog. Adrenaline was already flooding my system.

I honestly don't think I'd had a single night of proper sleep during the Games without the help of sleeping tablets. It's hard to explain the state you're in. Your body is exhausted and aching from every match, yet your brain won't stop. It replays every point: the good ones, the disasters, the 'what ifs'. You imagine the crowd, the pressure, the plays, the moments. Over and over.

Eventually, it was time to head to the stadium. Time to warm up. We waited backstage and were then called over by the officials to get ready to go into the arena. There was this loud noise from the stands. I peeked out, wondering what on earth was going on. Now, I've played in plenty of noisy, packed venues in Asia, but this was Athens. And what I saw is something I'll never forget: the stadium was full of British fans, waving Union Jacks and chanting, 'Gail and Nathan's Barmy Army!' There were beach balls, flags, even a

Union Jack lilo being passed around the stands, which were *full* of spectators.

Later, I found out that two flights from the UK had landed that day, and loads of passengers had come straight to the badminton when they heard we were in the final. This was back when real fans could still get tickets, not just corporate sponsors and a ballot system. Then we were announced inside the stadium. The roar when our names were called out gave me goosebumps. Walking into the arena, I couldn't help but grin. I think I even laughed. You can see it on the TV footage, I actually mouthed, '*Oh my f***ing God*!'

Let's talk about the first game. Actually, I don't want to talk about it, but I will. Zhang Jun came out in that first game like he'd been injected with some kind of turbocharged steroid serum. Honestly, the Hulk would've nodded in admiration. I couldn't see the shuttle; that's how hard he was hitting it. And sure, I was nervous, I was shaking. But I'd made it to the Olympic final by returning smashes like those, so how on earth was Zhang hitting it *that* much harder than anyone else on the planet?

They were reigning Olympic champions for a reason. They hit us with everything.

At one point, Nathan turned to me and shouted, 'What the f**k is wrong? Just hit it back!'

Oh right, *of course*, silly me, I thought I'd try out some reverse badminton in the Olympic final, you absolute knob. Literally, the next point, Zhang launched a smash straight through Nathan like his racket wasn't even there. I just looked at him and said, 'See? Not so f**king easy, is it?'

We were getting destroyed. The Barmy Army fell silent. There was an awkward hush. A few celebratory whoops from Chinese fans. And every time I missed another smash and Gao Ling barely had to break a sweat, the umpire seemed to slap on another point for fun.

All I could think was, 'This is mortifying. Get me off this court. Now!'

We lost the first game 15-1. It looked like we were just another warm-up act for the reigning champions. During the changeover,

Andy Wood came on to give us a talk. To this day, I still have no clue what he said. He has told me since, but I was deep in moody-teenager Emms mode and completely blanked it. In my head, I was saying, 'Well, at least it can't get any worse, eh?'

I walked back on to the court with one thought. 'I don't give a flying f**k anymore.' I was that ashamed of how I was playing. I even told myself, 'May as well close your eyes trying to return this smash; only way you have a chance.'

And so, I did. No joke. Zhang launched another monster smash, and as he jumped and shouted his war cry, I crouched down, shut my eyes … and swung. It hit the sweet spot in the middle of the strings and I nailed it. The shuttle shot back past Gao Ling, landed at Zhang's feet. Winner.

The Chinese looked genuinely puzzled. I did the Emms Strut. The crowd erupted.

And just like that, we were back.

Our attitude shifted. We played like we had nothing to lose. Suddenly, we were 6-1 up. Then 10-6. Zhang was rattled. Then came a moment I'll never forget: Zhang hit a shot clearly long, no question about it. The line judge called it out and then just changed their mind. Just like that. The umpire couldn't overrule. Nathan protested, but it was pointless. They got the serve back and clawed it to 8 against our 10.

Still, we dug in. We fought for every point, and when we finally got to set point, 14-10, it felt like a dream. Of course, they weren't done. They closed it to 14-12. My heart was thumping. Then, by some miracle, they sent a return long and we levelled the match 1-1. Game on.

The final set was the most intense, exhausting and emotional game of my life. They jumped out to a 3-0 lead. We fought back and took the lead, 5-3, then 7-3. We even got a line call in our favour (finally). The Chinese started time-wasting, every little trick in the book. I swear I aged five years during that set. They came back again, but we led 8-6 when we switched ends. They levelled at 8-8 but we pushed to 11-8. The crowd was behind us. We were flying. We were winning and closing in on the Olympic title.

But nothing comes easy in an Olympic final.

Zhang and Gao clawed it back. Reached match point at 14-11. Nathan saved it – absolutely ice-cold. Then it was 14-12. We still had a chance.

But, on the next serve, it was over. One shot. One mistake. And the gold was gone.

We had made history as the first non-Asian pair to reach the Olympic mixed doubles final since badminton was introduced in 1992. But in that moment, history didn't mean much. We were so close.

And the worst part? The final point was my mistake. A relatively simple smash at the net, and I pulled it too far down. The shuttle clipped the top of the net and dropped back on to our side. I take full responsibility. I always have.

In that final, I felt like the impostor. Nathan had already been in a world final. Zhang and Gao were Olympic champions. For me, though, it was my first major final. I honestly believe that if I'd had a stronger mindset in that match, if I'd truly believed I belonged there, we might've won. That's the margin at the very top of sport. It's not just about fitness, or power, or skill. It's a belief. And in that final, for just a little too long ... I didn't have enough.

I walked off the court and picked up my racket bag. You're immediately ushered towards the media. As I left, the Chinese pair were still celebrating, hugging, shouting, overwhelmed with joy. I felt ... nothing. Just numb. The kind of numb where you can feel the heat rising to your eyes, the tears threatening to spill, but stuck somewhere behind a wall of disbelief.

As we walked past the stands, Nathan stopped to hug his daughter Neve and his parents, John and June. My family was too far away. I couldn't even look for them properly, I was being pulled towards the media zone. I could already see the BBC interviewer waving at me, gesturing wildly to hurry over. I started walking slowly in his direction, but I didn't want to be alone. I wanted Nathan. I didn't want to talk to anyone without him next to me. I kept saying, 'Just wait. One minute. Please.'

What I didn't realise was that the cameras were already rolling. It was live. I completely ignored the frantic arm-flapping from the production crew. Finally, Nathan appeared, walking over just in time. The look of sheer relief on the interviewer's face was priceless. The TV light flicked on and, just like that, we were live across the country.

I started to cry. Not the quiet, dignified kind. The kind where your voice catches in your throat and your eyes well up before you can stop them. I apologised. I thanked everyone watching back home for their support. Later, we found out more than six million people had tuned in to watch our final.

Then came the medal ceremony. I went back to the changing rooms to get out of my sweat-soaked kit and into the official podium tracksuit. But once I was out of sight, the dam broke. I sobbed. Not just a few tears, it was full-body sobs that shook me. I was desperate to go back in time, desperate to fix it and win. One of the venue staff came in, telling me to hurry up. I caught a glimpse of myself in the mirror, eyes red and swollen, face blotchy, a total mess, and realised it was time to walk out and face the world.

I joined Nathan in the line-up. The ceremony music began to play. He took one look at me and said gently but firmly, 'No tears up there, okay? Be proud.' I swallowed hard, forcing the tears back down, and nodded.

Then it was our turn.

'Gail Emms and Nathan Robertson, Great Britain!'

The roar from the crowd was deafening. There were more cheers for us than for anyone else. It felt like a wall of sound holding me up. Laurel wreaths were placed on our heads. Nathan, trying to lighten the mood, whispered, 'I look like Jesus.' Honestly, he kind of did.

There were endless photos. So many hugs and kisses from family, friends, team-mates and fans. And then we returned to our team, a tight unit of maybe ten people: coaches, physios, psychologists, nutritionists, doctors. The whole support crew that had helped us reach that point. Everyone said the usual things. 'Unlucky.' 'You did great.' I couldn't hold it in anymore. I just blurted out, '*I want gold.*'

Standing on the second step of that podium burned. I didn't want silver. I didn't want to smile politely while the Chinese stood above us. I wanted that top spot. I *needed* it. There was a fire in me, and I knew I hadn't hit my ceiling. I hadn't peaked. This wasn't the end. It was just the beginning. And next time, I'd be the one standing at the top. I made a promise to myself right then: I would never again settle for second place. And I would never again feel 'honoured' just to share a court with anyone. I belonged there. I had earned it.

Steph: I can't imagine how it must have felt to have been the player that lost the match at that crucial point, and I sense you feel it was your self-doubt that let you down ... but surely you still deserved to celebrate a silver medal?

THE CELEBRATIONS

THE WEEK and a half after the final was a blur of hangovers, partying and chasing the next drink. I oscillated between drunk and hungover on a loop. The worst part was stumbling back into the Olympic Village at ridiculous hours, usually after a long night at Heineken House, the Dutch hangout that quickly became *the* place to be, and heading straight for the canteen McDonald's, hoping a sausage and egg McMuffin might sober me up a bit.

One morning, around 5am, I shuffled in, barely upright, clutching my tray with a hash brown and breakfast sandwich, trying to act normal. As I looked for a table, I spotted a group of Team GB athletes already eating. I thought, 'Perfect! My people!' So, I wandered over, ready to crash their breakfast. Except as I got closer, reeking of booze, I realised who the group was. It was the 'Awesome Foursome' rowers: Matthew Pinsent, Steve Williams, James Cracknell and Ed Coode. They were literally hours away from competing for Olympic gold. Too late to back out, I attempted a subtle escape, saying, 'Gooooood luck! You've got this!' while trying to slink away unnoticed. They were not impressed. Still, they went on to win gold, so maybe my drunken blessing worked? I'll take it.

The closing ceremony came around, and word spread quickly about the legendary *Sports Illustrated* party happening later that night. Apparently, it was the ultimate way to cap off the Games. Naturally, the badminton squad decided we had to be there. We managed to get the address, jumped in taxis and headed off on a 45-minute ride into the unknown. The cabs dropped us at the end of a long, dusty driveway, shouted something vague and sped off. Helpful. I was painfully aware that I'd spent far too much money by this point and was teetering on financial fumes. The thought of a pricey nightclub was mildly terrifying. But we walked down the drive anyway, half-laughing, half panicking. At the end, there was a building. We showed our athlete accreditations at the entrance, all nervous smiles and hopeful eyes. They waved us in. So far, so good.

As we stepped through the next door, I saw the bar and made a beeline for it. Turning to the girls, I said, 'I'll get the first round. How about vodka shots and we share a Red Bull?' – tactical thinking to stretch the budget. The bartender came over, and I asked her the damage. She smiled, paused, then said, 'Everything is free here.' I laughed. 'Even champagne?' 'Even champagne.'

Six glasses, please.

We each took a glass and turned to look around, and for five full minutes, none of us spoke. We just stared. Two swimming pools, a beach deck, a seafood buffet, a BBQ, a DJ spinning tracks … and, weirdly, Evander Holyfield on the dance floor. Everyone looked like they belonged on a magazine cover. Everyone was glowing, relaxed and euphoric. And everything was free. Honestly, if Carlsberg did Olympic afterparties, this would be it. It was the perfect, surreal way to end my first Olympics.

I'm not going to pretend the next morning was easy. Packing for the flight home while hungover is not something I'd recommend. But, as Olympic medallists, Nathan and I were upgraded to business class on the British Airways flight. So naturally … we kept on drinking.

Landing at Heathrow was another level. Photographers, fans, flags everywhere. By that point, all I wanted was my bed. When I finally got home and opened the door, I was stunned. The floor was covered with letters; there must've been at least 100. My phone wouldn't stop ringing. There were even TV satellite trucks parked outside my house waiting to do interviews. Popping into Tesco became a mission, people stopping me for autographs, hugs and congratulations. It was overwhelming.

I started carrying the medal with me. Not to show off, but because I loved sharing it with people. Letting them hold it, even wear it. I never fully felt like it was mine. And, to be honest, I still don't. So many people helped me earn that medal. It belongs to all of them, too. But I won't lie, it's silver. And in my head, that means Nathan and I lost the gold. People say, 'Wow, you won silver!' And I think, 'No, we lost the gold.' Don't get me wrong, I love my medal. I'm not going to sell it on eBay, but I'd say I'm about 90 per cent happy with it. That missing ten per cent is what kept me going. Every time I looked at it in the weeks and months after Athens, it reminded me: next time, I want *gold*.

More Partying

Back home in Bedford, I was suddenly the local hero. I took full advantage, rocking up to pubs wearing my Olympic silver medal and celebrating like a champion. After years of trying (and mostly failing) to blag free drinks, it turns out an Olympic medal is the golden ticket. I absolutely milked that silver for all it was worth.

How it's still in my possession is a mystery. It's been passed around by bar staff, bouncers, dancers and even bar managers. It's been dropped, drenched in champagne, and has generally lived a more exciting life than most people. It's scratched and battered now, but I love that. Every mark tells a story. Honestly, if reality TV had been what it is now, *Me and My Medal* would've been a hit series.

One night, I took my university mates out in Kingston. Julie ended up standing on a table, medal around her neck, yelling that she'd won it in gymnastics. Thankfully, no one believed her, because watching her attempt the splits would've been a traumatic experience for everyone.

I even hired a limo and treated the girls to a night at The Ivy. It was all going swimmingly until the limo was stopped on the way home by armed police. Apparently, someone had reported that the driver's phone looked like a gun. So, there we were: six drunk girls in the back of a limo being searched by two *very* attractive, heavily armed police officers. Not exactly your typical night out, but oddly fun. I even let them try on the medal.

That medal came everywhere with me. It was my VIP pass into clubs, my conversation starter and my ultimate party prop. No shame. No regrets.

Superstars and Ceilings

Straight after the Athens Olympics, I found myself swapping shuttlecocks for sprint spikes in *Superstars: The Revival*, filmed at La Manga in Spain. Nathan was already out there competing in the men's heats, while I arrived a bit later (the women's event was a straight final).

The show was hosted by Johnny Vaughan, and, I'll be honest, I arrived still half drunk from the Olympics afterparties and walked straight into the restaurant to find Nathan … who was also still drunk. It seemed to be the unofficial *Superstars* tradition that as soon as the events ended, all the athletes went straight to the bar. Super-fit, elite athletes turning into pub regulars by sundown.

That evening began one of the most surreal experiences of my life. Ten minutes after arriving, I stepped into the restaurant and was immediately scooped up into the arms of Liverpool and England football legend John Barnes, who shouted across the room, 'It's the better half of our badminton duo heroes!' I just stood there, suspended, wondering how on earth this was my life now. Later that night, while deep into karaoke and cocktails at the bar, Scottish rugby legend Doddie Weir picked me up, completely unprovoked, and pushed me up into the ceiling. I have no idea why. Maybe it was something in the lyrics being sung by Welsh rugby star Jonathan Davies, who was belting out karaoke on stage at the time. To this day, it feels like a fever dream brought on by too much sangria and possibly a cheese coma.

The events started, and it was time for the 100m sprint. This small blonde girl *can* move! (I may have mentioned this before.) I smashed it. As I crossed the finish line in first place, who was waiting at the end but Linford Christie. Actual Linford Christie! He ran over, gave me a massive hug, and, to my utter disbelief, invited me to go and play tennis with him. I thought he was joking, but he wasn't. Ten minutes later, I was on a court, racket in hand, trying to explain I played badminton, not tennis. He didn't care. He was trying to show me his tennis form, but turns out he wasn't quite as fast with a racket. I beat him easily. I still don't really know why he was there, as he wasn't competing. Just another odd detail in what felt like a very glamorous and bizarre hallucination.

I wish I could tell you I won the whole thing, but I ended up fifth out of eight. I'd love to blame it on the elite level of competition … but truthfully, the nightly bar sessions probably had something to do with it. That's my excuse, and I'm sticking to it.

What *did* come out of that week, though, was my first real chance to connect with athletes from other sports. We were all staying in the same villa complex, and in between events and hangovers, I had some truly eye-opening conversations. One that stuck with me was with Olympic rower Katherine Grainger. We were talking about training intensity, and she described how rowers often hit 95 per cent of their max capacity in training, collapsing off the rowing ergometers in exhaustion. As she spoke, something clicked. 'Had I *ever* pushed myself that hard in badminton?' she asked. I wasn't sure. She looked at me, confused, and simply asked, 'Why not?'

That conversation changed me. It was the first time I saw my sport and my limits through a completely different lens. I flew home with more than sore legs and great stories. I came back with a new mindset. Sometimes, all it takes is the right conversation at the right time, and ideally in a sun-soaked villa in Spain, preferably after karaoke.

Ready … Steady … Cook!

I can honestly say, I had never dreamed of being on the cooking programme *Ready Steady Cook*, but the invite came, and I didn't want to be rude.

Nathan and I were contestants on this legendary daytime cooking show. This was the true test to see who was the best. As we were introduced to the studio, in his usual exuberant fashion, Ainsley Harriott gave me the most unforgettable, eyebrow-raising line I've ever been handed on national television. With his signature grin, he announced:

'Ahh, the hand that has smashed a thousand cocks!' Erm, thanks Ainsley. The studio burst into laughter. I nearly dropped my salmon.

I was on the 'Red Tomato' team, proudly clutching my bag of ingredients: salmon and sweet potato, simple, but classy. The lines were drawn, the chopping boards were out, and it was game on. Now, I'm no professional chef, but I can hold my own in a kitchen, and I wasn't about to let Nathan win without a fight. There's something deeply satisfying about beating your badminton partner with a spatula instead of a racket.

While Nathan was getting flustered trying to flambé something (which I'm still convinced was unintentional), I was calmly creating a salmon dish with roasted sweet potato and a tangy yogurt dressing. I played it smart; I let my professional chef do all the work. Ainsley loved it. And, most importantly, the *audience* loved it.

When the votes came in, and the red tomatoes outnumbered the green peppers, I knew I'd done it. I'd won *Ready Steady Cook*. And yes, I still have the winning plate to this day. It's not tucked away in a trophy cabinet or polished behind glass. It's right in my kitchen, occasionally used, often smiled at, and always remembered. It's a symbol of culinary victory, and a gentle reminder to Nathan whenever he comes round for dinner.

They Think It's All Over ... It Is Now!

There are many surreal things that come with being an Olympian: standing on podiums, signing autographs in Tesco, people shaking your hand in the street, but nothing, and I mean *nothing*, prepared me for being blindfolded and felt up on national television. Yes, I appeared on *They Think It's All Over*. And yes, I was the mystery guest on the infamous 'Feel the Sportsman' round. Nathan and I were invited on to the show as a pair, the Team GB mixed doubles duo, ready to be, quite literally, manhandled for sport.

Hosted by the brilliant Nick Hancock, the show was part sports panel, part comedy chaos. The premise was simple. Two blindfolded team captains had to identify the mystery sportspeople by touch alone. You can probably see where this is going … First up was Rory McGrath, sent, blindfolded, to inspect Nathan. He gave it a solid go, having a good feel around Nathan's shoulders and arms, but clearly wasn't confident. Meanwhile, on the other side of the stage, Arsenal legend Ian Wright was tasked with figuring me out. Within about five seconds, and I swear this is a direct quote, Ian declared, 'I've got a girl!' Great detective work, Ian.

That's when things got interesting. Rory, clearly feeling left out of the action, abandoned Nathan and made a beeline over to me. There I was, arms awkwardly out like I was waiting for a hug, and now I had *two* blindfolded men feeling me up on national TV. It was one of those moments where your soul hovers above your body and says, 'Well … this is happening.'

I stood there as calmly as I could while the two of them gave it their best go, poking and prodding. It took them a *good* feel before someone finally blurted out, 'It's Gail Emms, so the other person must be Nathan Robertson!'

Despite the mild public groping, it was an absolute blast. Everyone on the show was brilliant. Nick Hancock was hilarious, Ian Wright was cheeky but lovely, and Rory … well, Rory got more familiar with my forearms than most of my opponents ever did. Looking back, it was one of the most bizarre TV experiences of my career – but also one of the most memorable. It showed the fun, slightly ridiculous side of being an athlete in the spotlight. You train for years to represent your country … and then, one day, you're on a game show being poked by a footballer and a comic in blindfolds. Only in Britain.

You Are … *Not* the Weakest Link

I had been in an Olympic final, but nothing prepared me for facing the queen of cutting comebacks herself: Anne Robinson.

Yes, I appeared on *The Weakest Link*.

Even better (or weirder?), I was on it with Nathan. For reasons unknown (perhaps a casting decision made during a particularly optimistic coffee break), we were entered as a *pair.* Just one slot on the show … but two brains, two voices and two athletes. Slightly unfair I think, but did we care? Absolutely not.

It turns out that two heads are, in fact, better than one. Especially when you're asked things like 'Who was the British monarch in 1605?' or 'What is the capital of Kazakhstan?' We didn't have these hard questions, though – it was a celebrity version. The questions were more like, 'What colour is at the start of a rainbow?'

Anne Robinson was just as terrifying in person as she looked on screen. That sharp glare, the frosty pause before delivering a zinger, you knew she was watching, listening, waiting for any slip-up. We walked on to the set with matching grins, and she gave us 'the look'. The one that says, 'I smell weakness.'

At one point, she raised an eyebrow and deadpanned, 'So you play together … and now you answer questions together? A bit needy, isn't it?' Nathan, bless him, tried to charm her. I just laughed and let her have the moment. You don't sass Anne Robinson, you survive her.

Round by round, contestants were voted off and, somehow, Nathan and I stayed put. Maybe it was the competitive instincts kicking in. Maybe it was all those years of tactical thinking and pressure-handling on the court. Or maybe the others just didn't want to vote off two people at once. Economical gameplay, I say.

By the final round, it was just us and swimmer Mark Foster. And yes … we won.

Anne's final words as we collected our winnings were typically dry, 'Well, I suppose badminton *is* a team sport …' We took that as a compliment.

A Question of Sport

There are TV shows you grow up watching, and then there's *A Question of Sport*, the holy grail for any British athlete. So, when the call came in that Nathan and I were wanted as 'Mystery Guests', and then later as panellists, it felt like the ultimate honour. In the world of TV, this was the top tier. It was *the* dream.

Our debut as Mystery Guests was ... well, unforgettable. We were cast as Sonny and Cher, tasked with serenading each other to 'I Got You Babe'. Cute in theory, but in practice, it was absolutely bizarre. It quickly dawned on us that in all our years of playing together, we'd never had to gaze into each other's eyes for more than a quick nod before a serve. Suddenly, we were singing love songs to each other, under blazing studio lights, trying to stay in character. Nathan's fake moustache kept sliding off his sweaty face, and I couldn't stop giggling. I'm fairly certain I was still mildly hungover from the night before.

That was just the beginning. I went on to be a Mystery Guest many more times, each disguise more ridiculous than the last. I've been a secret spy, a damsel in distress scaling the towers of Warwick Castle, cowgirl Dolly Parton punching in for her 9 to 5, and even Nessa from *Gavin & Stacey* (complete with line dancing at a Manchester men's club, alongside Lee Sharpe as Bryn for Comic Relief). As you do.

But the real highlight was finally getting to sit on the panel. My debut will always be one of my favourite moments. I was on Matt Dawson's team along with Pat Cash and I was buzzing the entire time. I even managed to get a fair few questions right, which helped. That appearance kicked off what became a long and brilliant association with the show; I ended up appearing 16 times in total.

Over the years, I met some incredible people: darts icon Phil 'The Power' Taylor, footballers Carlton Cole and Marlon Harewood, cricketer Chris Woakes and so many more. And, of course, there was Ally McCoist, an absolute legend, but Phil Tufnell stepped up brilliantly when he joined the team. His humour and energy were spot-on.

More recently, I had the pleasure of being part of *Sue, Matt & Phil Live: The Reunion Tour*, which was a stage show featuring the dream team of Sue Barker, Matt Dawson and Phil Tufnell. Honestly, the format *never* should have changed. The energy, the audience love, it was pure magic. It may have gone under a new name, but the heart of *A Question of Sport* was alive and kicking on that stage.

I've got nothing but respect for the line-up that replaced Sue, Matt and Phil – Sam Quek, Ugo Monye and Paddy McGuinness are all genuinely lovely people, but they had some big shoes to fill. And, truthfully, the chemistry just wasn't the same. It didn't land. Eventually, the show was axed, which was a sad end to a legendary era.

Still, I'll always be grateful I got to be a part of such an iconic British institution.

Let's Go to Denmark

There's a funny thing about partnerships: just when you think you've found your rhythm, life changes the tempo. During our time as a pair, Nathan fell in love with a Danish girl, Ditte. It was the kind of love that crossed borders – literally. Not long after we won our Olympic silver in Athens, he announced he was moving to Copenhagen to live with her.

At first, I wasn't entirely surprised or even upset. I remember people reacting with wide-eyed concern, saying, 'But he's moving to Denmark? Isn't this the end of Emms and Robertson?' I'd shrug and say, 'Honestly, we don't train together much anyway. We'd just annoy the hell out of each other if we played more than twice a week.' And, truthfully, I wanted him to be happy. A happy athlete plays better. And if Denmark made him happy, then so be it.

The unexpected silver lining? I got to play in Denmark, too.

I signed with a club in Copenhagen, in the Hvidovre district, and the club was named Hvidovre. See what they did there? It was also the same club that Nathan signed for. For context, club badminton in the UK wasn't exactly thriving. We didn't have a strong league system or much of a professional infrastructure at the time. In Denmark, it was completely different: thriving leagues, packed sports halls, real community. There was a badminton culture, something I hadn't experienced since my early days of county matches for Hertfordshire. Playing for a club like Hvidovre wasn't just about the matches; it was about being part of something larger.

That said, the logistics were brutal. The EasyJet 6.40am flight from Stansted became my regular commute, which meant 3am wake-up calls to leave my house in Milton Keynes. By the time I got on the plane, I was out cold. Then I'd wake up in Copenhagen, shuffle into the freezing Danish air and brace myself for another whirlwind stint abroad.

There was a particular warmth, though, in the friendships I made. Most notably with Solenn Pasturel, or 'Mini' to me. Solenn is a tiny powerhouse from Jersey who trained in an academy in Denmark. I stayed with her, in her flat in the Hellerup region, which was absolutely Baltic, and the bathroom was down a freezing hallway, but we made it work. Pasta, cheap chicken, gossip, giggles – we created our own version of home away from home. She kept me sane.

I wish I could say my Danish debut was one of glory. It wasn't. It was, in fact, one of the worst performances of my career. Nathan and I had just come off the high of our Olympic silver in Athens. Our signing with Hvidovre came with fanfare: posters, announcements, cheering fans in the sports hall. We were the big names. And we were about to crash spectacularly. Hungover from celebration and woefully undertrained, we stepped on to the court against two young Danish players we'd never heard of. It should've been an easy win. It wasn't. We were slow, disconnected, barely able to see the shuttle. It was a car crash in slow motion. The silence in the hall after the loss was deafening. Our team-mates couldn't even look at us. I remember walking off the court feeling cold, not from the weather, but from the humiliation.

And that's when I started to learn what Danish sport culture was really about. It wasn't about your name or your medal count. It was about showing up. About respect. About being part of a team. At Hvidovre, you didn't just play. You pitched in. You coached juniors. You helped with sessions. You passed on knowledge. I remember when I declined to help at an U11 session because I was tired. The look I got from the coach and players said it all: 'That's not how we do things here.' And they were right.

Peter Gade, world number one in men's singles at the time, would regularly coach kids, hit with pensioners and pitch in wherever he was needed. That was the Law of Jante in action, the Danish social code that no one is above anyone else, that you contribute, and that humility and community come first. Playing in Denmark taught me more about teamwork than anything I'd experienced before. In England, badminton often felt like an individual pursuit, even in doubles. You were fighting for yourself, for your place, for your funding. But in Denmark, I felt what it meant to be part of a sporting culture that saw the athlete not just as a performer, but as a human being with responsibilities to the team, the club and the next generation.

That shift changed me.

And yes, I grumbled. The weather was awful, the cost of living was absurd and I still have traumatic memories of those 3am alarm clocks. But I came away with something more lasting than a match result. A sense of belonging. A deeper appreciation of what it means to support others. A glimpse of the kind of sporting world I wish we had more of back home. If I'd been Danish, I'd probably still be playing. I'd be knocking around in the third team, or the over-40s league, turning up to help out at club nights and feeling like I was still part of something. But I'm not. And in the UK, that sense of community is harder to find.

Still, for a while, in a cold flat in Copenhagen, with Mini's laugh echoing down the hallway and the club team shouting, 'We fight for Hvidovre!', I had it. And I'll always be grateful. Apologies again for that really bad debut.

It's Just Badminton. How Hard Can It Be?

One of the best things to come out of Athens and all the TV appearances that followed was the shift in how people saw badminton. Before that, the most common response I got when I told people I was a professional badminton player was: 'Wait, that's a real sport?' Or worse: 'Bet I could beat you!'

They'd then proceed to tell me how they'd played for their Year 7 school team, or how they once smashed it about in the garden with their nan and, apparently, still thought they could take me down. Just to top it off, they'd do 'the mime'. You know the one: a lazy flick of the wrist with a smug look, like the sport was all just a gentle tap underarm and a polite trot around the court.

And don't even get me started on the classics: 'But you're just a girl' or 'You're tiny – how hard can it be? I'd lift it over your head!' Honestly, if any of my international opponents had gone in with that mindset, my life would've been a lot easier.

But something changed after Athens. Suddenly, people stopped me in the street to shake my hand. 'Fair play,' they'd say. 'That shuttle goes *fast*. Amazing to watch.' And just like that, for the first time, people respected not just me, but the sport. It meant the world. After years of having to defend badminton as a serious sport, I was finally being seen for what I was: a world-class athlete in one of the fastest, toughest sports going. (For those still unsure: yes, a shuttlecock can travel faster than a Formula 1 car, clocked at over 265mph. Beat that.)

Of course, I still got the occasional challenge, and I could *never* resist. One of my favourites came after I'd retired, and was about six months pregnant, no less. I was invited to play against some Manchester United players: Wes Brown, Michael Carrick and Danny Welbeck. Wes and Michael were surprisingly decent. Danny ... let's just say his coordination is definitely better suited to his feet. The warm-up, involving all four of us and a group of children from local schools who had come along to meet their heroes, turned into a proper match between Wes and me. The poor kids quickly stepped aside as things got, well, competitive.

Wes really made me work for it, and bear in mind I was pregnant and not moving at my usual speed, but I still didn't let him score. Zero points. Sorry, Wes.

There seems to be a real thing with footballers and badminton. More recently, I got dragged into a hilarious spat on talkSPORT between former Villa striker Gabby Agbonlahor and ex-Spurs striker Darren Bent. Both were arguing over who was better at badminton. And not just casually, they were actually debating the rules live on air. Next thing I know, they're both asking me for coaching.

So, naturally, we took it to the court. I played both of them and gave my official verdict to the producers. Gabby gets full marks for enthusiasm, but Darren, he is genuinely talented. In fact, he's now overtaken Wes as the 'Best Footballer I've Played Badminton Against'. Sorry again, Wes.

Every now and then, someone *does* manage to win a point off me. And one of the most memorable and painful instances was Olympic gold medallist sprinter Jason Gardener. We were at a Youth Sport Trust event when he challenged me to a match. Let's just say there's a reason Jason stuck to running in a straight line at top speed. His hand-eye coordination made it clear that anything involving a racket was a hard pass.

Still, I was nice, I gave him tips, showed him how to grip the racket, you know, coach mode. We agreed to play to 11. I raced ahead to 10-0, and then, *of course*, on match point, I served high. Jason swung, and by some miracle of timing, the frame of his racket clattered into the shuttle. It wobbled over the net, just clipping the tape, and dribbled on to my side. Even elite players struggle to return those. I gave it a lunge, but nope. Jason scored. He reacted like he'd just won another Olympic gold. Sprinting around the sports hall, arms in the air, total joy. I've honestly never seen someone so proud of such a fluky point.

It's taken a while, but people are starting to see badminton for what it really is: fast, fierce, technical and brilliant. And if they still don't believe me, I'll happily take them on court and let the shuttle do the talking.

Gail: There were parties ... and then even more parties. Appearances, talks, late nights, early mornings. TV shows, radio interviews, champagne and more champagne. Training sessions were often pushed aside for press events or last-minute TV appearances. At the time, it was all so new and exciting that we just assumed we could do it all – train like normal and handle this whirlwind of media attention at the same time.

Steph: Tell me what the 'whirlwind' felt like?

Gail: It felt incredible on the surface, finally feeling seen, celebrated and enough. That bit was really addictive.

Steph: I sense there's a 'but' coming.

Gail: Yep, slowly I think that phase began to consume me. I wasn't training like I used to. I wasn't grounded. I wasn't me. At some point, I realised the truth: I didn't just want to feel like a star, I wanted to be the athlete again. The competitor. The fighter. It was time to stop the distractions, reset and return to the court and the real me.

WORLD DOMINATION, MWAH HA HA

All England

I'll never forget my first trip to the All England Championships. I was about 11 years old, travelling with my junior badminton club to Wembley Arena, then the home of the oldest and most prestigious tournament in the sport. Even now, the memories are vivid. The smell of popcorn and hot dogs hit me in the foyer, but it was the moment I stepped through those doors and caught sight of the courts that something shifted. That was when I knew.

There were players from all over the world, all sleek in their white shirts and shorts, moving with a grace and power I had never seen up close. I remember watching Gillian Clark and Gillian Gowers – two English legends – before being completely awestruck by the ferocity of the Chinese, Indonesian and Malaysian men, smashing shuttles with a speed and sound that didn't seem human. The squeak of trainers, the authoritative voice of umpires perched in high chairs, the roar of the crowd; it all felt like a dream.

I sat there alone in the stands, dazzled by the lights and the spectacle, and allowed myself to imagine. I could see myself on those courts one day. I tried to focus on the daydream, but the matches were too exciting. On the coach ride home to Bedford, all of us swapped stories of our favourite players and points, riding high on inspiration.

Fast-forward eight years, and that little girl in awe was walking on to the court as a competitor. The tournament had moved to Birmingham's Indoor Arena by then, and I was playing in the qualifying rounds, in singles (a mistake entry, I can assure you), women's doubles and mixed. I was a nervous wreck, but somehow managed to win my singles qualifying match. That was my first All England victory. In singles, no less! I still think that would surprise a few people.

From that year onwards, I competed in the All England every single season. In 2001, I partnered with Simon Archer in the mixed doubles and felt my first real taste of success on that stage. There's a rich history for England in that event – Nick Ponting and Jo Goode winning in 1994, and Simon winning himself with Jo in 1999 – so there was an added layer of expectation. We scraped through a tight quarter-final against an Indonesian pair and, suddenly, I was an All England semi-finalist. My body ached, my mind buzzed and I barely slept that night, still hearing the roar of the crowd in my ears. It was like being a pop star. I was hooked.

But that year also marked the start of a complicated relationship with the tournament. In the years that followed, I partnered with Nathan, and while we enjoyed great success, the All England somehow became overwhelming. It was the pinnacle for British badminton. Our only home Super Series-level tournament. For most of the year, I could walk through life in relative anonymity, but not during All England week. Suddenly, I was public property. I couldn't go anywhere without being stopped for a photo, a chat or an opinion. I loved it, but it exhausted me. My senses were constantly overloaded. Eventually, I stayed in a different hotel just for some peace. I even started walking to the arena in a hat and sunglasses. It felt ridiculous, but it was the only way I could stay mentally steady. I hated hiding, but that tournament meant everything.

I remember one match, maybe 2002 or 2003. Nathan and I had just beaten a tough Korean pair, and I was debriefing with the English team. Finn Traerup-Hansen, our performance director, came over to congratulate me. I brushed it off with, 'Thanks, but I served into the net at 5-5 and my backhand still needs some work.' Finn slammed his hand down on the seat: 'Stop this. Stop this thinking, Gail. You will *never* be perfect.'

It caught me off guard. I thought he was being a bit dramatic, maybe even a little harsh. Then he added, 'Lower your number.' I replied, 'Lower my what?' 'Your number. You keep chasing 100. That's unsustainable. If you're always striving for perfection, the crash afterwards will be harder. It'll burn you out. Lower your number, and you'll level out.' So, in my best cocky athlete voice, I replied, 'Alright, fine, I'll drop to 95.'

That moment changed me. It was the best advice I ever got. I allowed myself to make mistakes. I gave myself permission to be human. And when I reached World Number One in 2003, it was with that new mindset. I never played a perfect match, but I was far more consistent. And happier.

At the start of 2005, after the wild celebrations post-Athens, we knuckled down. Nathan and I had a point to prove, and the All England was circled in bold red ink. No more parties, no distractions. Just badminton. The draw came out: a tricky second round against the Koreans who had just beaten us in Germany. Not seeded, so most people assumed we'd win easily. But we knew otherwise.

We beat the Scots in round one, and then came the showdown. Three sets. It was a brutal pace. The crowd sensed the danger and willed us on. Their energy lifted us, and we played one of our best matches ever. That win took us to the quarter-finals and, from there, everything clicked. The final saw us against the Danes, Thomas Laybourn and Kamilla Rytter Juhl. We were the favourites. The match was … not great at all! Scrappy, nervous, error-strewn. But I served to Thomas at match point, and we won. *All England champions*!

Our coaches, Andy Wood and Rexy Mainaky, flew off their seats. Nathan did his aeroplane run across the court. The crowd went mad. I saw Mum and Dad in the front row, jumping up and down. Dad waved a flag that read 'Gail Emms: The Best' – a classic Dad move. We high-fived half the arena before reaching the podium. The announcer barely got our names out over the roar.

We'd done it. We'd won the All England. For us, for British badminton, for every kid playing in cold school sports halls across the country.

We signed autographs for three hours. At one point, we were so tired that we accidentally signed each other's names. But I'll never forget that day. Ever.

In 2006, we had five match points in the final and lost. I still can't bring it up with Nathan as it haunts him. That was our last All England final. In my retirement year, 2008, we went out in the quarter-finals. No fairy tale ending.

Still, I look back with pride. That 2005 win was everything. Recently, I returned to the All England for the 20th anniversary of our win. I hadn't been back in years. Maybe because I wanted to keep those memories preserved, untouched. But I brought my youngest son, Ollie, his first All England, and he was the same age I was back at Wembley Arena. It made it all feel full circle. To watch the sport I love, with him by my side, in the place that gave me my proudest memories, it was perfect.

China Open

People often list mine and Nathan's career highlights: World Championships, Olympic silver medallists, European titles, Commonwealth Games medals, and they're right to, as they are huge achievements. But there's another one that rarely gets the spotlight it deserves: winning the China Open in 2005.

Now, that win meant more than just another trophy on the shelf. It was a victory earned in the most gruelling, unwelcoming of environments. And I say this as diplomatically as I can: playing in China, particularly back then, meant facing far more than just your opponents across the net.

Even before the shuttle was hit, the hurdles began. The red tape around entering the country was never straightforward, but the real challenges started on arrival. The bus from the airport always seemed to take the most circuitous route possible, dumping us at an accommodation that felt deliberately sub-par. Practice schedules were handed out at the last minute, and if we were lucky, our slot was at 6am or 11.30pm – usually on the worst court available. Throw in a hotel that was miles from anywhere with no Western food in sight, and you start to get a sense of the 'hospitality'.

And then came the tournament. In 2005, our first-round opponents were a pair of Chinese qualifiers. Now, in a country where more than 100 million people play badminton, if you're Chinese and playing in your national Open, you're *good*. Like, top-ten-in-the-world good. So, although on paper we had a favourable draw, in reality it was like facing a world-class pair. We scraped through that one, then beat another Chinese pair in the second round; again, not a familiar name, but tougher than the last. In the quarter-finals, we met Zhang Jun and Zhao Tingting, seasoned players from the national team, and our old 'friends' from Athens 2004. I remember that match so clearly. Everything clicked. I couldn't miss. We played some of the best badminton of our careers and absolutely thrashed them, much to the dismay of the crowd.

But the deeper we went into the tournament, the more the external pressures ramped up. By the semi-finals, both Nathan and I were running on fumes – food poisoning, sleep disruption, a constantly shifting match schedule. And then, the refereeing. The tournament was held in Guangzhou, which meant local officials, umpires, line judges, you name it. And let's just say, their interpretation of the rules didn't exactly favour the visiting teams. Anything we hit near the lines was called out. It was so blatant, we had to start aiming right down the middle of the court just to be safe.

Andy Wood, normally the calmest presence in the room, absolutely lost it. I've *never* seen him so angry. He was ready to swing for a Badminton World Federation (BWF) official as the Chinese coaches sat nearby, smug and chuckling. It was infuriating. But somehow, we won. Even the crowd seemed embarrassed by what they were seeing.

In the final, we faced a Korean pair – finally, not another Chinese team. But by then, the damage had been done. We were physically and emotionally drained, and we knew we had just a few hours to get to Hong Kong for our flight home. Badminton England had given our travel schedule to the organisers, and given that neither of the

Korean players had other finals to play, it made perfect sense for our match to go early. Instead, the mixed doubles event was scheduled *last*. Convenient, right?

After much protesting (and a few pointed conversations), it was eventually moved up to third. It was still going to be tight. And, of course, we couldn't even shower after winning. We got through the match in two sets, just about had time for the medal ceremony, grabbed our bags … and then got pulled for drug testing. I fully support anti-doping measures, but the timing here felt more than a little suspect.

Here's the thing about drug testing post-match: your body is dehydrated. You've just played an intense game, you're sweating buckets, and now you're expected to produce a *very specific* urine sample. Not just any wee, a certain volume, and the right colour too. Not too dark, not too diluted. Welcome to elite sport!

So there we were, desperately trying to hydrate and produce the goods. I've done it in 20 minutes before. The longest time took over three hours. The whole England team were willing us on like we were at match point again, just willing us to … well, *pee*.

And the final indignity is that you're watched. Not just monitored but closely observed. There's someone's face right down there, watching the whole thing, head centimetres away. For women, it's an ordeal. Naked from the chest down, someone crouched to make sure the sample is legitimate, and it's deeply uncomfortable. Honestly, when it comes to drug testing, blokes have it easy. Nathan was in and out (so to speak) before I'd even managed to get going.

But we produced the urine samples, we had won the China Open *and* we got on that train, exhausted, sweaty but victorious. That win wasn't just about badminton. It was about endurance, resilience and refusing to be broken, even when everything around you tries to wear you down. It's one of the proudest moments of my career, not because of the size of the trophy, but because of what it took to hold it.

Europe vs Asia

With badminton being so popular in Asia, it meant that many of the biggest tournaments were held there. At one point, I was spending nearly a third of the year in the Far East. The travel could be exhausting, not that I'm complaining, I promise! Occasionally, I'd get upgraded to business class, which felt like winning the lottery, especially when we had weekend travel and just a couple of days to acclimatise before competing. It could be a bit awkward, though, like the time I got the upgrade and Nathan didn't. I'm 5ft 3 and fit just fine into an economy seat. Nathan, on the other hand, is 6ft 3 and folds up like an ironing board. He wasn't thrilled.

We all had our own rituals for long-haul flights: travel pillows, earplugs, compression socks, and, if it was a night flight, sleeping tablets to knock us out and fight off the jet lag. It became a bit of a comedy scene. Picture an entire England squad, fast asleep, twitching and flinching mid-dream as we mentally replayed rallies in our sleep. We'd be spasming mid-air smash, our racket arms flying about. There was always a scramble for the window seat (seat A, if you were lucky). Most of us were right-handed, so sitting on the aisle meant you were guaranteed a few accidental slaps from your neighbour mid-flight. We'd often disembark with red marks from each other's flailing limbs.

That kind of thing becomes normal when you're in the badminton world. Explaining it, however, in a more ... *romantic* context wasn't so easy. 'Oh, by the way, you might get slapped in your sleep tonight,' I'd have to warn someone I was dating. Cue them waking up with mysterious bruises and a look of total confusion. And heaven forbid they insisted on sleeping on the right side of the bed – that was the danger zone!

There was always an underlying sense of 'Us versus Them' when we competed in Asia. Often, Nathan and I were the last European pair standing in the draw, and you could feel the tension when we upset the home favourites. I remember a special event in the Philippines – 'Europe vs Asia' – which was set up to showcase Asian dominance. But due to scheduling conflicts and, let's be honest, some financial disputes, the Chinese team didn't take part. The result was a weaker Asian team ... and a European victory. Whoops.

Growing up, I idolised players from Denmark, Sweden and England. Back then, European nations dominated mixed doubles with a more traditional, tactical style. Players like Nick Ponting, Chris Hunt, Simon Archer, Jo Goode and Julie Bradbury inspired our generation. They proved that British players could reach the top and didn't need to be intimidated by the Asian powerhouses.

Physically, European and Asian players were very different. On average, European men were taller and heavier, around 6ft, while Asian men were closer to 5ft 8. It was the same for the women: we were generally stronger and taller; they were lighter, faster and more agile on court. Over time, that gap began to close. The Asian players grew taller, something often credited to changing diets and a growing appetite for protein (and American burgers).

Like any sport, badminton had its darker side. There were rumours, whispers, along with the knowing looks. Doping and match-fixing were always lurking in the background, never entirely proven but never quite dismissed either. There were the occasional positive drug tests, though they were rare. More often, it was the sudden transformations from some Asian players that raised eyebrows: players vanishing for months, only to return looking like Marvel superheroes. Legs like tree trunks, voices deeper than before, it didn't take much imagination to suspect something wasn't right.

The silver lining with badminton is that, unlike some sports, it's not just about power. Skill, finesse, strategy – they all matter. So even if someone was 'enhanced', they could still be beaten. That thought always gave us some hope.

I'm convinced match-fixing happened. Especially in those suspicious 'China vs China' matches, where the younger pair would mysteriously lose without putting up much of a fight. It was widely believed that coaches would instruct them to defer to the older, more established team – know your place, take the loss. It was awkwardly obvious at times.

As gambling infiltrated the sport, things got murkier. You'd see top seeds drop a set to an unranked or clearly weaker opponent, and not in a competitive way, but in a suspiciously convenient one.

The problem is, when the prize money on offer is relatively low and someone flashes an envelope or bank transfer worth more than a player might earn all season, what do you expect? The temptation is huge. Sadly, many of the questionable results seemed to come from players in poorer Asian nations.

That's the danger – once it starts, where does it end? And how do you even begin to police it properly? I'll never forget one particular match I lost; it was in Denmark, and it was a match I *should* have won. Afterwards, a man came up to me and said my result had cost him £10,000. I just looked at him and told him to jog on. As if that was ever going to be my problem. How dare he say that to me?

I don't know how things are now, but I do know this: as long as money's involved, cheating in sport will always exist in some form. I could never have gone down that path. I feel sick thinking about cheating, whether it be doping or match-fixing. Not because I didn't care about winning, but because I had something far scarier to answer to. My mum. And believe me, disappointing her would've been worse than any ban.

There are countries I still miss playing in, especially Malaysia and Indonesia. The crowds were unbelievable. You'd have 10,000 seats but 25,000 fans crammed in, some practically hanging from the rafters. They loved the spectacle. If you made an error, the entire arena would erupt in laughter, all pointing at you in unison. The only way to handle it was to bow, smile and own the mistake. Show the crowd some love, and they'd stay on your side.

That said, things could get out of hand. Before one Indonesian quarter-final, I opened my bag in the hall to find one of my court shoes missing. I had packed it myself in the hotel room, but now it was gone. After a frantic search, it turned up in a bin outside. From that day on, I never let my bag out of my sight.

And the 'gamesmanship' didn't stop there. The conditions themselves were weaponised. In places like Malaysia and Indonesia, it was consistently 30°C outside, so the halls were heavily air-conditioned. This created the infamous *drift*. Depending on the airflow, the shuttle could veer wildly off-course. You'd aim for the sideline and find your shot flying into the stands, or your clears would zip long by miles. Sometimes, just as we'd swapped ends between games, the air con would mysteriously change direction, always favouring the home players. We'd lose the advantage we'd earned, and suddenly our attack was neutralised. Other times, someone would open a door on the concourse mid-rally, flooding the court with blinding sunlight.

And silence during play, like the tennis at Wimbledon, was never an option. Forget it. The noise would ramp up exactly as I was serving, with shouts and cheers designed to make me fluff my shot or set up a smash for my opponent. It wasn't subtle at all, but we learned to play through it.

Despite everything, there was always a sense of camaraderie among players. A friendly rivalry. The Malaysian squad spoke the best English and were the most sociable. Towards the end of my career, a few of the Chinese players even began to say hello. I really wish I'd learned Mandarin. It would've helped me build stronger connections with both the players and the media, and, let's be honest, it would have opened the door to more sponsorship opportunities. My business brain hadn't quite switched on at that stage, and that's one of my biggest regrets: not capitalising on my profile when I had the chance.

Indonesia was one of my favourite places to play. It came with its fair share of challenges. In the lead-up to tournaments, we sometimes experienced volcanic eruptions or earthquakes. I'd be terrified; the locals just laughed it off like it was a bit of rain. Once, we competed amid real civil unrest, with Christian/Muslim tensions peaking and even a bomb threat at our hotel. But the tournaments went ahead, and the love for badminton never wavered. The smiles from fans never faded.

Playing in Asia highlighted the contrast between how badminton is treated there versus back home. In Malaysia, Singapore and Brunei, we stayed in five-star resorts. In one Malaysian tournament, our rooms were perched on the edge of the rainforest. Every morning, monkeys would visit our balcony for fresh mangoes. It was magical.

So, when the Asian players came to Europe and we put them up in an Ibis next to a dual carriageway, I felt a bit embarrassed. Don't get me wrong, I love a budget hotel breakfast as much as anyone, but for players used to luxury and tropical heat, sitting in a cold dining room in rainy Germany or Holland probably made them question their life choices. This was when Europe had the upper hand. Many of the Asian players hated the cold, and the English breakfast buffet didn't help. I'll never forget the Malaysian team at breakfast, clutching bottles of chilli sauce, desperately trying to make sense of the blandest food they'd ever seen.

Looking back, it was chaos, laughter, stress, culture shock and unforgettable memories rolled into one. And I wouldn't trade it for anything.

Far East Experiences

There were a few places on the tour that I considered my 'bogey' destinations, Japan being one of them. I'd been so excited for my first Japan Open, but the moment I arrived, I felt completely out of sync. The sheer number of people, the slightly surreal atmosphere, the eye-watering prices, and, of course, the toilets that squirt water at your bum. I just couldn't relax. It didn't help that I always struggled with jet lag in Japan more than anywhere else. If you've seen *Lost in Translation* with Bill Murray and Scarlett Johansson – that was me. Staring at the ceiling, at 3am, wide awake, completely out of whack.

The real kicker was that mixed doubles usually kicks off the tournament schedule, and as the No.1 seeds, Nathan and I were often the first match on with a lovely 9am start time. That's fine if you've had sleep. Not so fine when you haven't and men are smashing shuttles at over 200mph straight at your head. You really need your eyes to be open – and working – for that. Eventually, we came up with a jet lag survival plan. Nathan and coach Andy decided the best approach was to wake me up at 5am, drag me around a local park to get my body moving (not literally on a lead, but close), and pour coffee down my throat until I could function. Once the match was over, I'd collapse back into bed.

After a couple of visits, though, something shifted. I warmed to Japan. In fact, I fell in love with it. The tournament in Tokyo was held in April, just as the cherry blossoms were in full bloom: it was breathtaking. I stopped fighting the culture and started embracing it. I discovered a love for sushi. I visited Disneyland Tokyo and wore Mickey Mouse ears without a shred of irony. I met the Harajuku girls and talked about fashion. I genuinely miss Japan now, and I think a lot of young people could learn something from the deep respect shown to elders that's woven into Japanese society.

South Korea was a very different experience. The tournaments were often hosted in cities deep in the country, far from the buzz of Seoul. I remember one time, Donna Kellogg (who had been my ladies' doubles partner since 2003) and I were walking to a shopping centre to grab some food. As soon as we entered, it became apparent that we were *very* tall by local standards. I'm 5ft 3 and felt statuesque. Donna is 5ft 10 and basically became a walking attraction. Within minutes, she was being pointed at and followed by many. Honestly, it was like the little green aliens in *Toy Story* spotting 'The Claw'. 'A stranger! From the outside! Oooooooh!' I couldn't stop laughing, which didn't help the situation at all. Donna was less than thrilled. Tall, blonde and very clearly foreign, she drew a crowd like some kind of celebrity apparition. In the end, we gave up on the food court and took our meals to go, retreating to the safety of the hotel.

The Korean Open was eventually moved to January on the calendar, which meant sub-zero temperatures. Sometimes it dropped to -10°C. The hall was freezing, so a giant industrial heater was wheeled in to warm the air before play started. All good until it began smoking and caught fire. Thick smoke, actual flames. The officials stood there for a while, watching casually, before eventually deciding to evacuate us. Luckily, the fire was brought under control and, believe it or not, play resumed less than an hour later – as if nothing had happened. The air still reeked of burning wires.

Despite our best efforts, Nathan and I never made it past the quarter-finals in either Japan or Korea. They remained the only two international tournaments where we didn't make a final. Maybe it was just bad luck for Nathan, because Donna and I *did* make the women's doubles final in Korea. Unfortunately, we had to withdraw. Donna's legs were so battered and covered in bruises and cuts from diving around the court that she couldn't bend her knees. Her skin had actually started to split from the pressure and pain. There was no way she could play another match.

Brunei ... now that was an experience. The Sultan of Brunei had a particular request: he wanted his son to compete in the men's doubles tournament. Realistically, this should never have been allowed. The Prince was a decent player, sure, but nowhere near elite level. He had no world ranking, but when you're the Sultan of Brunei, and let's just say ... significant funds are involved, doors tend to open. The match itself was one of the most uncomfortable things I've ever watched. Everyone was trying *very* hard not to win too convincingly, or show how out of place he was on the court.

In return for our cooperation, we were treated to a surreal trip around the Sultan's private amusement park, nestled within the palace grounds. Rollercoasters, carousels, the works. It had a Michael Jackson 'Neverland' vibe, only glossier. And yes, there was even a full-sized badminton court inside the palace, all gold-plated, no less. Because, of course, if you are the Sultan of Brunei, you can have a gold badminton court.

Hong Kong, on the other hand, was chaotic but captivating. Cramped, messy and noisy, but full of life and character. We played at the Queen Elizabeth Stadium, and our hotel was conveniently within walking distance. The downside was that it was right next to a sprawling, pungent fish market. The smell was something else – sensitive noses beware. We are talking full-on stench of fish guts sloshing into the street. It was intense. Still, I found the market fascinating. The fish were mostly still alive when customers chose them. They were then scooped up, beheaded and sold on the spot. Nothing was wasted, not even the heads. As Western girls wandering through, we must've looked completely bewildered, gawping at what, for them, was just a normal workday. And then there were the chickens ... live one minute, gone the next. Thankfully, they took them out back before doing the deed. I used to quietly say goodbye to the chosen ones – morbid, I know, but I couldn't help myself.

The worst part for me was the frogs. I have a full-blown frog phobia (it's called ranidaphobia, if you're curious), and I can't even look at them. But there they were, all laid out on ice at the market stalls. Half dead, stunned or maybe just cold, but every so often, one would twitch, flip or jump JUST as I walked past. I'm convinced they knew. Evil little things. For the record, I do like Kermit the Frog. He's the only frog I can tolerate. What really turned my stomach was that these frogs were skinned alive. Yes, *alive.* Even with my phobia, that stirred a bit of compassion in me. It was brutal.

On a lighter note, one evening Andy took me to the famous Felix Bar, perched above Hong Kong harbour. The view was spectacular, especially for the men, who apparently get to pee against a glass wall overlooking the city skyline. Only in Hong Kong. I loved the place, the buzz, the glamour, and then it got even better. Sting walked in. Yes, Sting! I went over to say hello, maybe get an autograph, but just as I approached, he turned to leave, and I, completely unintentionally, brushed his bum with my hand. Mortifying. So if you're reading this, Sting: I'm sorry. Complete accident.

Taiwan

I only visited Taiwan once. It had just been added back on to the international tournament schedule after a few years' absence, so off we went to Taipei. The city felt like China on two wheels, but swap bicycles for mopeds, multiply the noise and chaos, and you've got a sense of the place. What struck me most was our hotel. It was pure luxury, five-star to the extreme, the kind of place that makes your jaw drop when you walk in.

But what really made Taiwan unforgettable were two completely different experiences – one bizarre and unsettling, the other deeply beautiful.

The first experience was our visit to the infamous 'Snake Alley', or Huaxi Night Market. I'd heard about the legendary snake show: a performance involving a live snake, where the handler would eventually hang the creature from a hook, slit it open and collect its blood for people to drink. Yes, drink. For some reason, I was convinced I'd do it. I think I had Leonardo DiCaprio from *The Beach* in my head – this wild, brave tourist moment where I'd prove something to myself. So off I went, along with a couple of girls from the squad, to find a stall running the show.

The whole scene was surreal. There was a lot of shouting in Mandarin, the snake was presented and then, before we could really process what was happening, the snake was hung up and sliced open. I watched as its blood was drained into a glass, its movements slowing with each drop. Then came the bile. It was brutal. Horrifying, actually. And I felt an unexpected wave of pity for this poor creature. The bravado vanished. I was suddenly nauseous and desperate to leave. Safe to say, I did *not* drink the blood. We ended up drifting through a few clothing stalls afterwards, trying to shake the feeling. That whole experience stuck with me, and I'm glad to say this practice was finally banned in Taiwan in 2018.

The second memory, however, couldn't have been more different and remains one of the most beautiful moments of my badminton career.

Nathan and I hadn't made the finals. I honestly can't remember who beat us, but our coach, Andy, came over and said, 'There's a bus going at 4.30am tomorrow. I think you should be on it.' That was all he said. Now, I am *not* a morning person, but something about the mystery made me curious enough to set my alarm. I dragged myself on to the bus, curled up and tried to sleep for the hour-long ride.

When I woke up, we were somewhere completely different. The air was humid and the landscape green, almost tropical. It was quiet, so quiet, and we were clearly out of the city, nestled somewhere up a mountain. We got off the bus and were told to start walking. And then came the magic. Every 50m or so, as we curved around the mountain path, there were little huts. And each hut had a badminton court. Not fancy ones, just basic setups, but alive with people. Each stop was a mini club, filled with Taiwanese locals brewing tea, making breakfast, and, of course, playing badminton. We were welcomed like old friends. When they found out how good we were, their excitement was contagious. We were invited to play and played point after point, and they couldn't stop smiling, or feeding us.

As we climbed higher and the sun began to rise, I found myself grinning from ear to ear. It was one of those rare moments when everything made sense: the sport, the people, the connection. Playing with kids, elders, complete strangers who shared our love for the game … it was pure. Simple. Joyful.

We didn't head back until late afternoon. I didn't want to leave. That morning reminded me exactly why I started playing badminton in the first place. Not for medals, or money, or rankings, but for moments like that. Community, humility and gratitude. I only wish I'd taken more time during my career to experience things like it.

(Oh, and I Met Ed)

I had been in a few relationships before, but dating while constantly travelling the world as an elite athlete was never easy, especially with people who didn't fully understand the unique demands of my lifestyle. In the summer of 2005, my sister messaged me, saying she was heading out to some bars in Milton Keynes and there was someone on her course she thought I'd fancy and get along with. She was right. Enter Ed. Slightly younger than me (two years and three months to be exact, Ed), a good-looking police officer who loved sport and worked out regularly. We met that night, exchanged hellos, and while I remained sober in preparation for my flight to Jakarta the next morning, Ed was … getting *very* drunk. At one point, he took his shoe off on the dance floor and started trying to slap people in the face. I turned to my sister with doubts, but she laughed and promised me he was normally very sensible when sober.

The next day, I got a phone call from Ed, oblivious to the fact I was in Indonesia and how expensive international rates were, telling me he had fallen asleep in the middle of a dual carriageway, only to be woken by the police and escorted home. Not a conversation I was expecting, but, somehow, curiosity got the better of me, and we began dating. Ed was quieter and more introverted than anyone I'd dated before (only when he was drunk did he display outrageous behaviours), and especially compared to Nathan. His calm, dependable nature stood out. He really listened, gave thoughtful advice and quickly became a steady, grounding influence in my often-chaotic world. When Ed and Nathan eventually met, it ended in a friendly right hook from Ed that landed a bit too hard, resulting in a crack we all heard. Awkward? Absolutely. But we all laugh about it now … I promise! In 2006, Ed moved in with me in Milton Keynes and became a beloved cornerstone in my life. He was my 'Steady Eddie', my rock through the rollercoaster that was my sporting career.

Melbourne Commonwealth Games, 2006

I was ready for this tournament. Focused. Determined. I had my sights set on gold in the mixed doubles, and I genuinely believed Nathan and I could do it and make amends for not winning gold in Manchester. England had slipped a little in the rankings, so gold was ambitious, but a medal felt certain. The women's doubles was more of a wildcard; there were some strong pairs in there, which meant anything could happen.

What I hadn't prepared for was Melbourne's ridiculous heat. March turned out to be a furnace, and our team manager had earlier in the year decided we didn't need air conditioning in our rooms. Cue 40-degree heat storms, no sleep, and let's not forget the spiders. Absolutely massive. Hairy. Lurking. Watching. Australia, seriously, what is wrong with your wildlife?

We started strong, and England picked up silver in the team event. Then came the individual events and, with them, the relentless routine: early mornings on the bus to the venue, late nights trying to wash kit in laundry rooms (because, yes, still not enough kit). We were housed in brand-new accommodation that hadn't been properly finished, so no kitchens, basic fittings and floor-to-ceiling windows, some with no curtains. Perfect for a bit of accidental people-watching. Now, Donna and I may have discovered an unexpected highlight of the Games. Let's just say some of the male swimmers (who shall remain nameless) were fully aware that their lit windows and post-training strip-downs were visible to others. No full nudity, very professional and tasteful, but I will confess my admiration for swimmer physiques, so Donna and I may have enjoyed our cups of tea a little more each evening. Appreciation only, of course. On behalf of both of us, thank you, gentlemen.

Back to the less glamorous parts of the Games. The accommodation also came with limited plug sockets. Donna and I had just one between us. Midway through the tournament, I'd just showered and needed to dry my hair, but Donna was using our one plug. 'No worries,' I thought, 'I'll use one in the communal lounge.'

In the lounge, our analyst Hannah Behan had her setup on a table, but she wasn't there, and her laptop screen was blank. I assumed she wasn't using anything, so I unplugged one lead for a few minutes, cranked up some music and dried my hair. Just as I was finishing, I heard a scream that still haunts me:

'NOOOOOOOOOOOOOOOOOOOOOO!'

In burst Hannah, pale, panicked and seconds from tears. I stood there, towel-clad, hairdryer in hand, completely clueless. Turns out, by unplugging her external drive, I had accidentally wiped the entire England badminton team's opponent analysis. All of it. Gone. Two years of work. Dozens of match plans. Our entire playbook. Toast.

The coaches rushed in thinking someone had been murdered. Instead, they found me sheepishly holding a hairdryer. Hannah was inconsolable. We had to head to the arena for a match, and I was public enemy number one. No opponent prep for anyone. Silence at breakfast. Side-eyes in the corridor. Brutal.

Hannah eventually forgave me, managing to recover a small fraction of the data, but most of it was gone. My joke that we didn't need it anyway, especially after Nathan and I went on to win, didn't go down well. Too soon, Gail. Way too soon.

In the mixed, Nathan and I beat Singapore in the semis and cruised through the final against New Zealand. The air conditioning in the hall gave us a nice tailwind, so with the right side, you could unleash a monster smash. Even mine was thunderous.

In women's doubles, Donna and I lost the semis to Malaysia, but won the bronze match against Singapore. So, I finished with a full set of medals: gold, silver and bronze.

It was a strong showing overall, but I was gutted about missing the women's doubles final. I'd put so much pressure on myself to deliver in the mixed that I think I held back a little in the other event. It was a lesson. I wanted to prove to Donna that I could do both ladies' and mixed doubles. I told myself I'd never split focus like that again.

Truthfully, the Commonwealth Games were a grind. Not a happy grind. I was ready to go home. Most of the athletes stayed for the closing ceremony and flew back to Heathrow together. Donna and I boarded the same flight and, somehow, don't ask me how, we were assigned exit row seats. Right next to 6ft 7 boxer David Price. I was in the middle. Donna got the window seat.

Now, I did *not* request an exit row seat. At 5ft 3 (and a half), I don't need one. Donna, at 5ft 10, was thrilled. But as I sat down, I became the target of every tall athlete walking past. 'Are you joking?' 'How's *she* got an exit row?' 'She's the *smallest* on the team!'

Over. And over. Again. What really got me was how no one even addressed me directly. Just comments flying around as if I were invisible. Not one polite request to swap. Just muttering, swearing and exaggerated sighs, by the 90 per cent of Team England who were taller than me.

Eventually, a stewardess came over and asked if I wanted to move. At that point, I had had enough of everyone being mean. No chance. They could all sit on their long legs and sulk. So, in retaliation for me saying no, the netball team decided to stand in front of me, chatting loudly, stepping on my feet, making a point, the *whole flight home*. It was like being back in school. Eventually, the crew told them to sit down. I flinched every time someone 'accidentally' trod on my foot, only to be met with, 'At least *you* can stretch your legs.' Ah, yes. The sweet, supportive camaraderie of elite sport …

European Championships, Netherlands, 2006

Just one month after the Commonwealth Games and, boom, we were straight into *another* major championship. No rest, no reset. The schedule kicked off (yet again) with the team event before the individual matches. I think we picked up a bronze but, honestly, by then the fatigue was starting to bite.

Nathan and I were both playing two events within the team competition, before the individual events took place, and the workload was taking its toll. He was absolutely shattered. And when we lost to Germany in the quarter-finals of the mixed doubles, it was a full-on shock. It was *the* upset of the tournament.

I was livid. I couldn't contain my disappointment. I was *raging*. 'What the actual fuck?! Are you kidding me?!' I was ranting to anyone who would listen (or even those who wouldn't), convinced Nathan had just given up on me. In my head, it was all on him. Of course it wasn't, I was knackered too. But when you're in the middle of it, tunnel vision takes over. How could he not find the extra energy to push through?

And then it hit me. As I was mid-rant, something clicked. I had to deliver in the women's doubles with Donna, or I was going to be all talk and no action. The partner who is quick to moan when it doesn't go her way. I decided that wasn't going to happen. Time to put the big girl pants on. No moaning. No excuses. Just get it done. And we did. *Gold.*

Donna Kellogg is an absolute legend; she was *phenomenal.* Together, we dug deeper than ever. The rallies were *endless.* Seriously, I think we set a world record for the longest point. The final was against the Germans; those girls were machines with the stamina of ultra-marathoners, but we outwitted them. Stubbornness. Grit. Refusing to give up. That was our game that day, and it paid off. Donna and I were crowned European champions.

Afterwards, I cried. Not out of emotion or pride, but just from sheer exhaustion. Everything ached. Everything. But there was barely time to breathe, let alone rest. Training for the World Championships in Madrid was just around the corner.

I needed to deliver in Madrid. The pressure was on.

Donna Kellogg – the Duchess of Derby

If there's one other person I need to pay tribute to in my badminton journey, it's my ladies' doubles partner, the one and only Donna Kellogg. It is very easy to write a book on my mixed doubles achievements as, for me, it was the most exciting event to play. I had grown up playing against boys, always proving a point on the opposite side of the net, getting their smashes back, so it was always my first love among the disciplines. Ladies' doubles, in comparison, is slower, with more patience needed, and it took me a while to fully understand the game and learn to love it.

Donna was affectionately known on tour by many names: the Duchess of Derby, Crazy Kellogg, and, in particularly intense matches, The Hulk. But behind the nicknames was a player who had the unique ability to change the momentum of a match in a single shot. At 5ft 10, with legs that seemed to go on forever, Donna could cover the court in a way that left opponents, especially the tactically astute Asian pairs, completely thrown off. Her reach and anticipation were game-changing, and her skill level was off the charts.

But Donna was never just about the shots. She had fire. Sometimes, *a lot* of fire. Her emotional reactions during a match became part of her legend. Let's just say she didn't always choose the calmest moments to 'Hulk out', but that was part of her magic. Her yellow card tally even prompted a letter from the Badminton World Federation suggesting she go for 'anger management' classes.

One time at the Swiss Open, the tournament organisers had placed delicate artificial flower baskets between courts to try to spruce up the venue. Lovely idea. Except Donna, mid-match and mid-rage, golf-swung one clean off the court, the flower heads flying everywhere like confetti. Another time, she squeezed a shuttle so hard in frustration that it crumpled in her hand before being launched directly at the tournament desk. It was *art*, in its chaotic way.

Then there was the Japan Open, hosted (bizarrely) in a disused air hangar. Great for cameras, but not so great for shuttle speed.

With thin air and no air flow, the shuttle slowed to a crawl. We found ourselves stuck in a match against a Japanese pair with world-class defence. After what felt like an eternity (25 minutes, in fact), it was still 2-2. I started to cry, right there on the court. 'This is *not* why I play badminton,' I sobbed to Andy Wood, our coach. Donna, also physically and mentally at her limit, followed suit. We lost that match and our minds, but years later, it became one of our best shared stories.

Then came Singapore. Another Japanese pair, this time with an ear-piercing celebration squeal – 'Eeeeeeeeeee!' – every time they won a point. Imagine the sound of a guinea pig being strangled. Now repeat it. For a full match. Donna was *not* okay with it. It got so bad, we started making the noise back at them. Four grown women are now squealing at each other across the net. It was absurd. And yes, we lost again. It still haunts us.

But despite the madness, or maybe *because* of it, Donna was the kind of partner you'd go to war with. Her dives became iconic, though often accidental. At the Danish Open, she launched herself across the court, tumbled a few times, and ended up butt first in a kit basket at the side of the court, legs kicking in the air like an overturned tortoise. I couldn't stop laughing. We lost the point. Totally worth it, though.

She never held back from speaking her mind either. Once, in Asia, surrounded by officials and opponents all under 5ft tall, she loudly proclaimed: 'I look like a bloody *freak* here!' Donna didn't do subtle. But she *did* have honesty, grit and relentless drive.

She played through injury after injury; back, feet, you name it. If modern sports science and medical support had been around earlier in her career, I genuinely believe Donna Kellogg would've collected even more medals and titles. Because talent-wise, she was one of the best players England ever produced.

Walking out on to the court with Donna was never boring. Her game was unpredictable, brave and full of heart. She brought drama, laughter, dives, pirouettes and unforgettable moments. More than anything, she brought fight. She's a testament to mental toughness and overcoming adversity. A powerhouse in every sense of the word, and an incredible friend. I will always be proud to say I played alongside 'Craaaazzzzzzeeeeee Kellogg'. It was a privilege to share that journey with her.

On Top of the World – World Championships, 2006

If 2005 in Anaheim, USA was the heartbreak, then 2006 in Madrid, Spain was the redemption tour. At least, that was the plan.

Let's rewind. The 2005 World Championships were meant to be *our* year. Nathan and I were playing brilliantly, top seeds, in form and full of belief. We were ready to conquer California and claim that elusive world title. That is, until British Airways went on strike, one week before the tournament. Of course they did.

Suddenly, our preparation turned into a logistical nightmare. Flights cancelled, chaos everywhere. Somehow, by what I can only describe as divine sporting intervention, Nathan, Donna Kellogg and I managed to blag the last few seats on one of the remaining direct flights to LA. Others weren't so lucky. Some team-mates had to detour via Vegas. One group even got a limo from Vegas to LA because it was the only transport left. It was less 'elite sports team' and more *Race Across The World: Badminton Edition*.

Anyway, we made it. The tournament was being held in the Anaheim Ducks stadium, minus the ice, of course, and we were feeling good. The draw was perfect. We had our training slot, and we were ready. And then … it happened. Ten minutes into practice, after a few light rallies and a couple of drop shots, Nathan went down. Not in a heroic, slow-motion sporting way. He just … *crumpled.* I looked at him lying on the court and rolled my eyes: 'Oh, come *on*, get up, you idiot.' (Or something slightly stronger.) But Nathan didn't get up.

And then I saw it. His right ankle had ballooned to almost double its size. Just like that, *boom* – the dream was over. One day before our first match. The pain was real for him, physically, and, for me, emotionally. We were top seeds! We had the draw! We had the momentum! And now, all we had was crutches, an ice pack and a lot of swearing.

But that's sport. It can be cruel, chaotic and completely out of your control. You just have to breathe and move on. Donna and I salvaged the trip with a run to the quarter-finals in women's doubles and then, because when life gives you lemons, you hire a convertible, we did an epic California road trip. Vegas, San Francisco, Santa Cruz. Sun, sea and saloon bars. The kind of recovery only America can offer.

So, Madrid 2006 turned into unfinished business.

Nathan and I came into the tournament focused, ready and with something to prove. Our draw this year, however, was brutal. Every round felt like a final. But we navigated it one match at a time:

First round – Scotland – win.

Second round – Korea – win.

Quarter-finals – Laybourn/Juhl of Denmark – win. (Old rivals from the All England final.)

Semi-finals – Sudket/Saralee of Thailand – we scraped through, 25-23 in the third game. Absolute heart-attack territory. My parents nearly combusted in the stands.

And then … the final. But this came with a twist, as our opponents were our *team-mates*. My roommate Donna Kellogg and Nathan's roommate Anthony Clark. Best mates. Shared dinner the night before. Shared breakfast the morning of. Shared dreams of gold.

We did what any pros would do: smiled, nodded and quietly agreed to emotionally detach. 'Right,' I said to Donna, as we gathered our kit. 'You go your way, I'll go mine. See you on court.'

The national coaches weren't allowed to coach us. It was just us four. Team GB civil war. The weirdest kind of showdown. Playing against friends is always strange. You know their game inside out. You've seen them struggle, rise, break and recover.

Anthony was tense. I could feel it. He wanted this badly, probably a bit too badly. His shots were snatchy and rushed. Donna was trying to get involved in the game, but we kept the pressure on Anthony. We won the first game, and halfway into the second game we had a lead and the momentum. I remember looking across the net and seeing it in Donna's face; she knew. Nathan and I had it. We were going to win. And win we did.

The moment the final point landed, I felt … nothing. No explosion of joy. No screaming celebration. Just … *relief.* We climbed the podium, gold medals around our necks, national anthem playing, and I remember just wanting a nap. My soul had left the building. Everyone asks what it's like to become a world champion. And yes, it's incredible. But in that moment, I was just done. I was mentally fried and emotionally emptied out.

We had a celebratory dinner that night with champagne, laughs and lots of photos. But I wasn't really there in spirit. I watched my parents beaming, socialising and toasting the win. I slipped away to bed before midnight. No party. No fuss. Just silence.

Steph: Can you tell me more about that feeling of 'emotional numbness'?

Gail: It's just survival mode. You go into autopilot. Our schedules were ridiculous, but you could never moan. You're lucky to be there and doing what you're doing. Oh my God, it's so hard mentally to keep winning over and over and over again. Your brain hurts. You're in the middle of Korea or somewhere. You're missing your best friend's wedding. You can't sleep, so you're on sleeping tablets constantly. You're on so many diclofenac tablets, trying to keep your body together. Your shoulder is screwed, and your knees are strapped up. You're missing real life. But you are 'living the dream'. So, you become numb.

Steph: It's natural that your brain shuts down and feels numb to protect you when your nervous system is overloaded. It's helping your brain calm itself when you're overwhelmed. The problem is, over time, if you keep shutting off, then it's going to have consequences, physically and emotionally.

Gail: If you're numb, you can't be fearful.

Steph: You know how some animals play dead when they're traumatised?

Gail: Yeah …

Steph: It's called the flop trauma response. And this is what was happening to you.

Gail: So, you're comparing me to a goat pretending to be dead? I think I have seen that on TikTok.

Steph: (laughing) What I am saying is this is your body's natural way of dealing with stress. It works for you because you're mentally and physically unresponsive when you do that, so you don't have to go there, where it is painful. And by the way – good use of humour again to deflect what's uncomfortable for you.

It took me weeks and weeks to process that I was actually a 'world champion'. I finally found myself looking at the medal. It glinted in the light. And I finally let it sink in. We had done it. We were gold medallists. We were number one in the world. What was so strange was that as soon as those feelings landed, I started to question how long I wanted to continue playing badminton for. In 2006, we had the World Championships, Commonwealth Games and European Championships. All in one year. I was exhausted. I remember someone coming up to me at the National Badminton Centre and saying, 'Make sure you win a gold medal at the 2008 Olympics in Beijing, otherwise I won't have a job.' They said it a bit tongue in cheek, but it got to me. I thought, 'There must be more to this.' I remember turning to Andy and saying, 'After the Olympics in Beijing, I'm going to stop.' I don't think he believed me when I said it. But I knew. Mentally, I had gone.

Ed and I were in a serious and committed relationship, and we were talking (privately) about wanting a family. Physically, I could have carried on playing badminton for much longer, as my body never had any bad injuries, but I wanted to stop at 31 years old. A short professional career, really. The end of elite sport for me was in sight.

THE LAST HURRAH – OLYMPIC GAMES 2008, BEIJING, CHINA

THE CLUE was always in the name … Beijing. China. Badminton. We were heading straight into the lion's den. Everyone knew the Olympic Games in Beijing was going to be the toughest test. It was home soil for the strongest badminton nation in the world. And for Nathan and me, the two years since we had won the World Championship had been decent: semi-finals, the occasional final, but not outstanding. We were not in world-beating form. Not podium form.

The real issue was Nathan's right ankle; it had never been 100 per cent right since that fall in the 2005 World Championships. The pain and joint restriction were starting to seriously affect his movement, especially his reach into that forehand rear corner, where so many critical rallies are won and lost. He was tentative, unsure and the uncharacteristic errors were creeping in.

And, truthfully, so was the tension.

I could sense it in his game, in his body language, in the way he snapped back when we tried to talk about it. He'd brush it off with 'it is what it is', or something vague and deflective, like a man pretending everything was fine as the house burned down behind him. I didn't want him giving me vague answers. I wanted plans. I wanted commitment. I wanted my partner, the confident, combative, razor-sharp Nathan I knew.

Eventually, the decision was made that he would have surgery. The ankle needed to be cleaned up and sorted. And we'd just have to hope; to pray, really, that he'd be back in time, and in form, for the biggest tournament of our lives.

Meanwhile, our Olympic seeding hadn't exactly done us any favours. Nathan and I were ranked No.5 in the world. Anthony and Donna were No.6. Both solid positions, but just outside the top four, which meant … no protection in the draw. And that's when fate, disguised in a Team GB blazer, stepped in. Sir Clive Woodward, fresh into his shiny new role as chef de mission for Team GB, drew our opponents out of the hat. I wish I could say he had the magic touch. He didn't. He pulled out the worst-case scenario for both British pairs. I mean, spectacularly bad. Almost comically.

Nathan and I drew the No.2 seeds: Gao Ling and Zheng Bo of China.

Donna and Anthony got the No. 3/4 seed: He Hanbin and Yu Yang, also of China.

To make it even more ironic, we had better records against *each other's* opponents. Honestly, when I saw the draw, I just stood there thinking: 'S**t. S**t. F**king s**t. Thanks a lot, Sir Clive.'

Gao Ling. The same Gao Ling who had beaten us in the final in Athens four years earlier. A legend. And now partnered with Zheng Bo, who could smash a shuttle faster than most of the men on the circuit. We had never beaten them. Not once. They were the poster pair of the 2008 Games, China's Olympic darlings, and playing in front of a home crowd that expected nothing less than gold.

And yet, despite all of that, there's always that flicker of belief. That little whisper that says: 'But maybe …' That's what sport does to you, doesn't it? It feeds you this stubborn hope. Even when logic says, 'You're not the favourites to win,' your heart says, 'Yeah, but there's always a chance.'

If Nathan had been fully fit, if we'd had the perfect Olympic preparation, maybe I'd have believed more than just a flicker. But we had to work with what we had. I had to train like never before – Andy Allford pushed Donna, Anthony and me to our limits, and Nathan joined in when and where he could. We adapted. We worked. We fought. And slowly, but surely, Nathan's ankle healed. The prayers had worked, and with just a few weeks to go until we left for the games, Nathan was at a good level of fitness.

And spare a thought for Anthony … he even gave up junk food. Now, that was a bigger shock than any Olympic draw. Let's be clear: if there was one man who had *not* eaten a green vegetable since 1997, it was him. He was a man powered by chicken nuggets, but he gave it a go. He signed up for the most intense nutrition programme of his life … and his body loved it. His *personality*, however, did not. He became a miserable sod. A proper moaner. It was endless. The complaining. The cravings. The existential despair over broccoli. After about eight weeks of it, the rest of us snapped. We practically begged him: 'Please, for the love of all things holy, just eat some f**king chicken nuggets!' He did and, just like that, happy Anthony was back. Some things, it turns out, are better than vegetables.

Punch-ups, Pool Cues and Princess Anne – Macau Training Camp

The Team GB pre-Olympic training camp was in Macau, a place I'd never been before. Known as the 'Vegas of the Far East', it felt slightly surreal to be doing shuttle drills somewhere usually more associated with roulette wheels and suspiciously cheap martinis.

For most of Team GB, China was still new territory. There was support on hand, translators, nutrition advice, tips on local etiquette, basically a small army of people making sure no one accidentally offended anyone or poisoned themselves with a dodgy meal. For me, though, it just felt like another stop on the seemingly endless circuit. I did a quick count and realised this was going to be my 25th trip to Beijing. Twenty-five. I'd been to Beijing more than I'd been to my local pub. That's how long I'd been chasing shuttles across Asia.

Macau itself was … interesting. Lots of neon and not much badminton history. But the real highlight, at least according to our strength and conditioning coach Andy Allford, was the fact that the USA basketball team, aka 'The Dream Team', was also in town.

Now, Andy, bless him, is a massive basketball fan. Possibly still grieving the fact that he never quite hit the 6ft mark to make a bigger impact in his basketball days. When he heard we could get tickets to watch LeBron James, Kobe Bryant and Carmelo Anthony in action, he was like a kid on Christmas Eve with a Red Bull drip. He was practically vibrating with joy. I think he did wee himself a bit, but I didn't ask too many questions.

We got there, great seats, atmosphere buzzing … and I fell asleep. Yep. Out cold. Drool and everything. To this day, I may be the only person on Earth who has watched LeBron James dunk and thought, 'Meh, nap time.' In my defence, I had serious jet lag and zero emotional investment in basketball. Sorry, Andy. Truly.

The rest of the camp went surprisingly smoothly. Training was sharp, the food was bearable and other sports were filtering in too. The boxers, for one, added a whole new level of entertainment. Back in Athens 2004, Amir Khan had been the lone GB boxer. Now in 2008, the squad was stacked, and lively as hell. I loved them. They were all completely different sizes and had accents from every corner of Britain; Scouse, Cockney, Manc, Geordie. It was like a live-action episode of *EastEnders* meets *Gladiators*.

The boxers' favourite pastime was pool. Not swimming – snooker-style pool. The kind played in a communal area with slightly sticky cues and an unspoken 'winner stays on' policy that somehow always ended in chaos. Every time I walked past, there was a new argument. Loud, creative and occasionally threatening.

Picture this: Billy Joe Saunders, a wiry welterweight with a sharp tongue, accusing David Price, an actual human skyscraper of a super-heavyweight, of a dodgy shot. Voices rise, pool cues clutched like medieval weapons. I genuinely once saw a flyweight square up to someone triple his weight. It wasn't just sport, it was theatre. And I had front-row seats.

Then word came down the corridor like an Olympic game of Chinese whispers: Princess Anne was about to pop in and say hello. Now, in theory, this shouldn't have been a problem. In practice, there was an escalating boxing civil war going on over a disputed foul, and those pool cues were starting to look less like sports equipment and more like jousting lances. It was about to kick off, and royalty was walking straight into it.

I ran in like someone possessed and shouted, '*Princess Anne is coming*!' Now, I don't know what I expected … but I certainly didn't expect every single boxer to instantly snap to attention like a synchronised platoon. Pool cues down. Hands by their sides. Silent. Immaculate. Like naughty schoolboys mid-fight who just heard the headteacher's footsteps in the corridor.

Moments later, in walked Princess Anne. She looked around the room, raised an eyebrow and, with immaculate dry wit, asked, 'Who's winning then?' David Price, not missing a beat and clearly still buzzing from his last shot, replied, 'That would be me, Ma'am.' Cue a room full of boxers seething in silence, stewing at the injustice but too royal-terrified to speak. Princess Anne smiled, nodded graciously, wished them all luck, and off she went.

Then, as if nothing had ever happened, they all instantly returned to their original positions, picked up their cues and resumed arguing. Same volume. Same insults. Same threatened uppercuts. I just sat back down, sipped my water and thought, 'This is better than anything on telly.'

Murrays and Messi

We arrived at the Team GB headquarters in the Olympic Village, where the flat allocations had already been sorted. This time around, the badminton team was sharing a flat with Andy and Jamie Murray. Yep, *those* Murrays.

I'd met Jamie a few months before, but Andy, the rising star of British tennis, was still just a name in headlines, with the occasional grumble from the British media for his dry humour. They weren't due to arrive until later, though.

In the meantime, I was busy walking around the village feeling … ancient. At 31, surrounded by baby-faced athletes with Instagram-confidence levels (before Instagram was even a thing), I felt more like a team chaperone than a competitor. Gone were the wide-eyed nerves of Athens. Everyone here walked with purpose, earbuds in, no time for eye contact. I remember thinking, 'Did I ever look that assured?' Probably not.

Sir Clive Woodward was the first familiar face we bumped into. He greeted us with a smile that said, 'I hope you've forgotten that terrible draw I gave you.' I hadn't. I stared at him: '*You*!' He got in before I could open my mouth, 'I'm so sorry.' At least he *knew*. That alone earned him a fraction of forgiveness.

Clive had also introduced a new rule: the 'GB kit colour schedule'. Every day in the village was designated red, white or blue, and we were all expected to match. It felt like being in the world's fittest cult. You couldn't even sneak to breakfast in a rogue T-shirt without getting side-eyed by a synchronised swimmer in full kit.

This time, I got to do something I'd missed in Athens: walking in the opening ceremony. Standing in line, I found myself next to a 13-year-old Tom Daley, who, despite still being at an age where most boys were discovering Lynx Africa, was already a mega-celebrity in China. Fans were screaming his name, leaning over barriers just to get a glimpse. I stood next to him, feeling like a hired babysitter.

It was humid. The waiting was endless. We were hot, sweaty, dehydrated and borderline hangry. But the moment we entered the Bird's Nest stadium and heard 'Team Great Britain' echo around that vast arena … goosebumps. The lights, the crowd, the camera flashes, wow, it was the only time in my career I was truly jealous of the athletics and football teams. That entrance was the dream.

Of course, once the lap was done, we were penned into the middle of the stadium like battery hens, still no water, still no food, and surrounded by increasingly energetic Chinese dancers. I was on the brink of collapse, staring blankly ahead, when I noticed two absolutely massive figures next to me, trying desperately to blend in. *Kobe Bryant and LeBron James.* Two of the tallest men on Earth … attempting subtlety in a stadium of 5ft-somethings. It was like hiding giraffes in a petting zoo.

When the (possibly CGI) fireworks ended, we legged it out of there. Food. Shower. Bed. Then the Murrays arrived. And let's just say … they were not in the Olympic spirit. They strolled in with their own gear on, Team GB kit still crumpled in a bag, and looked around like they'd just walked into a very enthusiastic summer camp. 'So, what's this all about then?' Andy asked, genuinely baffled.

No. Nope. I wasn't having that. Absolutely not.

I sat them down and gave them the crash course in 'What The Olympics Means'. I explained how, for most of us, *this* – the Olympic Games – was the absolute pinnacle. We weren't squeezing it in between Wimbledon and the US Open. We lived for this. Trained our whole lives for it. And all we asked was that they put the bloody Team GB kit on.

To their credit, they did. They were probably a bit shocked, but they got changed, zipped up their GB hoodies, and Donna and I took them to the food hall, basically the social hub of the entire village. It is three football pitches in size. A huge all-you-can-eat buffet. Every cuisine imaginable, with athletes of every shape and size from every corner of the planet. Andy looked like he'd just walked into Willy Wonka's factory. I had to show them how to get a tray and guide them to the right counters. It was like taking two awkward nephews to their first school cafeteria.

Then Andy discovered pin badges. '*This is amazing*!' he shouted. 'You can swap with all the countries!' We rolled our eyes. He was like a child at Disney. And so began the unofficial 'Badminton vs Tennis Pin Badge Swap Challenge'. Andy strode up to some athletes from a Caribbean island, beaming and holding out his GB pin. The look on their faces was pure confusion, followed by a polite-but-clear 'no thanks.' Andy was crestfallen. Apparently, being a semi-famous tennis player didn't mean much in the Olympic Village. Jamie, Donna and I laughed mercilessly, but that only fuelled him more. He went on a mission.

Donna and I lost. Badly. Andy came back like a man possessed with badges from everywhere. Turns out, he was better at pin trading than tennis that week. Which leads us to the match. Andy and Jamie went out in the first round. As they were unprepared, they were out of sync. They came back to the flat sheepish, apologetic and visibly gutted. 'We didn't give it enough respect,' they admitted. Four years later, in London, Andy Murray won Olympic gold. You're welcome. I'm taking *all* the credit.

The food hall was still my favourite place. You could just sit there, cuppa in hand and people-watch the most fascinating human zoo on Earth. The weightlifters looked like literal tanks. Gymnasts barely cleared 5ft. Basketball players made adult furniture look like nursery toys. It was a rainbow of tracksuits, body types and meal trays. I played a silent game of 'guess the sport' every day.

One morning, I wandered in solo. I got my cereal, maybe some porridge, and looked for a free spot. I saw a gap next to a group of Argentinian athletes, and sat down beside a short, quiet guy. His tracksuit said 'Argentina', so I tried some friendly miming.

'What sport?' I asked. He mimed back, 'Football,' while kicking under the table. He asked me about my sport. I replied, 'Badminton', while arm and wrist flicking, the action that people do to me, that I hate. We smiled, nodded and wished each other good luck in our respective mime languages. I finished my breakfast, said thanks and headed off. Nathan found me later, looking slightly baffled. 'You know you had breakfast with Messi, right?'

Lionel. Actual. Messi.

I mimed badminton to *Messi* ... I guess it's just another day at the Olympics.

Emms/Robertson vs Gao/Zheng. Play

It was the biggest match of my life. No exaggeration, just truth. This was the one. A defining moment, a make-or-break type of match that sticks to your soul long after the sweat has dried. Backstage, warming up with Nathan, I was trying to focus on tactics, but, with my brain, you can't give me more than two or three things to think about or I'll start mentally redesigning the Olympic logo and wondering what's for dinner. So, I picked my two key focus points, clung to them like a lifebuoy and tried not to pass out.

Then came the announcement:

'Representing Great Britain – Gail Emms and Nathan Robertson!'

It was showtime.

We walked out. Nathan first, then me, looking like the warm-up act for the real headliners. The crowd offered us a little polite applause. A few claps here and there. And then, there it was, *the unmistakable sound of my mother.*

'Go Gail! Wooooo! Go Gail!'

For God's sake, woman. There I was, about to play the match of my life, trying to enter a zen-like state of sporting readiness … and my mum's out in the stands doing a one-woman rave. I swear she was bouncing more than the shuttlecocks. Security. Please. Do your job.

And then … the home favourites arrived into the hall.

'From China – Gao Ling and Zheng Bo!'

The crowd *exploded*. Ten thousand people simultaneously lost their minds. I'm not sure if it was a badminton match or a boy band reunion. Horns, flags, screaming … meanwhile, Nathan and I looked like two uninvited guests at someone else's surprise party.

The Chinese coaches were so intense, I half expected them to remove their tracksuits to reveal boxing robes. The vibes were *not* gentle. This was war on a badminton court.

Now, fun Olympic fact: it's a weird feeling knowing that 99.9 per cent of everyone in the building wants you to fail spectacularly. They want you to miss or fluff every shot, and implode. Maybe even cry. They don't care about your years of training, but that's sport. You've got to show up anyway. Smile politely, and then try to ruin their day.

Play starts, and game one, we were *on fire*! We won it 21-16 and were basically strutting around thinking we'd just solved badminton.

Game two. Oh, right. Their turn to be on fire. Damn. We lost that 21-16, and it felt like we'd woken a dragon.

It went down to game three and, oh my God, we were *down 17-12*. Five points behind. And yes, I know five doesn't sound like much. But in Olympic badminton terms, that's like being in a three-legged race and realising the other team has four legs *and* jetpacks.

Then I looked at the scoreboard, the big, digital, LED-fabulous score, and thought: 'No. *No*. I'm not bloody losing this match! My mum has flown all the way from Bedford. She will bloody kill me if I lose this!'

We dug in. One point. 17-13; Another; 17-14. Zheng Bo started to twitch. Gao Ling was giving him *that* look. You know the one: 'Pull yourself together or you're toast.'

Momentum is magical. Suddenly, the wind was blowing our way. Not literally, but metaphorically, we were sailing. We clawed it back to 17-17. Then a little wobble, they edged ahead, but we kept going. 19-19. And then … 20-19 to us.

Match point. And whose serve was it? Mine. Of course. My hand was shaking. My *toes* were shaking. I could feel every nerve in my body screaming, '*Don't mess this up*.' I served. A short one. Perfect height. Zheng couldn't attack it. Hallelujah.

Then Nathan took over like a man possessed.

Smash.

Return.

Smash again.

Back it came.

Third smash to Gao Ling.

Down it went, landing on the floor at Gao Ling's feet.

We. Had. Done. It.

We had beaten the Olympic favourites in their own backyard. The 10,000-strong crowd was suddenly silent. Not even a polite clap. I could hear the metaphorical gasps echoing through China.

Sir Clive Woodward was in the VIP seats with the British Olympic entourage. After the match, he said it was one of the best sporting comebacks he'd ever witnessed. I told him that made us even for that dreadful draw he had handed us. We were square now, Clive.

Nathan and I were bouncing. Our coaches were jumping, hugging, doing the most unBritish public displays of emotion imaginable. My mum was still in full '*Go Gail!*' mode, now crying and chanting in equal measure. I practically rugby-tackled Nathan in celebration.

Security came over, presumably to protect us from 10,000 disappointed fans or maybe just to escort us straight into the media zone where the story was already spreading.

Gao Ling wasn't going to get her third Olympic gold. Not this time. Not on our watch.

And my mum? Oh, bless her. Later, she told me, completely deadpan: 'Wasn't it lovely that the Chinese crowd were chanting your name?' What…????? No, Mum. They weren't saying 'Gail'. They were saying 'Jiayou', which means 'go for it' or 'keep fighting'. But to her, they were my fans. Honestly.

We were buzzing on the way back to the village. Everyone was hyped up, chatting about how we might actually be on the path to Olympic gold. But deep down, we knew this was *just* the round of 16. The first step on the ladder. There were bigger battles to come.

Still, what a start!

Quarter-Finals: Emms/Robertson vs Lee/Lee

Quarter-finals of the mixed doubles. Nathan and I, versus the South Korean pair: Lee Yong Dae and Lee Hyo Jung. We'd beaten them before. They'd beaten us before. It was a 50:50 match, but after our first-round win, I liked our odds to beat them. Lee Yong Dae was just 22 years old – young, fast, practically floating across the court like a badminton angel on Red Bull. And Lee Hyo Jung was a solid brick wall with a killer smash. The game plan was simple: make Lee Hyo Jung move. Keep her shifting, pull her out of position to create gaps.

We went into the match confident. The warm-up was good. I was feeling sharp. Nathan was raring to go.

In game one, we played well, but the Koreans nicked it 21-19. Close. Cruel. The kind of score that makes you want to break a shuttlecock in half with your teeth.

Then … game two.

Let me tell you something about sport: sometimes, it just isn't your day. Not because you didn't prepare, not because you weren't good enough, but because fate decided to play a part in the result, and you were not the winning outcome.

Lee Yong Dae was a wizard that day. He hit the net cord so often, it was like he had a secret magnetic force attracting the shuttle to it. We were playing well, Nathan was doing everything right, but every time we hit a good shot, they'd do something outrageous in response, like they'd swapped rackets for magic wands.

We lost the second game 21-12.

We were out. Officially fifth place. Not exactly the Olympic ending I had written in my head. We had beaten the favourites in the previous round but, now, the dream was dead. The Koreans went on to win gold, so we didn't lose to just *anyone*. We lost to the best. Still ... that didn't make it sting any less.

I watched them cheer – *really cheer* – as we stood there, hollowed out. It was like watching someone throw a party inside your broken dream. All I could think was: 'Please tell me this isn't happening.' Nope. No such luck. It was painfully, excruciatingly real.

Then came the next phase of Olympic heartbreak: media interviews. You can't hide. It's in the contract. You lose, you cry, but you still have to walk past 30 cameras and pretend your soul isn't currently leaking out of your tear ducts. We trudged into the media zone. And who's waiting for us, under the brightest light in China? Rowing legend, Sir Matt Pinsent. Four-time Olympic champion. And now: bearer of microphones. He turns to me and asks, live on the BBC, 'So, Gail, how are you feeling right now?'

Oh, Matt. Matt, Matt, Matt. I love you. I respect you. But that has to go down as one of the most ridiculous questions I've ever been asked at that time. How do you *think* I'm feeling? I've just had my Olympic dreams smashed to bits in front of 10,000 people and about a billion people had watched on TV. I opened my mouth to answer politely ... but, instead, out came tears and snot, along with pure Olympic despair. It was not a graceful moment. Poor Nathan had to stand there awkwardly while I ugly-cried on national TV. He soldiered through the interview like a champ. I just tried not to drown in my own feelings.

Then came the press line. A conveyor belt of microphones and sympathetic nods. Nathan and I got separated and had to face the questions solo. Just me, some damp tissues, and a growing desire to escape to the Olympic Village and hide under a duvet.

I was *nearly* free. Just a few interviews left. And then ... *him*.

A man in his 30s. He had clearly been sent to badminton as punishment by his editor. He looked at me with the eyes of someone who had googled 'badminton facts' 30 seconds ago and was absolutely winging it. He asked the usual, 'Tough loss, how do you think the match went?' I mumbled something semi-coherent. Then he paused. His brain was clearly doing gymnastics. I saw the moment it panicked, trying to find any follow-up. And then … he hit me with it.

'So … are you going to have babies now?'

…?????

I'm sorry, *what*?!

Not 'What's next?'

Not 'Will you continue competing?'

Not 'How do you feel about your Olympic career overall?'

Nope.

'*Babies*.'

I looked at him angrily. I couldn't believe it. So I said, deadpan, 'Yeah. I'm starting tonight, actually. Cheers.' And walked away.

Honestly, I'd just poured my guts out on court, cried all over the BBC and this guy thinks that asking about motherhood is the best question for me. The audacity. The timing. The complete lack of *any* emotional intelligence. I guess in the minds of some people, once a female athlete has literally just finished a match for our country, we just turn into baby machines, as that is all we are good for. Classic.

So there it was. No medal. No fairy tale ending. Just heartbreak, tears and a deeply inappropriate interview. But that's sport. Sometimes you lose. Sometimes your dreams die on live television. And sometimes a man with a press badge asks if your uterus has immediate plans. All part of the Olympic experience.

I picked up my bag, barely knowing what I was doing. I felt … lost. Not just lost in the Olympic sense, lost as in disconnected from everything. I stood around, unsure where to go or who to be in that moment.

Then I saw my mum. She'd come down from the stands and was making her way towards me. The second I saw her, I just broke down. I couldn't hold it in anymore. The tears came like a flood. All I could feel was this overwhelming sense that I'd let her down.

She gave me a huge, grounding hug. And in that classic mum tone, I swear to God, she asked, 'Did you try your best?' I pushed her away, gently but sharply, and snapped back,' Of course I did, Mum. It's the Olympic Games. Of course I tried my best!'

Suddenly, I was a teenager again. Full Kevin and Perry. 'You don't understand. You're so embarrassing.' I wasn't angry at her, I just didn't know what to do with the wreckage of my dream.

Eventually, I sulked off and made my way to the Olympic Village shuttle transport. A bus was leaving in two minutes, and I legged it to catch it. Nathan was already on it, and it was rammed; not a single seat in sight. I made my way to the back, desperate to find one. I couldn't face standing for 45 minutes with everything aching, physically and emotionally.

And there it was. A lone seat. Glorious. Empty. Mine. I looked up at the person sitting next to it. It was Andy Murray. He and Jamie had come to watch our match and cheer us on. I remember him looking at me, his face still slightly frozen from watching me sob my way off the court. He clocked me, clocked the tears still on my cheeks and panicked. You could *see* it in his face. 'No no no no no,' he muttered, scanning the bus for another seat. Too late. I dumped my bag down next to him and said, 'You. I'm sitting here. And you're going to talk to me about anything but badminton. Got it?'

That poor guy looked like he was about to pass out. But credit where it's due, Andy stepped up. He talked absolute nonsense to me the entire ride back. Told me about his new house in Roehampton, how he'd moved to be closer to the tennis centre. He gave me the full life story of his dog, Maggie. Anything and everything to steer me away from the fact that I had probably just played my last match for Great Britain.

We got back to the village and still didn't quite know what to do with ourselves. Andy helped me with my bags, and we headed straight for the food hall. I didn't want to go back to my room. I wasn't ready to be alone with that grief. We walked in, me, Nathan, Jamie and Andy, and found a table. Andy wandered off to the McDonald's counter (yes, there's a full McDonald's inside the Olympic Village;

thank you, IOC sponsorship deals) and came back with a box of chicken nuggets for me. It sounds silly now, but that little act meant everything. I couldn't move. I couldn't speak. I just sat there, stunned. But Andy saw that. And he did what any true team-mate would do: he showed compassion. Quiet, unspoken compassion. Athlete to athlete. He placed the nuggets in front of me. I started crying again. He looked at me and said, softly, 'I had no idea that was your last match … I'm so sorry.'

And so, we sat there, eating McNuggets. And I mourned the dream that never happened.

After Athens, when we won a medal, the world wanted to talk to us. The calls didn't stop. Interviews. Sponsorships. Events. But Beijing? Fifth place? The silence was deafening. No one says this out loud, but it's there. The subtle shift from being a national hero to being a footnote. The unspoken line: 'If you don't medal, you didn't succeed.' The British Olympic Association would never say it's only about medals, but let's be honest … it felt like it. That was the difference between 2004 and 2008. In Athens, I was celebrated. In Beijing, I felt like a failure.

Everyone tells you that just qualifying for the Olympics is an achievement. And I know that's true. But it didn't feel that way. Not when you've worked your entire life for a dream that ends in a 45-minute bus ride, a box of nuggets and a quiet goodbye to your sport. I know I shouldn't compare the two games, but I'm human. And in that moment, all I felt was this crushing truth: I didn't win a medal. I didn't do what I came here to do. And in the eyes of the world, that meant one thing.

I had lost.

Aftermath

After our quarter-final loss, I was asked to attend a few sponsor events – Lenovo Computers and B&Q were supporting me at the time. One evening, I was invited to watch the athletics with Tony Blair. It was the night Christine Ohuruogu won gold in the 400m. I found myself in a box with Tony and Cherie. All very surreal.

Unfortunately, I kept calling their son Liam instead of Leo. Well done, Gail. Smooth.

What made things slightly more amusing (for me, not him) was, when we stepped out into the main stadium, people started pointing, waving, asking for selfies. Tony clearly thought it was all for him, he is a former prime minister, after all, but, actually, it was me they recognised. Turns out I was pretty well known in China at the time. Let's just say I don't think that sat too well with him.

When you needed a break from the Olympic Village, Team GB House was the place to go. It was a place where athletes could reconnect with loved ones, as friends and family weren't allowed inside the Olympic Village. It was private, as it was off-limits to the media and the general public, and had a lounge, food and a bar, which was essentially a Team GB version of *Cheers*, where everyone knew your name. It was close enough to the village and main stadium to be convenient, but just far enough to offer a peaceful escape from the noise, pressure and intensity of the Games.

Because badminton was one of the first sports on the schedule, we got to pop in and see friends and family early on. But as medals started rolling in, the rules changed and only medallists were allowed in on certain days due to capacity. It became a bit of a club, and if you weren't wearing a medal, well, good luck. One night, I desperately wanted in. I ended up asking Ed Clancy, one of our gold medal cyclists, if he could sneak me through. It was so painful to have to ask someone who had achieved what you hadn't to help you get in … but that's how it was.

That same night was the infamous 'Bradley Wiggins-on-a-taxi-roof' incident. Let's just say the drinks had been flowing and Brad got a bit … excitable. It got sorted quickly, but it's what happens when athletes finally let loose after months, or even years, of relentless discipline. Celebration, commiseration … either way, the release has to happen.

I stuck around Beijing for a few more days, tried to soak in the Olympic atmosphere but, honestly, my heart wasn't in it. One day in the food hall, I spotted French tennis star Gaël Monfils. Maybe

I'd had a drink or two by then, but I thought it was hilarious that we had the same name. I marched right up to him and said, 'Alright *Gaël*, I'm *Gail*!' He didn't find it nearly as funny. In fact, he told me, in no uncertain terms, to 'F**k off!'

Charming. Later, I tried sneaking into the tennis event with some friends. As athletes, we had passes that allowed access to lots of venues, within reason. The trick was to casually cover the part of the badge that said your sport. The goal was to blend in and get through security. So off we went, me, Donna, Hannah (our analyst), and we arrived at the tennis venue, fingers strategically placed over our credentials. Hannah and Donna got waved through. I didn't. A volunteer moved my finger, saw 'badminton', and said, 'You're not coming in.' Just then, who walks past but my old mate Gaël Monfils. So, still trying to salvage the situation, I called out, 'Gaël! It's Gail again! Remember me?' He didn't miss a beat. 'She is not with me. I do not know who she is.' And off he walked. Cheers, Gaël.

Donna and Hannah, meanwhile, ended up accidentally sitting in the athletes' warm-up area … surrounded by the likes of Roger Federer, Rafael Nadal and, yes, Monfils. They later told me, in disbelief, how much better the tennis warm-up area was than ours. Pool tables. Bean bags. Fancy snacks. Sofas. Badminton? We had water and a bench. Eventually, they got rumbled and were politely (ish) asked to leave.

The next mission was to watch some athletics. Donna and I had managed to sneak into the 100m final in Athens and thought, 'Why not try again?' So, same trick – finger over 'badminton', flash the pass, act casual. It worked this time. We were in. We wandered around pretending to be 400m runners, throwing in some stretches for good measure. We found some seats just before the 100m final and started chatting with a group of Brits nearby. 'So, who's going to win?' we asked. One girl looked at us like we'd landed from Mars. 'You see that really, really tall guy in lane 5?' We nodded. 'He's from Jamaica. He's going to win.' Donna, trying to build rapport, replied: 'Oh yeah, Jamaica, they're quite good at sprinting, aren't they?' Nailed it, Donna.

Of course, that guy was Usain Bolt, and we had a front-row seat to his first Olympic gold in the 100m. He won by a mile. And we were there for it, pretending to be runners, totally blagging it.

A few days later, I'd had enough. Fifth place wasn't what Team GB wanted, and I felt that loud and clear. So, I booked an early flight home, skipping the closing ceremony. On the bus to the airport, I ended up sitting next to Dave Brailsford, the performance director of British Cycling. We chatted, and when I mentioned I was retiring from badminton, he asked me how much I could squat. I told him. Apparently, it was more than Victoria Pendleton. His response was to invite me for a test. 'Fancy a trial in track cycling?' And for a second, my ego took off. Could I? Should I?

But the truth was that I wasn't ready to make any big decisions. I politely declined and never went to the Manchester Velodrome.

A part of me still wonders ... *what if I had?*

I sat on the plane home, alone. Not just alone in the literal sense, but in that 'quiet after the storm' kind of way. My Olympic dream was over, and I was doing my best not to think about what came next. But deep down, I knew reality was waiting, and I couldn't avoid it forever.

Steph: So, you didn't have a plan for what to do when you retired?

Gail: No, no plans whatsoever. Other than rule the world, obviously. I didn't understand why no one had offered me a job.

Steph: A Gail with no meaning and purpose spells danger to me! You know, it's impossible to replicate the adrenaline and dopamine hits you got from competing in sport at such a high level. Real life will always be a poor second best compared to that.

Gail: I wish more athletes were aware of this before they hit the wall like I did.

Steph: No surprise you hit the wall because you chose to conceal it all so well to the outside world, and it's a really heavy feeling doing that, basically pretending that everything is fine when it isn't.

Perfecting the pout at an early age.

Mum in her football days pre me.

I think the racket is bigger than me.

Talent oooozing out of me.

Trying to get sponsorship deals early on. Didn't work until 20 years later. Thank you Carlton.

Lisa and me aged two and five. Already proving my sister is not as cool as me.

Why is my sister licking my baby brother's head?

Yes I am topless. Only photo you will see of me this way. On holiday in Torremolinos.

Family holiday with my nan and grandad in the Algarve. Hired a villa. Ants attacked it and got in the Frosties. I took the photo. Obviously.

Bradgate Road Junior Club! I'm at the front. Pink tracksuit!

C&A pink tracksuit finest.

The standard awful school photo – Dame Alice Harpur School for Girls.

Bedfordshire U16 county team for ICT. I was 12. There's the balloon shellsuit.

Nathan and I winning the Yorkshire U18 aged just 16 years old because we were bloody good.

Girls' trip to Ibiza aged 18. Left to right: Hazel, Sunny, Lisa, Me, Anne, Jenny, Megan.

England U18 European Junior Squad in Slovakia.

Uni mates at a pub in Kingston. Near Emms passage. Left to right: Duffy, Lorna, Me, Lordy.

My first flat in Bedford with my brother Adam and sister Lisa.

Crazy Kellogg and me winning the ladies' doubles national title.

On the podium with our Athens 2004 Olympic silver medals. Nathan doing his best Jesus impression.

TIME TO SAY GOODBYE

I RETIRED at 31 years old. Some people dream of retiring at that age, don't they? No more early wake-up alarm calls, no more national pressure, no more protein shakes. But, for me, retirement at 31 didn't feel like freedom; it felt like an identity crisis.

One day, I was Gail Emms, Olympian, one of the best badminton players this country (and dare I say, the world) had seen. And the next? I was just … Gail. No kit, no match schedule, no Team GB hoodie. Just me with a CV that basically said: 'Can hit a shuttlecock very well. A bit feisty. Must exercise or will get angry.' A bit like a Gremlin instruction kit.

Honestly, I didn't *have* to retire. I wasn't injured, bankrupt or past it; in fact, I was in great shape. The medal from Athens had made life a lot more comfortable. But something inside me said it was time. Maybe I thought there'd be a glittering new chapter waiting for me, complete with exciting opportunities, a meaningful new purpose, and, dare I say, *closure*.

The spoiler alert is that there wasn't. I was so naive, in hindsight.

I approached retirement like I was still in training. Determined. Relentless. Like a hammerhead shark sniffing out the next challenge. I thought, 'Right, I've completed badminton. What's next? Conquer the world? Reinvent myself? Do *Strictly Come Dancing*?' (I didn't, sadly.)

But here's the truth no one tells you when you leave elite sport: it's not a fresh start. It's not a gentle glide into the next chapter. It's grief. Full-on, gut-punching grief. It's like someone tears out a chunk of your soul, the bit powered by dreams, competition and adrenaline, and throws it in the bin. You mourn not just your career, but your identity. The '*you*' that you've trained, built, sacrificed for … is now all gone. And it's not dramatic to say that you have to learn how to be a whole new person. A civilian.

I hoped I was leaving on a high, maybe even with people saying, 'Oh, Gail should've carried on – she had more in her.' You want to exit like a rock star leaving the stage, fans still cheering. But let's just say not *everyone* was devastated.

Nathan, my long-time mixed doubles partner, my on-court partner in crime, my badminton husband – I honestly thought he'd be lost without me, that he'd turn up at my door, bouquet in hand, sobbing, 'Please don't leave me! I can't play without you!' Instead … he found Jenny.

Yes, Jenny Wallwork. Tall. Young at 21 years old. Brunette. New kid on the block. She arrived on the scene with suspicious speed. I blinked and suddenly there she was, taking my place, doing interviews, training with Nathan and tapping his bum on court. It was like watching your ex parade around with his shiny new girlfriend while you're still sobbing into your pasta bake. The pair started dating too. Now, I didn't go there!

I'd smile in interviews and say how supportive I was of the new pairing. 'They're doing so well, aren't they?' I'd say through a smile. But deep down, I was praying they wouldn't do better than Nathan and me. I know, I know, it's petty. It's all ego. But that's the truth. I wasn't ready to be replaced. I certainly wasn't ready to be replaced *so well*.

In the end, what I've come to realise is that retirement isn't a clean break. It's messy. It's emotional.

And there are the darkest, most awkward days. You're learning how to be a human again after living as a high-performance machine for decades.

Steph: Do you think you have ever properly grieved the loss of your career?

Gail: No, because no one talked to me about it. I didn't understand any of the emotions I was feeling. I now know it was grief. I had no control. I was waiting for someone else to take care of the situation. I was stuck in a narrative of: 'Someone save me.' But I didn't want to say that because that's not how a sportsperson acts. To show vulnerability? I only know how to fight. I still dream about playing, I replay points I missed, and there's also the scenario of being late because I have missed the bus, or I can't get to the court for some reason.

Steph: Because you never processed the trauma of the ending properly, it's still real for you now. This is why things trigger you all the time and pull you back, and why you still dream about playing and reliving points. Your brain is stuck on repeat, and it will keep serving up your past until you learn from it.

Grief and Going Cold Turkey

The first few weeks after retiring were absolute elation. Pure joy. A big *woo-hoo! Here we go*! No more brutal 6am training sessions, no more dragging my body through the gym while someone shouts at me to 'dig deep'. Instead, I gleefully said hello to burgers, late nights, lie-ins, and the sheer luxury of doing what I wanted, when I wanted. No more being told what to do, how to move, what to eat or when to stretch. It felt like freedom.

But then … reality arrived. Quietly at first … then like a slap in the face with a big fish.

About three months in, the novelty wore off. I realised that while I'd spent my life chasing gold medals, the rest of the world was chasing mortgage approvals and utility bills. And guess what? The real world didn't care that I'd been a world No.1. The sporting spotlight had faded, and now I was just … Gail. And that real world runs *very* differently. In sport, if something needs doing – you do it. No fuss. No dithering. No emails about emails. But out of sport, oh no. Everything takes *forever*.

A decision? That'll need a meeting.

A follow-up? Book it in for three weeks' time.

Approval? Not your department – ask Sandra. But Sandra's on annual leave until the 14th, so … hold tight.

I couldn't believe it. Why all the talking? Why no doing?! Meetings about meetings. Brainstorms about brainstorms. And don't even get me started on 'circling back'. Honestly, the world could run *so* much more smoothly if it borrowed just a little of sport's get-it-done energy. Because out here, I felt like I'd gone from elite performance … to elite patience.

I was slowly going insane.

Steph: I think because you never got an option to stay connected with badminton in any way, it was like going cold turkey; well, freezing turkey actually; you were throwing everything you loved and valued professionally and socially in the bin. Being able to give back to the sport would have been therapeutic and rewarding for you. The junior girls could have learned so much from your experience.

Gail: I would have loved to have worked with the girls. We don't have enough female coaches. We don't have a mixed doubles mentor for girls to talk to about what it's like on that court when the guy is smashing a shuttle at 250mph at your face. But coaching, I don't think it was really me. But something would have been better than nothing. I was filled with a desire to give back, share my experience, my passion and everything I'd learned at the highest level. I saw so many opportunities to create lasting circles of support where former athletes could stay involved, offering expertise in coaching, mentoring, media, governance and beyond. But in truth, I don't think badminton quite knew what to do with me. I felt like an outsider to the sport I'd given my life to. No path, no plan, no invitation. It left me wondering … whose problem, was I? Because I wasn't sure if I was completely done with badminton … but it seemed like badminton was done with me.

I had no clue what I wanted to do next. If I'm honest, part of me genuinely expected the phone to ring with job offers – something glamorous, maybe sporty, definitely important. I mean I was an

Olympian. A world champion. Surely someone out there had a role with my name on it? But no. Silence.

So, after enduring what felt like an endless cycle of *meetings about meetings*, I eventually landed a job with the Youth Sport Trust. It sounded promising, going into schools, inspiring the next generation through sport. Perfect, right? At the interview, they asked me, 'Do you have much experience speaking in schools?' I smiled confidently and said, 'Absolutely. I've visited loads. I've spoken to talented kids, future stars, gifted and elite young athletes. I've told them how I got my medals, how hard I worked, the power of focus and determination …'

Then came the curveball. 'Well,' they said, 'you'll actually be working with kids who are disengaged from sport. They don't like it. Some have low self-esteem, others have anger issues. Many have never even been picked for anything.' I blinked. Wait. What? There are kids … who *don't* like sports?

It was genuinely a new concept to me. I walked out of that interview in a daze, thinking, 'How on earth do I relate to someone who doesn't know the joy of winning? Or the pain of defeat? Or the comfort of knowing you can get better at something if you practise?'

Even with the doubts, I took the job. And on my first day, I was faced with a group of girls who were withdrawn, unsure, full of uncertainty, the complete opposite of the performance-driven bubble I'd lived in. I had to find a way to connect, to make them see that sport could be *theirs* too, not about medals or glory, but confidence, belonging, fun.

And in that moment, something clicked.

Steph: You are a natural connector, Gail. No coach could train you to do that. You had found a new niche and something you could potentially be really good at. Can you understand why this role motivated you?

Gail: I actually think it was the challenge of getting through to these girls. It was like a competition where I was the underdog but I came out on top.

New Challenges

If you can talk to 12-year-old girls who hate you, you can talk to anyone. Think Catherine Tate and Vicky Pollard characters, all saying to me, 'Who the hell are you? What are you doing here? I ain't doing no sport, Miss, I ain't messing up my make-up. What is it that you do, Miss? Like, play badminton? I could beat you at it.' (Extra points for those of you who had the character voices going in your head.)

Despite all the confusion I was feeling post-retirement, the identity loss, the aimlessness, I realised I had *something* to give. Maybe I didn't know who I was outside of badminton just yet, but I knew I could help these girls feel seen. Valued. Strong. And maybe, just maybe, that was the start of finding myself again. But it was never going to be that simple.

So, what really happens when an Olympian tries to re-enter working life?

The downside of my school visits was that I inevitably always ended up playing male PE teachers in draughty school sports halls across the country. Once upon a time, I was taking on the best in the world – China, Korea, the Far East powerhouses of badminton. Now, it's Mr Davies from Year 10 PE. The classic story.

I started visiting schools to showcase badminton, inspire kids and support sport in education. Inevitably, there's always the resident male PE teacher hovering by the court, brimming with quiet confidence. 'I used to be decent actually … played a bit of county badminton … football … rugby too … would've gone pro if it weren't for that hamstring/knee/shoulder/back/ego.'

Right then. Time to play nicely. We warm up. I smile sweetly, hit soft taps across the net. Sometimes I even switch to my left hand just to keep things light. I fluff a shot into the net. You can practically see the gleam in their eyes. 'I've got her,' they think. The underdog story is writing itself.

Then … boom.

I summon the crowd (otherwise known as the Year 9s), and get them lined up by the court, chanting my name like it's the Olympics.

I play my part – all sweetness and smiles. Meanwhile, the PE teacher is peacocking.

Let's be clear, he hasn't played in years. And yet there's this lingering belief: *it's only badminton*. That funny little sport with a 'feather cock thing'. How good can she *really* be? She's only small.

One rally in, and he hasn't seen the shuttle. Two rallies in and he's tripping over his own feet. Three rallies in and the kids are screaming for more. Me? I'm playing like my entire Olympic career was simply a warm-up for this exact moment. Forget Athens. Forget Beijing. This is it: a cold, echoing sports hall somewhere in Lancashire, floor so hard it doubles as an ankle assassin, net hanging on by a thread, a shuttle so worn it's forgotten how physics works. The markings on the floor are so chaotic it's like trying to play badminton on a map of the London Underground. And don't get me started on the temperature: we would have been warmer playing in a walk-in freezer.

But I get to show the kids my sport, and how hard I have worked at it. It never leaves you.

A Gymnast, a Badminton Player and a Paralympian Walk into a Bar ...

The Youth Sport Trust had gathered quite a line-up of elite athletes to deliver talks in schools – Olympians, Paralympians, Commonwealth legends, all sports, all backgrounds, all corners of the UK. Every now and then, we'd have a conference or event, which gave us the perfect excuse for what we all really looked forward to: a night out. There's one particular evening I'll never forget. Newcastle. We were staying overnight (code for we are 100 per cent going out), and the local tour guide for the evening was none other than Craig Heap: gymnast extraordinaire, proud Geordie, and absolutely buzzing to show us around his hometown. Craig had *that* gymnast energy – like a puppy that knows how to cartwheel. You couldn't miss him, literally flipping out on the pavement with excitement.

Our little squad for the night looked like the start of a bizarre reality circus show:

Me: Gail Emms, badminton, 5ft 3, blonde, already in heels I'd regret.

Craig Heap: Human spring.

Tom Davis: Heavyweight judo, 100kg-plus, built like a fridge (a very lovely, gentle fridge).

Kevin Simpson: Wheelchair tennis player with a dry wit and a brilliant laugh.

Tim Prendergast: New Zealand Paralympian, 800m/1500m runner, 95 per cent visually impaired.

Now, somewhere along the way, Tim asked me to be his guide for the night as he needed a responsible adult. Let me just say this clearly: I am not the person you want guiding someone who can't see. I mean well, but I get distracted. I tell stories. I overshare. I think I'm hilarious. What Tim *needed* was someone calmly describing kerbs, bollards and uneven paving stones. What Tim *got* was me, narrating God knows what, while completely forgetting to mention a large tree branch at head height.

Still, after dodging various minor disasters and gathering momentum like a rogue parade float, we rolled, bounded, tripped, wheeled and *eventually* made it to Vodka Revolution. Drinks were flowing, spirits were high, and, of course, Craïg couldn't resist. Two drinks in, and he's walking on his hands across the dance floor like it's the Commonwealth Games. The rest of us soon joined in with the fun on the dance floor. We boogied. We laughed. We twirled. It was joyous.

About 20 minutes later, I flopped back on to a bar stool, catching my breath.

Then it hit me. 'Tim.' Oh God. '*Shit. Tim.*'

I knew something had felt … off. I did that subtle, panicked 'cool walk' back to the dance floor, trying to make it look like I hadn't just abandoned a visually impaired man mid-Cha Cha Slide.

And there he was. Still dancing. Loving life. Not a care in the world.

I slinked over slowly, pretending to talk to someone else nearby. Casually sidled up.

'Oh wow, gosh! Dancing's exhausting, isn't it? Shall we head back to the table?' Tim turned to me, cool as anything, 'How long have I been here on my own, Gail?'

'Alone? Noooo. You weren't alone. Dancing. We've all been … dancing.'

'Gail. *How long*?'

'… Ten. Fifteen minutes tops.'

Let's just say he never quite let me live that one down. And rightly so. Sorry, Tim.

School Reality

Working with the Youth Sport Trust on their Living for Sport programme was one of the most meaningful experiences of my post-retirement life. They're an incredible charity doing life-changing work, and I'll always be grateful I got to be a part of it. What struck me the most, what stays with me even now, was realising just how lucky I'd been to have sport as a constant in my life. Like myself, for many of the young people I met, sport is their lifeline.

There was one school in Luton I'll never forget. I arrived early, before the school gates had even opened, and there were already students waiting outside. Eager to get in. Not because they were particularly keen on maths or couldn't wait for PE, but because school felt safer than home. What hit me hard was something so simple, so human: the shoes these students were wearing. So many of the children were wearing those cheap black plimsolls you can pick up for a couple of pounds at Primark. But their toes were pushing through the ends, their feet clearly too big. No one had been able, or perhaps allowed, to get them the next size up. For more than half the kids in that school, this was the norm.

I cried. On the spot. Just stood there and cried. I offered to donate my fee to buy new shoes. The staff gently declined. As kind as the gesture might have been, they explained some parents or carers would be angry or, worse, they might sell the shoes. I felt completely helpless. This wasn't some far-off, distant story. This was happening just a short drive from where I grew up. It was a reminder that while teachers and schools do their absolute best, many children are fighting battles the moment they leave the school gates. And sometimes, all we can do is show up, listen and do what little we can.

There was another school, somewhere near Stoke-on-Trent, I think, that had a quote up on the wall. One of those motivational slogans they use to inspire the students, sandwiched between the school values. I can't remember the exact wording, but it stopped me in my tracks. It said something like:

'Life is s**t. But we'll give you the tools to deal with it.'

Honestly, I thought it was bloody brilliant. Raw, honest and exactly what some of these kids need to hear: that yes, life can be tough, unfair and heartbreaking, but there's strength in learning how to fight back.

Well said, Stoke.

I truly believe it's time more schools started teaching real mindset tools, the kind that help young people approach life with resilience, honesty and grit. We need to stop sugarcoating how hard things will be. There will be countless moments when no amount of money can solve the problem, and I say that from experience. At the fee-paying school I attended, I often saw money used as a quick fix, a safety net. But what happens when that money runs out? I've faced that reality more than once. Instead of focusing solely on a rigid curriculum, maybe it's time schools focused on developing resilient human beings and teaching them how to cope with failure, how to adapt, how to find purpose beyond perfection. That's the kind of education that truly lasts.

London Marathon, 2009

In September 2008, I got a call from the charity SPARKS, a fantastic children's medical research charity now linked with Great Ormond Street Hospital. They asked if I would run the London Marathon for them in April 2009. You know when something's been on your 'should probably do that before I die' list? Well, that was me and the London Marathon. Freshly retired from badminton, it also felt like a good way to stay in shape. So, of course, I said yes.

There's a bit of marathon legacy in my family: as mentioned earlier, my dad used to run them as a way to lose weight, so I knew it would be tough. But I genuinely had visions of transforming into this svelte, lean machine. The reality was that I lost a grand total of 2lb over months of training. My body basically said, 'Nice try.'

What no one tells you is just how mind-numbingly dull the training is. Endless, repetitive runs in the freezing cold of winter. Romantic notions of sunrise jogs and personal breakthroughs quickly vanished. It was just me, my sore legs and the same bloody pavement. Day after day.

Come race day, I found myself on the celebrity starting line; oh yes, I was deemed a 'celebrity' alongside none other than Katie Price and Peter Andre. They were surrounded by photographers. Apparently, it was supposed to be an 'honour' being next to them. I stood there thinking, 'What on earth are you doing here?'

Like most sporty people, I had that magic sub-four-hour goal in my head. I'd heard people call it the 'best day of their lives'. But no, not for me. I got elbowed constantly (being 5ft 3 in a sea of giants doesn't help), couldn't see a thing, tripped over discarded water bottles and was just generally in a state of 'why am I doing this?' for most of the race. It was the second hottest London Marathon on record, and I stopped at least ten times, not for injury, not for rest, just out of pure boredom.

I crossed the finish line in three hours and 47 minutes. Respectable. But not enough to beat my dad, who smugly reminded me that he still holds the family record at 3:42. I've never seen a prouder, smugger grin.

The BBC grabbed me right after for an interview. And I lied. Boldly. On live TV. 'Oh, it was amazing!' 'Such an incredible experience!' 'Yes, Steve Cram, I'd love to do it again next year!' Let me be clear. No. I would not. Ever. Again. The medal was nice, the charity meant something, and I suppose I can now tick 'run a marathon' off the list. But let's never pretend it was some life-changing joyride.

Still ... Dad was pleased. So I guess someone won.

Royal Ascot

One of the perks of being a Team GB athlete and winning a medal is that there are some really amazing invitations that come your way. One of those was the highest accolade – to join the esteemed esquires and certain members of the royal family at Royal Ascot for a day. The invitation was for myself, Nathan, Andy and his lovely wife Suzy and it was to attend in the box next to the Queen. We all said yes immediately and arrived around 11am, all looking extremely posh – well, as posh as we could, in top hats and tails for the men and Suzy and I donning hats, dresses and heels. We looked gorgeous, if I do say so myself.

On arrival, as the Bollinger was popped and poured very generously, it was clear that this was not going to be a sober day. By the time we sat down at the table for some food, I was already feeling the effects of the bubbles. The food was, as expected, out of this world, and my accent was getting posher and posher, with my little finger now permanently sticking out as I drank my champagne.

We were giggling, placing bets, drinking, eating, more drinking, it was a goooooood day. Just before 2pm, a lady wearing a beautiful suit that I could tell cost more than my car tapped me on the shoulder and said, 'Good afternoon, Miss Emms, I thought I would introduce oneself. My name is Lady Henrietta (I can't actually remember if this was her name, but it was very similar if not), I will be your aide for the day, so do let one know if I can be of service. Oh, and we will be requiring your services in about an hour. Thank you.' My services … well, I didn't read that part of the invitation. S**t. I was about two bottles of Bollinger in now. I started to pray it wasn't anything too demanding of me.

An hour later, Lady Henrietta tapped me on the shoulder and said, 'Miss Emms, please join me and let me escort you to the parade ring for you to judge 'Best Dressed Horse'. I stood up and duly followed her and her very expensive outfit out of the box, and then held on for dear life to the stair rail as we made our way over to the parade ring. As I was going down the stairs, a few things came into my head:

- My outfit only cost £150 and that included the hat. Lady Henrietta's button on that suit jacket probably cost that amount.
- I had drunk waaaaaaay too much champagne.
- What the hell is 'Best Dressed Horse'?

We got to the spot that was waiting for us and the horses were paraded around in front of me. A grey one, a brown one and a dark-brown one. Amazing. I had no idea; they all looked the bloody same, just different colours. Lady Henrietta, discreet as only someone who is incredibly posh is, leaned over and whispered into my ear, 'Would one like one to help one on this matter?' Yes, one would bloody like some help, thank you, Hetty darling.

To be fair to Henny/Hetty, she did point out the tails and plaits in the mane that were the handywork of the stable boys and girls, and we decided to pick a horse. Well, Henny/Hetty did. I nodded in agreement, and the prize money was handed to the stable boy or girl responsible. I now know that this is an esteemed honour and a good amount of money. Who knew, eh?

After the envelope was handed out, I was very glad to be led back to the comfort of the box and my champagne glass handed back to me, full up. Wooooo hooo! Let's get back drinking!

I must have put some bets on, though don't think I was winning at all, and after three or four races, Lady Hetty/Hen-Hen was back by my side, and said, 'Miss Emms, it is time to present the trophy to the winning stables of the next race. Would you like to follow me down to the presentation area?' I thought I was out of my duties; now, a good three bottles of Bollinger in and sounding (and probably looking) like Patsy from the TV show *Absolutely Fabulous*, this was going to be one hell of an effort from me. I staggered down the stairs, walked as straight as I could to the presentation area. There was a trophy there glistening in the sunshine and about 50 photographers lined up. I was sweating a little, and then the winning stables was announced. 'From Godolphin Stables, His Highness Sheikh Mohammed bin Rashid Al Maktoum', and I saw the very famous owner walk towards me.

Now, here is where the combination of panic and alcohol went to town in my head. I thought, 'How the bloody hell does one greet a sheikh?' – which is a perfectly legitimate question to ask, really. Is it a handshake? Is it a kiss on the cheek, once or twice? Or is there a no-contact rule? Then I thought, 'If I walk towards him, he will come to me either with his hand out or arms out, so I know, I will be guided by him.' Genius.

The slight flaw in this was the fact that as I walked towards Sheikh Mohammed when he was getting close to me, my stiletto heel decided to dig right into the grass and get stuck so, as I took the next step, I stumbled and lunged forward to try to get my balance. However, Sheikh Mohammed had reached me by this point, so as I was in my forward momentum, I grabbed him to stop myself from falling on to the floor. His waist and backside were the right height for this, which meant my face was in his groin.

There are some looks from people you never forget in life. Sheikh Mohammed's look of revulsion as he picked me up by the scruff of the neck and tossed me aside is one of those. He then walked towards the trophy, picked it up and stormed off, leaving me to pick my stiletto out of the grass and gather some sort of decorum.

The 50 photographers all had the shot. Drunken Gail Emms's face in Godolphin owner's groin. Not one photo made it into the papers. I guess I have to thank the Sheikh for that.

The rest of the day went without any mishap, but I definitely eased up on the Bollinger. I thanked Lady Hetty, and we went into Windsor, where we were staying.

I was never invited back.

Still nursing my hangover two days later, I found out I was pregnant. Ed and I were going to be parents. I was going to be a mum. I prayed that Bollinger was good for foetal development.

Member of the British Empire

I was awarded the MBE in the Queen's Birthday Honours in June 2009. The letter came through the post, and I was a little shocked, but incredibly moved and flattered when I read it. It is an extremely high honour to know that someone has nominated you for this prestigious award, and then that nomination has been accepted, which means a lot.

I believe that sportspeople shouldn't get honours straight after retirement. I mean this, because I feel it's our job to play the sport; we get funded and supported to win medals for Great Britain, but it is still appreciated.

The ceremony was held on a late November day in Buckingham Palace, with Princess Anne giving out the awards. I was six months pregnant by then, but I looked like I was about to give birth any day. The Buckingham Palace staff looked at me uneasily, and I am sure one was walking round with a bucket and sponge, expecting my waters to break at any moment. I reassured everyone that I was only six months pregnant and smiled the best I could when inevitably they made a face to imply I was breeding a giant and that I was the size of a whale.

I had three invitations for people to watch me receive the award, which I gave to my mum, my dad and my partner Ed. The week before, I realised that my mum's wardrobe consisted of tracksuits, ripped jeans, T-shirts and my old badminton kit. I have caught my mum on numerous occasions walking out of my house with various items hidden under her jumper. I still believe the real reason that mum changed her surname back to Emms a while after her divorce from her second marriage was not 'because I want it to be the same as my children', as she protests, but because she can then wear my 'EMMS' England/Team GB badminton kit down at the badminton hall on club nights.

I had to get Mum an outfit. It was like making a toddler dress up in something for an occasion, and they really don't want to wear it, and will be the moodiest and stroppiest that they can be to stop it happening. I picked out lots of lovely outfits in Marks & Spencer, only to be met with: 'Don't know why I can't wear jeans.' 'Because it is Buckingham Palace, Mum, and there is a dress code. That's why.' We got there in the end. A dark-grey jacket and skirt, with a pair of shoes that I am sure were too big for her, but we got there.

Thank God for that. That was a bigger achievement than winning the bloody award.

On the day, Mum, Dad and Ed were ushered into the ballroom and shown to their seats. It was such a lovely sight, seeing them in the crowd. As much as I say that I don't feel like I fully deserve an MBE, my parents do. The award is for them. For the sacrifice they had to make to get me to where I am. There were tears in my eyes as I saw them sitting there, nervously fidgeting, my mum still not used to her suit. Mum and Dad were sitting in Buckingham Palace because of me, and it all started to get emotional.

I went back into the room, took a few breaths and decided to make conversation with others who were receiving awards. I looked around and realised I was the youngest in the room by about 30 years. Not a problem, as I introduced myself and asked, 'So how come you are receiving an award today?' Now, I may have mentioned I am a little bit competitive – not that receiving an honour should be competitive – but talk about becoming aware that your achievements are nothing in comparison to others. The list was along the lines of:

- 'I have been cleaning streets and woodlands voluntarily for 50 years.' Yeah, that's better than mine.
- 'I have been fostering disabled kids for 45 years.' Yep, got me again there.
- 'I have been finding homes for injured pets and also nursing them back to health all my life.' Oh God, I can't compete with that.
- 'I have been working with special needs kids and given all my savings to help them get an education.' Seriously, these people are angels.

The list went on and on. It was humbling, to say the least. Then a lady in her 80s, Dorothy, turned to me and asked, 'And what about you, dear? Why are you receiving an award today?' 'Well, Dorothy, I am good at hitting shuttlecocks over a net.' They all looked a bit confused, but basically that's what it was. I can play badminton well.

And got paid, funded and supported to do so, which felt rubbish in comparison to the wonderful voluntary work that these awesome women were doing. (I did explain that I was a pregnant Olympic silver medallist in badminton and the UK was not handing out awards to fat sportspeople as it looked like at that moment in time.)

We lined up and were introduced one by one to Princess Anne. Now Anne is an Olympian herself, and I have met her a few times at various Olympic events. She recognised me as I walked over, laughed at my huge bump, and it was heartwarming and personal. I curtseyed the best I could without looking like a Weeble and I waddled off. Mum, Dad, Ed and I had a celebratory drink afterwards, but the emotion of the day took its toll on me. It was overwhelming, and I wanted to go home. I used the pregnancy as an excuse, but it all got too much, in all honesty.

If I could go back in time, I would, and take that day and plan it better to honour what my parents did for me. Even with all the heartache and problems they went through, they found a way for me to navigate the stresses and rollercoaster that is elite sport. I feel guilty that we didn't celebrate it properly.

Celebrity Mastermind, My Almost Moment of Glory

I was heavily pregnant with Harry when the call came in. 'Would you like to do *Celebrity Mastermind*?' Well … I wasn't exactly busy. Waddling around, eating biscuits, not working much, so I said yes. Then came the question: 'What's your specialist subject?'

Now, let's be clear, I didn't *have* a specialist subject. But I had time. So, I thought, what could I genuinely enjoy swotting up on? A TV series. Easy to binge, entertaining, low risk of falling asleep. *Gavin & Stacey*. 'And yes,' I told the producers, 'I'll even include the Christmas special.'

Fast-forward to the studio. My fellow contestants:

- Paul O'Grady (The Life and Times of Gypsy Rose Lee – never heard of her).

- Musician Goldie (Films of P.T. Anderson – no clue).
- Loyd Grossman (18th Century English Art and Artists – oh come on, Loyd).

Then it was my turn. The famous black chair. The dramatic music. The blinding spotlight. My baby is kicking like mad. I was more nervous than in the Olympic final. Every fear of looking like a total idiot screamed, '*Run*!'

First question: 'On what date does Pamela send out her Christmas cards?'

'November 1st.' Boom. I was off. I ended that round with 19 out of 20 – the highest ever celebrity score on a chosen subject. Take *that*, 18th-century art.

Next came general knowledge. Paul and Goldie struggled, even combined they couldn't beat my specialist score. But Loyd was good, very good. He sat in that chair with the confidence of a man who's sold a lot of pasta sauces … and he nailed it. Ended up with 32 points.

I needed 13 points in the general knowledge round to win. Just 13.

First question: 'If you supported the Gunners, what football team would that be?' 'Arsenal.' Off I went. Some answers I knew, others I guessed. Guessed *correctly*, thankfully. I could feel it … I was close. The buzzer sounded. Tension in the room. All eyes on the scoreboard.

I had 31 points. Just one short. Loyd wins.

Apparently, 31 would've won *any* of the other *Celebrity Mastermind* episodes that year. But no, I had to go up against a posh culinary encyclopaedia.

And no, I haven't bought a single Loyd Grossman pasta sauce since.

MOTHERHOOD

Baby Time

Harry was due on 26 February 2010. It was now 7 March, and I was getting bloody annoyed, and so large that it was ridiculous. One Sunday evening, Ed and I decided to go and get a burger with friends Natalie and Graham, at Gourmet Burger Kitchen, in The Hub area of Milton Keynes. I ordered a chilli burger – anything to get this baby out of me. Halfway through, and I felt the need to go to the toilet, and, as I stood up, my first thought was, 'Oh my God, I have wet myself!' and off I waddled to the toilet. I got to the disabled toilet downstairs as I wasn't going to make the upstairs ones and, as I did, there was quite a puddle, as my waters had broken. I waddled back out and we left to go home and get ready for the hospital. I didn't get to finish my burger.

Steph: I can only imagine that motherhood was a huge shock to the system. Being an elite athlete is the most selfish of occupations, whereas being a mother demands being selfless and putting someone else before you all the time. That's quite a contrast.

Being a Mum

With all the good wishes of my sporty friends – some even talking to the bump, including Denise Lewis, Mark Foster and even Shane Warne amongst many – I imagined Harry being born with muscles and ready to catch a ball as he was being delivered. The reality was that he really didn't want to be born at all, but when it was *finally* time, two weeks after his due date, he was so bloody big that after 36 hours of excruciating labour and getting absolutely nowhere, I was rushed to get a C-section.

If ever there was a baby who had a pissed-off face because they had been very happy where they were, it was Harry. It took three surgeons to pull him out of me; he was so big, weighing in at a whopping 9lb 2oz. He looked like a grumpy old man, and as Ed and I were revelling in this birthing marvel, Harry went back to sleep. In fact, Harry slept so much, I had to wake him to feed him.

I had no idea what I had done, but I had pleased the baby gods, and I ended up getting more sleep with Harry than I have ever had before. Morning naps, afternoon naps, and then he slept through the night at five weeks old. Ed and I started to lie about it as we realised how bad it was for others. We were soon found out when we met up with our NCT (National Childbirth Trust) friends and all the couples were struggling with crying babies, and Ed and I were just sitting there, chilling with a drink.

If you are thinking, 'Ah, you can't be that lucky again with your next child', actually, Ed and I were. Ollie had to be cut out of me three weeks early, as his predicted weight was going to exceed 10lb at the rate he was growing. However, he was only just under 9lb in the end. And Ollie, not quite as grumpy-looking as Harry, slept well and went through the night at seven weeks old. I can count on one hand the number of 'bad nights' of crying I had with the babies, and I, as someone who adores my sleep and who gets cranky if I don't get enough, am eternally grateful for this.

I joke to the kids that the family motto is: 'Thou shalt be a sporting legend.' I was trying to act all cool as a mum, and inside I was secretly hoping my boys were going to be sports sensations from an early age.

Ed, their father, is not an Olympian. Nor was he ever a pro sportsman. I'm going to have to admit it, this slightly pained me on the genetics side. Though his trial for Colchester United U14 Academy apparently was 'a very big deal', and basically like trying to get into Manchester United. Well, that's what he told me anyway.

Parenting is hard. In fact, it's harder than being a professional athlete, no question. There are moments when I genuinely forget I'm responsible for two actual human beings. Not in the 'I've-left-the-baby-in-a-shop' kind of way, but in the 'How am I supposed to keep two other people alive when I'm barely managing it myself?' kind of way.

I'm writing this while on holiday in Cyprus, where just yesterday something happened that still has me in stitches, and the boys are 15 and nearly 12 now. It hadn't been the sunniest of trips, the wind had picked up, and we'd decided to head to the tennis court to play some pickleball. On the way there, Harry said he wanted to put some suncream on his face. Innocent enough. Both boys stopped to do the same. I turned around just in time to see them generously applying *my* face suncream, factor 50. 'What's the issue?' I hear you all ask. Well, this particular suncream also contains fake tan. And they weren't just dabbing it on; they were *slathering* it everywhere.

Next thing I know, I'm standing there staring at two bright-orange boys asking, 'Is it rubbed in yet?' I couldn't breathe from laughing. I actually ended up rolling around on the grass, tears streaming down my face. Ollie was the worst; he'd used loads, and the cream wasn't absorbing at all. Harry caught on quickly, asking, 'Do I look like Ollie?' which only fuelled Ollie's fury. He stormed off, orange-faced and raging, while the 'Oompa Loompa' song played on a loop in my head.

Once I'd recovered enough composure, we managed to get to the court. The wind made any normal rally impossible, so we invented our own game: I'd tee up the pickleball like a baseball and the boys would take turns trying to hit a target. It was all going well until it wasn't. Let's just say, there's a reason Harry plays in defence when he's on the football pitch; his aim isn't exactly surgical.

I tossed the ball up perfectly, Harry swung, connected sweetly, and the wind gave it an extra boost … straight into Ollie's face, nailing him right in the eye as he looked up from collecting his ball. He dropped like he'd been shot. I ran over, trying to be the concerned mum I'm meant to be, but the sight of Ollie, with orange tears carving rivers down his cheeks, sent me into another uncontrollable fit of laughter. You honestly couldn't make this stuff up.

My boys are brilliant. I actually like them. I want to hang out with them. I will be very honest and say I found it very hard in the beginning … it makes me realise we, as a society, are *not* set up for family living anymore. There is so much pressure on families and parents – not many are able to be stay-at-home parents, and the support system is completely f**ked now we don't have community-style living anymore.

There was a definite divide where I lived – the working mums and the non-working mums. I was trying to juggle everything, and I really felt judged and I didn't fit anywhere. I went into motherhood thinking I could do it all. Don't know where I got that attitude from (?), but inside I was struggling.

Steph: So, was there a bit of frustration about how you were being perceived as a mum?

Gail: I just still wanted to be me and do my own thing as well as be a mum. You're made to feel guilty – society says you, as the woman, drop the kids off, then have a part-time job 9.30am until 2pm, bake some cakes, skip in meadows with your kids, and so on. And when you don't fit into that mould, you feel ostracised. I was doing my best, trying to fit in and put that superhero supermum cape on, all the time saying, 'It's fine. I can do it. I can do this!' Then the realisation … It's not possible … How can I be the best mum and best me?

Steph: But what did the 'best you' look like in your eyes?

Gail: I craved my independence, that time away. That's when I could reset and be the best me. I needed to be selfish. It was what I was used to. And I was bloody good at it.

Steph: But you weren't used to putting in maximum mothering effort and getting no reward or, worse still, feeling like you were failing?

Gail: Looking back, I wish I had been able to lower my expectations. I couldn't be amazing at everything while being a mum.

Just 'Harry's Mum'

It was the summer of 2012. Harry was at the village nursery and their sports day had an Olympic theme to celebrate the upcoming London Games. I was chatting with some of the other mums, including Kelly, Tommy's mum. Harry and Tommy were good mates, and we were all happily watching the chaos unfold when one of the nursery staff stepped forward and announced, 'We'd like to invite Gail, Harry's mum, to say a few words to celebrate the London 2012 Olympics!' Kelly looked at me, genuinely puzzled. 'Why are they asking *you* to speak?' Before I could answer, her then-husband rolled his eyes and muttered, 'She *used to be* an Olympian, Kelly.'

That moment pretty much summed up my experience of motherhood at the time. As I walked up to the microphone, I caught the confused expressions on several other mums' faces, quickly followed by their partners whispering hurried explanations. The looks turned into wide-eyed shock: 'Oh my God! I didn't know you were an Olympian! I thought you were just Harry's mum!'

And that's why I mention it. Not just to give a shoutout to Kelly, who is genuinely lovely and deserves a mention, but because that phrase, *just Harry's mum*, stuck with me. It stung. It still does. So many mums hear it, or feel it, and it becomes a label that quietly chips away at who we once were.

That word '*just*' is deceptively sharp. It implies that everything you were before no longer counts. As if every achievement evaporates the moment you become someone's mum. I hated that feeling, that erasure. But I also didn't quite know how to fight it, because on the other hand … wasn't that exactly what I had to become? I wasn't an Olympian anymore. I was a mum. But was I *just* a mum?

And why did that bother me so much?

It triggered something deeper: memories of my own mum. She was '*just a mum*', left on her own after my dad walked out, with no financial support, raising kids while her own dreams faded into survival. For her, being '*just*' a mum turned into something far more painful and isolating than she ever expected. I saw what that title came to mean, and I knew it couldn't be enough for me. It wasn't an option.

Part of me regrets feeling that way. I wish I'd been able to embrace motherhood more fully. But the truth is that I couldn't afford to. Ed was in the police, and despite the incredible work they do and the crap they put up with, the pay just didn't stretch far enough. (And let's be honest, he had to deal with *me*, so he deserved a pay rise on that alone!) He worked overtime, a lot of it, to keep things afloat.

But it often felt like everything else was on me. The nursery drop-offs, school pick-ups, the appointments, the shopping lists and, on top of it all, earning half the household income. It was as if society looked at women and said, 'Well, you wanted it all, so here it f***ing is!' and dumped the entire load of working-mum chaos in our laps.

Who on earth designed the school day to be 9am to 3pm? Honestly, what job fits into that window? And don't get me started on after-school clubs; they cost as much as a second-hand car. And if you're late collecting your child? The fine goes up faster than a black cab fare after midnight in Soho. The stress was suffocating. I've never run for so many trains in my life. Forget the gym, I was doing full sprint workouts just to make it back to Milton Keynes, jammed into a packed four-carriage train with thousands of commuters, paying ridiculous prices for the privilege of being crushed into someone's armpit.

It wore me down. I became someone I didn't like; snappy, impatient, exhausted. There were no breaks, no time to breathe. Life felt like a relentless conveyor belt, and I never got the chance to enjoy the ride. Motherhood is often framed as the most natural role for women – the nurturer, the carer – but when you've come from a life built on ambition, competition and performance, that role can feel like a foreign country. My mind screamed, 'I am better than this. Anyone can do this life!' And that's when the Emms stubbornness kicked in: head down, blinkers on, prove to the world I could do it all.

But the truth is … I wasn't living. I was surviving. And slowly, I was losing myself.

Steph: When you were playing badminton, you had found your tribe where you belonged, but motherhood felt uncomfortable in comparison to that. Sport is so much more straightforward – you know exactly where you are in the rankings, and where you are in your matches. Motherhood is so confusing. There's no rulebook, and, even if there were, children don't play by the rules.

Gail: I definitely hadn't thought it through. Winging it was my style.

Trying to Fit In

I'll be honest, I struggled to fit in with some of the other mums. I had my crew – Natalie, Belinda and Kelly, who kept me sane and laughing. But despite being an extrovert and fairly confident, I'm also a bit guarded when meeting people for the first time. I'm not instantly warm and fuzzy. I'm definitely not a 'girly girl', and that can come across as standoffish. Some of the mums thought I was aloof, maybe even arrogant, as if I thought I was better than them. The truth was that I wasn't being aloof because I thought I was better than them. I was just trying to work them out and see if they were 'my people'.

I called a group of mums the 'Yummy Mummy Gym Bunnies'. You know the type. All arriving at school in giant 4x4 Range Rovers they couldn't park to save their lives, blocking half the road. Wearing the latest Sweaty Betty gym gear, even though they lived less than a mile away and had clearly driven rather than walked. They'd gather at the gates, loud enough for everyone to hear: 'Oh my God, I've got such a busy day today! I just don't know how I'll fit it all in!' And then proceed to list: manicure, gym session, Ocado delivery. Right. So busy.

I used to get irrationally wound up, probably mostly by the gym kit. Until one day, I decided to wear my Olympic medals on the school run, just under my jacket. I walked Harry to school, medals proudly around my neck. And I felt bloody brilliant. I highly recommend it. Wear a medal on the school run. It's like armour. No Yummy Mummy Gym Bunny can touch you after that.

I did consider going one step further and wearing my full Team GB kit *and* medals for Harry's first sports day at Middleton Primary. The plan was to rock up for the Mums' Race and make a bit of a joke of it. But word must have got out and, mysteriously, the Mums' Race was quietly removed from the programme. Someone snitched.

Probably the same mum who booted me out of the Middleton Mums WhatsApp group for 'inappropriate behaviour'. Inappropriate behaviour was a bit of a stretch. Well … maybe. But it was clearly a joke. Someone had posted about a mum's birthday drinks night: one said she'd bring wine, another said she'd bring snacks. I replied, 'I'll bring the strippers and drugs.' I laughed to myself, imagining the flood of laughing emojis, maybe some cheeky banter. Instead, there was tumbleweed. Absolute silence. A WhatsApp graveyard. And then, *poof*, I was gone. I was removed. Fine. Party for one then. More prosecco for me.

But the weirdest experience by far was something that still freaks me out to this day. Harry was in Year 3, and I was working in Watford, when my phone rang. It was the school, and every parent knows that sinking feeling: school doesn't ring unless someone's sick, injured, or there's a form you forgot to sign. I picked up, bracing myself. 'Hi Gail, it's Miss ——. Nothing to worry about with Harry, just wanted to talk to you about the email you sent yesterday …' I blinked. 'Sorry, what email?' She went on, 'Just regarding why we give extra work to certain children. So, it's based on ability, not favouritism …' I stopped her. 'Hang on, I haven't emailed you. I don't think I've ever emailed the school, actually.' She paused. 'I have it here … from' … and she read out an email address to me.

'That's not my email address.'

Silence. Then she *swore*. On the phone. She said she'd call me back and hung up.

Cue panic. My mind immediately jumped to the worst-case scenario, because when you're a parent, that's what happens. And with Ed working in police surveillance with organised crime, it escalated fast in my brain. Suddenly, I was imagining a Hollywood plot – someone impersonating me, a kidnapping, Liam Neeson-level drama. I called Ed. We were both in the headteacher's office within the hour.

The school showed us the email. Aside from the fact it wasn't mine, I was personally offended by the grammar. It was sloppy, passive-aggressive and signed off with 'All the best, G.' I mean, come on. I'm a 'Kind regards, Gail' type of woman. Let's maintain some standards.

The school took it seriously, called the police and determined it was technically fraud. The rumour mill fired up again, and eventually the school narrowed it down. They were confident they knew who did it. I told them I didn't want to know. I honestly didn't trust myself not to explode. I'm not a fighter, but this messed with my head. Someone pretending to be me and messaging my child's school, causing fear, stress and dragging Ed and me into panic over absolutely nothing, all because their child wasn't getting enough attention and they assumed I had some kind of 'celebrity' advantage.

For the record: I don't. But being called a celebrity? I didn't *hate* that part.

Harry and Ollie

I've never really understood the whole 'competitive parenting' thing. Maybe it's because I've already had my moment in the sun, so I don't need to live vicariously through my kids. Honestly, a lot of it feels like unresolved issues from failed dreams being repackaged and dumped on to unsuspecting children. At the school gates, it's like a full-blown insecurity circus; parents brimming with anxiety that their kid isn't the best at absolutely everything, as if that somehow reflects badly on them. It's total nonsense, of course, but it's the reality we've created.

That said, I probably wouldn't have had this perspective if it weren't for my eldest, Harry, who, let's face it, came out coated in gold dust. He was the lead in the nativity play, reading ahead of schedule and scouted for the MK Dons U8 football academy. I won't lie: I swanned about like royalty. Parents' evenings were an ego massage. I was smug. Smug and breezy.

Then Ollie arrived.

It was as if my body had used up all the 'golden child' ingredients and just scooped up whatever was left over. And oh, what a glorious chaos emerged. Ollie slept like a dream – credit where credit's due – but in return for Harry's serene glow, Ollie got all the red-hot rage. The Incredible Hulk would take one look and say, 'You okay, mate?'

We nickname him 'Mariah Carey' for his diva-level meltdowns. Logic was left somewhere in my uterus, and his emotions are unfiltered, volcanic and theatrical.

Exhibit A: Ollie storming around the kitchen, slamming cupboard doors because there were *still* 154 days until Christmas.

Exhibit B: Getting us kicked out of David Lloyd Milton Keynes because I beat him 11-4 at badminton and he smashed everything in reach, including Harry.

On his first day of school, he was found halfway up the fence trying to escape. He is either destined to be a multi-millionaire … or end up in prison. There is no middle ground with Ollie. Teachers went from saying, 'I wish I had a whole classroom of Harrys!' to 'So … Ollie's not the ringleader exactly … but he doesn't stop the chaos either.'

But then, he'll throw his arms around you in the world's best hug. He's incredibly sensitive, a fantastic goalkeeper and has finally started to play badminton regularly – although, yes, I still beat him 11-4 and, yes, the rage still follows. That's Ollie.

Harry, on the other hand, is a mini-me. The Emms gene runs strong in that one. Ollie has his dad's side. What I love most is that both of them have inherited my sense of humour – sharp, silly and just rebellious enough to get chucked out of future parent WhatsApp groups. Honestly, I'll be proud.

They're growing into young men now, and I'm doing everything I can to prepare them. When we go out, they order at the restaurant, ask for the bill and speak to staff with respect. I want them to be confident. I want them to respect women, but not be walked over by those who might take advantage. I want them to feel close to me but not *need* me. I want them to stand on their own two feet and provide. They have a good life, maybe too good sometimes, but I want them to understand the world won't always be kind. All I can do is be there, guiding them the best I can.

The other day, I asked them, 'Boys, I'm writing my book, and I'm at the section about you two. If someone asked you to describe me, what words would you use?'

Their responses: 'Crazy.' 'Chaotic.' 'Spontaneous – sometimes in a good way, sometimes not.' 'Funny.' They know me well.

But one comment from Ollie remains my favourite. We were out walking the dog, and I asked him a random question: 'If everyone in the family were an animal, what would we be?' He didn't hesitate. 'You'd be a monkey.' I laughed. 'Why a monkey?' And he said, 'Because you're always smiling and laughing.' That's the version of me I want my boys to remember most.

Gail: I was different and special as an athlete. And it sounds really bad – I don't feel special or unique as a mum. That's been the hard thing for me to accept: being a mum is actually special, and I'm just doing it in my own unique way.

Steph: Comparing yourself to other mums is never helpful. Who knows what was really going on for them anyway? How could any of them relate to what you were experiencing? They had never been an Olympian, and that was the filter through which you showed up in the world.

Gail: I thought, 'I should be working, doing something really high profile.' But no, I've got to come home, look after the boys and cook fish fingers.

Steph: But now the boys are older, I hope you can appreciate how much of an inspiration you have been to them, because of your unique experience of being an athlete and the journey you have been on. Gail, let me tell you, you are a special mum.

Gail: Heehee yes, I am special – sorry, couldn't resist there. But you can't show off as mum.

Steph: (Eye roll)

BACK ON THE BOX

Total Wipeout

There are two moments in my life that genuinely scared the living daylights out of me. One was hurtling down an Olympic bobsleigh track in Latvia after signing a waiver that basically said, 'If you die, that's on you.' The other was filming *Celebrity Total Wipeout*.

With the bobsleigh, at least there was a professional driver at the front and another at the back controlling the brakes. Ed and I were just wedged in the middle, heads flailing like dashboard bobbleheads, doing everything we could not to black out. The G-force was so strong I couldn't even scream. My brain went straight into survival mode: *just stay alive, just stay alive.* It was 50 seconds of pure, unfiltered terror. And yet, even after all that, I would still choose that death-ride again over another go at *Total Wipeout*.

Let me set the scene. We were flown out to Buenos Aires (business class, darling), and the plane looked like a surreal dream line-up: glamour model Nicola McLean, *Big Brother*'s Brian Belo, Roxanne Pallett from *Coronation Street*, *Strictly*'s Camilla Dallerup, comedian Simon Day, Ricky Groves from *EastEnders*, presenter Charlie Stayt, the iconic Julie Peasgood and Olympic high jumper Dalton Grant. Ten hours, endless champagne and nerves slowly bubbling to the surface.

So, why Argentina? One word: regulations. Health and safety rules are … let's say, more *flexible* over there. I'd only had Harry a few months before, so I was still trying to make peace with my post-baby body, something made harder by being surrounded by impossibly toned women. But I was just thrilled to be doing *something*. And, honestly, we all bonded quickly, probably out of sheer fear. Because make no mistake, the course was dangerous. Way more brutal than it looked on telly.

The big red balls are evil. They look like fun. They're not. You get launched, winded and dumped in disgusting, dog-pee-infused water. The mud was like wet cement, and I swear I stepped on more bits of rusty metal than I did solid ground. It was like trying to survive *Gladiators* on a building site.

During one round, I was sprinting from a moving platform to a static one, and my leg just … gave out. I hit the water hard and the pain shot through me like lightning. I genuinely thought I'd broken something. Roxanne saw me flailing and flung herself in like a *Baywatch* extra, but accidentally *landed on my leg*, turning my injury into a slapstick sketch. No first aid appeared. The producers just shrugged and said, 'Man up and carry on.' So, I did, hobbling through the next rounds and somehow making it into the final three.

I finished third, behind Ricky and Dalton. Bronze. I'll take that. At 5ft 3, slightly out of shape and with one leg barely working, I was just proud I didn't get booted out earlier. My competitive streak wouldn't have allowed it.

We didn't get to see much of South America, just the hotel and the muddy chaos of the course, but I do vividly remember the steak. And the Malbec. They made it worth the bruises.

Eternal Glory

In 2015, ITV approached me with an intriguing proposition: would I like to take part in a new TV show – *Eternal Glory* – a kind of 'sports science *Superstars*', pitting eight ex-professional athletes against each other in a brutal series of physical and mental challenges designed to test all-round fitness, resilience and grit. Naturally, I said yes.

Once I'd made the final cut, I ramped up my PT sessions with Riley Kumi to get fighting fit. I didn't know who else was taking part, ITV kept the contestant list tightly under wraps, but I had a quiet confidence. Racket sports like badminton demand cardio, speed, agility, reaction time, flexibility, tactical awareness … more strings to the bow than, say, long-distance running. I figured I'd be competitive.

After some intense sports science lab testing, I landed in Croatia and met the line-up: Olympic rowing legend James Cracknell, long-distance queen Liz McColgan, 200m Olympian Christian Malcolm, long jump star Jade Johnson, football icon Matt Le Tissier, Welsh rugby great Shane Williams and javelin Olympic medallist Fatima Whitbread. Representing badminton, I suddenly felt like the underdog. Shane looked seriously in shape; he was doing triathlons at the time and my money was on him.

Our host, Richard Bacon, and sports scientist Professor Greg Whyte welcomed us. The first event was introduced:

'Balance on one foot atop a pole in the sea.' We all thought, *nice gentle start.* Wrong. Standing on a narrow pole, waves smashing into your legs, wind trying to blow you off, this was anything but easy. When the buzzer went, chaos erupted. Bodies toppled like drunk flamingos. Within seconds, only Christian and I were left standing. He hopped about valiantly, then fell. First win in the bag. Good start, Emms.

The events ramped up: obstacle courses, underwater rock retrievals, heart rate control and, one of my favourites, wall sits. Greg looked straight at me and said I was the favourite. No pressure. My power-to-weight ratio from lab testing was apparently the best.

Wall sits were part of my badminton training, so I knew how to suffer through it. As thighs began shaking and groaning around me, I kept my cool. Liz McColgan and James Cracknell held out longest, but then it was James and me in a psychological face-off. At 6ft 5, James has serious mass – great for rowing, not for lactic acid build-up. Still, his pain threshold is elite. He lasted to around the six-minute mark before tapping out. I kept going, just to prove a point, and passed the eight-minute mark while singing 'Let It Go' from *Frozen*. Final time: eight minutes 34 seconds. Not bad for a 'retired' badminton girl. Those thighs still had it.

We grew close as a group, and it was hard seeing people go. I clicked with Liz – she's brilliant – and Christian, whom I already knew. But I also bonded with Matt Le Tissier, who always had a crossword or puzzle on the go and casually dropped the word 'discombobulated' into conversation (which I now use regularly, thank you, Matt). Shane was lovely, and he and Matt led nightly sing-alongs of One Direction's 'Steal My Girl', a tribute to their daughters. I can't hear that song now without picturing our villa in Croatia and those two belting it out like proud dads on karaoke night.

Eventually, it came down to me and James Cracknell in the final. David vs Goliath; 5ft 3 ex-badminton player vs 6ft 5 Olympic rower. The decider was a best-of-three reaction test. Tied 1-1, we reached the final round: the two of us holding on to a fixed rope, five rods lined up on a table between us, one would light up at random, and the first to let go of the rope and grab the rod would win. We stood facing each other in the dark, studio lights the only illumination. We waited … and waited.

The tension built. No movement. I was getting twitchy. Ten minutes had passed. Then, suddenly, the middle rod lit up. My right hand flew off the rope and grabbed it, milliseconds before James lunged forward.

Fireworks exploded. I'd *won*.

James didn't exactly burst with joy at my victory. In his defence, he'd fractured a bone in his hand trying to snatch that final rod and muttered that the challenge was 'designed more for someone like you'. I got it, he's used to winning. With two Olympic golds and a cabinet full of titles, second place probably feels alien. For me, it was sweet, sweet validation. I'd pushed myself harder than ever and won. I was proud to show what I could do and maybe prove something to myself in the process.

I carried that trophy all the way home … on my lap, on the plane, right next to James. Two months later, my boys managed to break it. Into the bin it went. I'm sure James would be pleased to hear that.

Steph: How was motherhood at this point?

Gail: I was a bit bored, if I'm honest. Ed went to work. I was stuck at home. How much coffee and cake can you have?

Steph: Not so much adrenaline with a child.

Gail: That's why I went off to Kilimanjaro.

CLIMBING MOUNTAINS

Mount Kilimanjaro

I never pictured myself on a mountain. Ever. I'd seen the Comic Relief Kilimanjaro climb on TV once – celebrities in the sunshine, laughing, posing with epic views in the background, and I remember thinking, 'That actually looks fun.' So, when I got the call asking if I'd join a charity trek up Mount Kilimanjaro for Laureus Sport for Good, led by the tennis legend Martina Navratilova, I said yes on the spot. I figured, if Cheryl Cole and Chris Moyles can do it, then, no offence, but so can I.

There was just one small detail: I had an eight-month-old baby. Harry was still in nappies and, yes, there were a few raised eyebrows when I announced I'd be disappearing to Tanzania for a couple of weeks but, truthfully, after months of nappy changes and teething, someone could've offered me three weeks on the moon and I'd have packed a bag. My spirit needed something wild. Something physical. Something that wasn't another episode of watching IgglePiggle in *In the Night Garden*.

So off I went to Kilimanjaro … with Martina Navratilova … and a group made up entirely of women. At first, I didn't think much of it. Then it hit me. *Ah. It's a lesbian trek.* Not that it mattered, but the penny dropped when I overheard some very personal conversations, and I remembered who was leading us. The group found it hilarious that I'd only just clocked it, and I made it clear I wasn't on the trip for that reason. They laughed, welcomed me in, and soon we were sharing stories. Many of the women had only recently come out, after years in straight marriages. Some were on a journey of self-discovery. I was there just trying to escape my bottle steriliser.

Before the trek, we visited a Laureus-supported sports camp in Nairobi. The poverty was shocking. There were kids playing football barefoot in the dust. But when we handed over the kit we'd brought, their faces lit up. It reminded me how powerful sport can be, and how a little can go a long way. Being a mum made it hit even harder.

The trek began the next day. And, of course, it started raining. While I was in Africa. Not a light drizzle. Torrential, relentless, biblical rain. I'd expected blue skies and rolled-up sleeves, like the celebs on TV. Instead, I was head-to-toe in waterproofs, trudging through mud. Even the Tanzanian guides were baffled. 'We've never had rain like this,' they said. Of course.

Morale dipped. Martina was keeping to herself, the group needed a lift, and I was doing my best to keep the energy up with our team leader, adventurer Mark Kalch. But on day three, Martina sat down on a rock and refused to move. 'I ache,' she said. 'This isn't what I expected.' I nearly gave her a motivational slap around the face. 'My shoulders and neck hurt so much!' Martina complained.

I'm not sure why I did what I did next but, at the same time, it seemed logical, so I went and stood behind Martina and started massaging her neck and shoulders. If this wasn't a commitment to the cause, I don't know what is. She started making appreciative noises: this wasn't my first neck and shoulder massage, ladies and gentlemen, and these fingers and wrists have had years of badminton training, making me both strong yet delicate. I was going deeper into Martina's aching muscles, and really getting into my role, when it dawned on me what I was doing, and I started to feel awkward as f**k. Martina was loving it. Seriously loving it. 'Oh yes, Gail, right there! Keep going!' I was starting to regret this act of kindness and now feeling beyond uncomfortable.

Mark caught my eye and started p**sing himself laughing as he saw the situation unfold and Martina, now moaning like the scene out of *When Harry Met Sally*. I had to stop, so I rounded up with a kung-fu chopping technique that I had seen somewhere and announced, 'Right, no excuses now!' and ran away to the communal tent, trying to process what had just happened.

A quick side note: I was sponsored by *British Turkey*. Yes, really. Turkey is not just for Christmas. My gear proudly displayed 'I ❤ British Turkey', which led to one of the Tanzanian guides pulling me aside to ask, 'What is this? Is British Turkey a place? Like the British Virgin Islands?' I explained, 'No, it's a bird. You eat it. Like a big chicken.' He paused, looked thoughtful, then said, 'So … you love big chickens?' For the rest of the trip, I was known as 'Big Chicken Lover'. Cheers, British Turkey.

Martina didn't last another day. She was mentally and physically drained and quietly left with two guides. In hindsight, she was dealing with personal issues and struggling with the altitude. I gave her a lot more empathy after that. The rest of us soldiered on … still wet, now cold, and then I got hit with altitude sickness. Let me be blunt: altitude sickness is the worst thing I've ever experienced. And I've been through 36 hours of labour. It was like the worst hangover of your life, but without the option to curl up on the sofa with Lucozade. Instead, I had to walk five miles up a mountain in freezing rain, and every step was agony. But, the good news for me was that we were doing one of our planned descents in altitude that day to reach camp – the idea of them is to help climbers acclimatise – and the lower elevation worked wonders. I collapsed into bed and woke up the next morning feeling human again.

By now, the rain had turned to snow. A few members of the group had to stop due to illness and soaked gear. It was a smart decision; altitude gets more dangerous the higher you go. You need to be sharp.

Summit day began at 2.30am. It was pitch black but, for the first time, we saw stars. No rain. No snow. Just a clear African sky. I paired up with a woman called Karen, and we moved together in a rhythm: '1, 2, 3, stop … 1, 2, 3, stop …' It was the only way we could physically keep going. The air was thin, every breath a struggle, and I started hallucinating from the exhaustion. After a quick soup stop, we pressed on.

I don't distinctly remember reaching the top. Just the famous wooden sign, the camera flash and the guide's face saying, 'I need to get you down. *Now.*' I was shaking, nearly blind with exhaustion. My body was done. He took my bag and pushed me into descent mode. Coming down Kilimanjaro is like skiing on scree. There's loose volcanic gravel. It's steep, slippery and unforgiving. I was running on empty and my legs were like jelly. The guide practically dragged me down. But finally, *finally*, the sun came out.

It took a mountain, a rainstorm and a group of extraordinary women to remind me of who I was. Not just a mum, but an athlete. An adventurer. And, apparently, a big chicken lover.

Everest – Laughter, Ice and Apples

I signed up for 'Trek to Everest Base Camp' after seeing an Instagram post. I clicked. Registered. And then … forgot about it. It wasn't until two months before departure in the spring of 2019 that the email came through with the full kit list, logistics, dates, and I thought: 'Oh shit. I haven't told my family!' Cue some very surprised faces when I casually announced I'd be heading to the Himalayas.

I was nervous at first, turning up alone, not knowing a soul. But that didn't last long. Within hours, I'd found my tribe. We clicked instantly, and then came the first true test: the flight to Lukla, known as one of the world's most dangerous airports. We boarded a tiny propeller plane and I closed my eyes for the entire landing. From there, we were off. Hiking through the Himalayas, bound for Base Camp. The rope bridges were nerve-wracking enough, but we'd also been warned about the yaks, which charge through with zero awareness or etiquette. Basically, move fast or be flattened.

At night, the stars were unlike anything I've ever seen. The sky looked like it had been dusted with diamonds; quiet, infinite, humbling.

But it was freezing. I mean *really* freezing. It dropped to -15°C at night, and even sleeping in all my clothes, I couldn't get warm. Every breath turned to mist. Every morning, my boots were stiff with ice.

But the scenery was utterly surreal. Dwarfed by towering Himalayan peaks, I felt both insignificant and deeply alive.

And then ... there it was. Everest. Not the postcard-perfect image from afar, but raw and looming in the flesh. Black. Majestic. Almost intimidating in its stillness. We made it to Base Camp, where the Khumbu Icefall stretched out before us. It was beautiful, but dangerous. Its deep-blue glacial cracks still bore scars from past earthquakes. You could see why lives are lost here, just trying to cross it to start the actual summit climb. Helicopters buzzed in and out, ferrying wealthy climbers to and from camp like it was a ski resort.

Among the scattered boulders and prayer flags were stones etched with names, memorials to those who never made it back. Standing among them gave me a moment of stillness, a time to pause, reflect and remember what really matters.

And yet, it wasn't all solemn. Far from it. There was joy, too – so much of it. Laughter echoed in the cold nights, especially during our rowdy games of Cards Against Humanity. I formed a little crew with Mick, Jeremy and Abid. We'd keep each other going, laughing until our faces hurt. One day, we were talking about the food we were most looking forward to when the trek ended. Mick, Jeremy and I dreamed of steaks, burgers and Sunday roasts. Abid, quietly but confidently, said, 'An apple.' Who craves an apple? Abid, obviously. That moment will stay with me forever. Abid was the kindest, sweetest soul. He passed away a few years ago, but I carry his memory with me. That trip wouldn't have been the same without him. He left a quiet, lasting imprint on all of us.

Everest wasn't just a mountain. For me, it became a symbol of life – vast, unpredictable, beautiful and brutal. The simplicity of the Tibetan way of living, the peace of the silent peaks, the disconnection from phones, feeds and constant noise; everything about it reminded me to live more slowly. To step back from the trivial and be present. Nature, after all, doesn't care about your inbox or your social media 'likes'. Standing beneath Everest, you realise just how small you are. And how wonderful life can feel when you *open your eyes to appreciate.*

The Big Three

As you can see, for a few years I had a bit of a habit: spot a challenge, sign up immediately and deal with the consequences later. If it looked tough, slightly dangerous or mildly insane, I was in. Like a magpie for madness. Then, a few weeks before the event, panic, followed swiftly by 'Ah well … f**k it', and off I went.

That's exactly how I ended up at the start line of RideLondon, a 100-mile cycling event, which Skoda had sponsored me to take part in. I had never ridden a road bike before. My longest ride up to that point had been maybe 20 miles, and that one involved pub stops. But here I was, Lycra'd up with only three weeks of wobbly training under my belt. Brilliant, Gail. Really solid prep. I managed to complete it, so all is fine.

But there was a bigger goal. Since I'd already run the London Marathon and finished RideLondon, all I needed was to swim two miles in the Serpentine to complete the infamous 'London Classics' and earn the coveted 'Big Three' medal. I do love a medal. That shiny chunk of metal was dangling in front of me like a carrot, and I couldn't resist.

So, I signed up for the swim. I'm a pretty average swimmer, but I figured I'd be fine. Bought a wetsuit. Got in the water. That's when I realised open-water swimming is an entirely different beast. Especially when you're surrounded by swans, ducks, geese and God knows what else. I flat-out refused to put my face in the water, so it was breaststroke the entire way.

I was doing alright, pacing myself … until about 200m from the finish. Suddenly, everything started to go dark. I'd been in the cold water too long and my body started shutting down. I don't remember much about the last stretch. I just know I somehow made it over the finish line and was immediately helped out by the event crew.

First, they stuck me in a hot tub, still shivering uncontrollably. Then came the emergency foil blankets, and the medical team parked me in front of a heater. I was five minutes away from being carted off to the hospital with hypothermia. Thankfully, my core temp finally stabilised, and I avoided the ambulance.

But the most important thing? I got the medal. Because, obviously, that's what matters.

Steph: I wonder if you can see a pattern emerging with the way you lived your life over this period?

Gail: I guess it was one adrenaline hit after another.

Steph: And do you think it was really just about the adrenaline or something deeper?

Gail: Tough to admit, but I guess I was filling a void.

Steph: Bingo.

TALKING FOR A LIVING ... WHO KNEW?

Motivational Talking to Microphone Drops

One thing I've always been grateful for: I'm not shy. I can get up on stage and talk to a room full of strangers, so when the dust began to settle after my retirement from badminton, motivational public speaking became a steady source of income for me.

Sure, I get nervous (every single time), but deep down ... I love it. There's something about walking into an event and getting announced; it's like a chance to show off, and I lean into that.

Still, it blows my mind that people *book* me to speak. They want the 'secret' to success. I always say the same thing: there isn't one. It's stubbornness, resilience and hard graft. That's it. I've told the same message to schoolkids and CEOs; I've just dressed it up a little differently depending on the crowd. Same truth, new outfit.

Now, my talks didn't start off as polished performances. I've had help shaping the content, working on delivery and getting feedback. One of the best bits of advice I ever got was to do a stand-up comedy course. I thought, 'Why not?' (Classic me.) I googled and found one at The Comedy Store in Camden. Six weeks, ending with a five-minute live performance at Bethnal Green Comedy Club. Easy, right?

Wrong.

Let me tell you, if you've ever sat on your sofa watching *Live at the Apollo*, thinking, 'I could do that, I'm well funny at work drinks,' ... think again. It was the most terrifying thing I've ever done in my life. And I've played badminton in an Olympic final. I still have the certificate from that course. I treasure it more than some of my medals. That's how real it got.

I went in cocky (shock, I know). The comedians running the course clocked me immediately. 'Stop being a presenter,' they said. Turns out, comedy isn't about delivering lines. It's about living them. It's real. Raw. You can't hide behind slides and soundbites. You have to be present, flaws and all. So, I learned how to shape a story, how to time a punchline. How to just ... stand still and own it.

The show night came. The group was split across three performances and I was first up in the third group on that final night. I watched people go on before me; some smashed it, some froze, some fizzled despite being naturally hilarious. Then it was my turn.

The lights dropped. 'And now ... Gail Emms!'

Spotlight. Microphone. Heart pounding. Showtime.

'Good evening, Bethnal Green! Now, I am a *little* bit famous ... I know, I know, I'm an Olympian.' Cue heckler: 'YOU GOT BRONZE!'

Fantastic.

'Bronze?! Don't call me bronze. Silver, babe. Means I came second ... which wasn't always ideal in the Olympic Village bedrooms ...'

And off I went. Condoms in Olympic welcome packs. Gold means you come first. Silver second. Bronze ... well, *three's a crowd*. I kept the theme going. Yes, Olympic athletes are at it once their events are done. Full-on carnage. And you *can* tell what sport someone's from by how they have sex.

Gymnasts? Want a score afterwards.

Sprinters? Done in under ten seconds.

Boxers? Three rounds, water break, back in.

Badminton players? Well ... we like cocks. Not balls.

Relay teams? Watch the baton.

It was going well. The crowd was into it. I doubled down.

'I probably scare the shit out of men in bed. Most women go for candles and slow tunes on ... I've got Lucozade Sport, a heart rate monitor and a defib on standby. It's not foreplay, it's a warm-up.

Stretching *is* advised. I don't want pulled muscles and excuses. No pain, no gain. Tears? That just means we're getting started.'

I clocked three guys in the front row, in their 20s, wide-eyed, somewhere between terrified and intrigued. They thought I was making it up. But no. That's the thing about comedy: you've got to keep it real.

I brought something different to that stage. Eventually, I got the flash from the back, it was time to wrap it up. 'You've been amazing, Bethnal Green! I'm Gail Emms. GOODNIGHT!' Mic in the stand. Walk off stage left. Boom. I was *buzzing*! High fives. And such relief, *I didn't die* on stage. I mean, no one's calling from the Apollo … but I held my own. I got the laughs. I did the thing.

But just like my one and only marathon: been there. Smashed it. Never. Again.

Fighting Talk – 17 Years of Wit, Chaos and Cult Radio Glory

I like to think I'm funny. People have said I am. One ex-boyfriend even admitted he couldn't handle the fact I was funnier than him. He was supposed to be 'the funny one', bless. Honestly, humour has gotten me into trouble more times than I can count but, every now and again, Emms the Comedian earns a solid round of applause.

And that brings me to BBC Radio 5 Live's *Fighting Talk*, a cult Saturday morning sports panel show where wit meets wisdom, and points are awarded for both insight and insanity.

My journey with *Fighting Talk* started back in 2008, not long after I retired. I got the call (thank you, Elly Oldroyd, I think you had a hand in that) and was invited on to what became the show's first all-female panel, alongside Sue Mott, Hazel Irvine and Elly herself. I wasn't really sure what I was getting into. I just knew it was live radio, it was about sport and it involved being funny. I was in.

Then host Colin Murray asked: 'Which female athlete do you fancy? Who does it for you?' I replied, 'You can't go wrong with a Swedish blonde – Carolina Klüft. And she's got multiple skills.' I think Colin actually dribbled. And just like that, I became a regular.

If you are intrigued to know how it all works, four panellists go head-to-head for an hour, either live on air or recorded 'as-live', earning points for being clever, creative and just plain ridiculous. People always ask me about the show, more than they ask about the Olympic Games now. You get a call from the producer, booking you in. Then two days before the show, you're sent the questions. It may sound spontaneous on air but, trust me, there's prep involved. You have about 24 hours to write your answers; ideally clever and hilarious, but sometimes you just land in the 'bang average' category and hope the delivery carries you through. The day before the show, you send your answers in. This is to avoid four panellists giving the same punchline (awkward). If someone else has your killer joke, then tough, you have to think again. The host doesn't know any of the answers beforehand, so those reactions you hear are genuine. That's the beauty of it.

Over the years, I've been on *Fighting Talk* with legends like Steve Bunce (who gives the best hugs), Bob Mills (like the best funny dad), Jim White and John Rawling. There's a real camaraderie between regulars that makes the whole thing magic.

But sometimes ... the vibe's off. This happened on a show with Bob Mills and Charlie Sloth. Charlie turned up wearing a huge puffa jacket, better suited for a ski expedition. Bob looked at him and asked, 'Are you going to take that off?' Charlie, deadpan: 'Man's not hot.' Bob was unimpressed. The tension was real, and I sat between them, praying for comedy gold and ending up with radio silence. Even the studio air was awkward. Of course, 'Man's Not Hot', the parody song, went viral not long after. Bob and I missed an opportunity there.

The other awkward show I encountered was with Adam Richman, him of TV show *Man v Food*. He's a *big* Spurs fan, a *big* TV star and was a *big* disappointment. He turned up with an entourage (never a good sign), didn't say hello and clearly hadn't researched the show. As we tried to rescue the segment, he gradually realised what the show *actually* was about, but only five minutes before it ended. He finally went, 'That was so f**king awesome!' and tried to high-five us all. Mate, too late. I was devastated. Never meet your heroes, I guess, and as someone who loves eating copious amounts of chicken wings, I was hugely disappointed in him.

I have had some of my favourite moments of all time while on *Fighting Talk*. I've racked up 50-plus appearances over the years, with hosts including Colin Murray, Josh Widdicombe, Georgie Thompson and now Rick Edwards. The questions are often gloriously ridiculous: 'Sportspeople as desserts.' 'Who's got the best legs in sport?' 'If sports stars were TV shows …'

That last one is still my all-time favourite. I was on with Dougie Anderson and Tom Davis. Dougie (in his lovely Scottish lilt): 'Sheep Shearing with Alan Shearer.' Tom Davis (deep Cockney): 'On the Couch with Peter Crouch.' Me: 'Wife Swap with John Terry.'

We were all in stitches. Even the producer corpsed. Moments like that are *Fighting Talk* at its finest.

Out of all those shows, I've only made it to the Champion of Champions final *twice*. The first time was with Colin hosting, and I wore a green dress, but I was so nervous I sweated through the entire thing. So much sweat that Colin deducted points for it. True story. I wasn't even wearing Charlie's puffa jacket. Just 'too hot to handle', apparently.

I've just recorded the 2024/25 Champion of Champions show, live at the BBC Theatre, in front of 350 people. It was me, Bob Mills, Dougie Anderson and Danny McLoughlin, the same night as the Europa League Final between Spurs and Man United. Danny's a United fan. He may have lifted the *Fighting Talk* trophy, but Son Heung-min lifted the real one for Spurs. So technically … I win.

It's not about the appearance money (it really is a very low amount), for me, it's about the chaos, the challenge and the crackling energy of live radio. The moments that go brilliantly and the ones that crash and burn. It's addictive. Even now, when I get the call, I get that same buzz, because *Fighting Talk* is more than just a sports quiz. It's about being bold, being cheeky, and showing up with your game face and your best gags.

It's me. It's sport. It's chaos. It's *Fighting Talk*.

*Steph: I had absolutely no idea you had done all this stuff! You were obviously playing to your strengths, and most athletes would be absolutely s**t at all of this and you've made a career out of it. Tenacious, versatile, funny ... this is a very different version of the story you originally told me about how your career post-sport has been 'a bleep-bleep disaster'.*

Gail: Oops ...

Steph: Maybe it's time to stop being so self-deprecating? You have just given yourself the evidence that your thought patterns are outdated. Please can you find some new ways to talk to yourself about what you have achieved more positively? Sorry ... now I feel like I've told you off.

Gail: I needed telling, Miss.

Come On You Spurs

Tottenham Hotspur have finally won a trophy. Let that sink in. *Seventeen* years of glorious 'nearlys', crushing 'almosts', and existential Premier League crises ... all worth it for one shiny Europa League (or whatever it's called) trophy. We finished 17th in the league – but who cares?! We're back in the Champions League, and there's finally something in the cabinet that isn't dust and broken dreams. My boys and I celebrated long into the night, tears of joy, but so proud of the team. And a little surprised that we had a defence ... where had that been hiding all season?!

I don't get to see Spurs live as much as I'd like but, when I do, it's memorable. Like back in 2005, when Nathan and I were invited pitch side for Spurs vs Newcastle as Olympic medallists, promoting the London 2012 bid. Paul Coyte, the voice of Spurs, was set to interview us pre-match. As we waited near the halfway line, Alan Shearer started warming up nearby, casually pinging balls about ... until one came flying directly at my head. I swear my peripheral vision and Olympian reflexes kicked in, and I channelled full Keanu Reeves in *The Matrix*, leaning back as the ball whizzed past my face, smashed into the advertising boards and landed at my feet.

I picked it up, handed it back, and, ever the comedian, quipped, 'Phew, close one, Alan. Good job, your aim's off today, eh?' Not even a smirk. No apology. Just pure Shearer: cold, clinical and clearly not a fan of banter. Spurs won that match, and he got subbed off for being rubbish. I like to think that is karma for nearly killing me.

Then there was 2010, when I was invited to the Emirates Stadium to watch Arsenal vs Spurs as a thank you for work I'd done with Premier League 4 Sport. Lovely gesture, but terrible venue. I was ushered into the Directors' Box, which was very posh indeed, but at half-time we were 2-0 down. Standard Spurs.

Then came the comeback: Bale, Van der Vaart ... and finally Kaboul with the winner. I was sitting on the aisle, right next to the home supporters. After Bale's goal, I let out a subtle cheer. Van der Vaart equalised. I couldn't help, it, I squealed. By the time Kaboul made it 3-2, I was on my feet, fists in the air, before Ed wrestled me back into my seat hissing, 'Shut up. Seriously. Shut. Up.' The Arsenal fans were not amused. Thank God I'm a woman; if I'd been a bloke, I think it would've kicked off. But what can I say? It was Spurs' first win at Arsenal in 17 years. A little giddy joy was justified, but I will always remember not to be such a d**khead next time.

I've got a photo of myself and Harry Kane proudly up in the lounge. I'd gone to a match with rugby sevens legends (and fellow Spurs fans) Tom Mitchell and James Rodwell. Post-London 2012, we were treated to some hospitality ... which I took very seriously. I got absolutely hammered. Then someone decided it was photo time with the man of the match, which happened to be Harry Kane. I staggered up for the pic, leaned in on Harry and, bless him, he held me up. You can see it in the photo. That smile on his face is 50 per cent 'nice to meet you' and 50 per cent 'if I let go of this woman, she's going down'. Cheers, Harry. One of our own.

Spurs have some brilliant people behind the scenes. Say what you like about Daniel Levy, but the new stadium is next-level. The staff are unreal, genuinely welcoming, whether I'm there for a corporate do or go-karting with the kids. Recently, for Harry's 15th birthday, I took him and Ollie to see Spurs vs Bournemouth. Paul Coyte, hero that he is, got us into the H Lounge, where we met Ledley King and Micky van de Ven and got photos with them. It was a total surprise. The joy on Harry's face – that's what football is about. We chatted with Paul about how important these little moments are, especially for kids. Not every player loves the media stuff, and I get that; it's tiring. But those five minutes can have a lifelong impact. Harry and Ollie were still buzzing at school the next day.

I also had a cracking chat with Ledley King about dodgy knees and stiff hips, true bonding stuff. He told me he'd watched me at the Olympics. Honestly *made my day*!

Tottenham Hotspur is a team that tests every emotional limit but somehow still holds your heart. Whether it's a trophy drought, last-minute winners, awkward encounters with Alan Shearer or drunken photo ops with Harry Kane, I'm Spurs through and through.

And now? We've got silverware. We've got stories. And we've got delusional hope. (Again.)

COYS.

Millwall Till I Die ... Nearly Literally

I love the new Spurs stadium – it's shiny, sleek, with spaceship vibes – but I've also got a real soft spot for the old-school, gritty grounds. You know the ones: rusting corrugated iron, dripping with history, wedged right in the heart of the community. So, when my mate Jamie and his dad Len, both hardcore Millwall fans from Bermondsey, invited me to The Den to watch Millwall vs QPR, I couldn't say no.

Naturally, I leaned into the stereotype and joked to friends, 'If I make it out alive, it's a win,' and 'Millwall till I die!' Well ... turns out that came alarmingly close to being a self-fulfilling prophecy. It wasn't a punch-up, to be clear. It was a sausage roll.

Half-time rolled around, and I went to grab a pint and a snack, my classic football behaviour. I took one bite of this innocent-looking, surprisingly soft, deceptively flaky sausage roll ... and, suddenly, I couldn't breathe. A rogue shard of pastry lodged itself right in my windpipe. Cue choking, coughing, spluttering – the works.

Jamie leapt into action like a slightly panicked St John Ambulance volunteer, smacking me on the back repeatedly, while shouting something unhelpful like, 'Don't die here, for f**k's sake!' The first few thumps didn't work. I was now sweating, wheezing and making that terrifying silent gulping noise that says, 'This might actually be it.' Jamie was just about to go full Heimlich when, miraculously, the demonic bit of flaky pastry dislodged itself and projectile-launched on to the floor like it had a grudge. A stunned silence … then laughter. Then the slightly surreal realisation that I had just nearly choked to death on a sausage roll at Millwall.

Millwall till I die? Almost happened. Over a f**king pastry. You can imagine the eulogy at my funeral. Still, Millwall won 2-1 and their fans were obviously delighted. They decided I was their lucky mascot, but only if I'm willing to risk choking to death again at every match. Hmmm… I'll think about it.

So yeah, I survived The Den. Not the violence. Not the fans. Just the sausage roll. Iconic.

My Mum and David Ginola

You'd think I'd be the golden child in my family with Olympic medals, telly work, the lot, but no. The only time I've ever truly seen that sparkle of awe in my mum's eyes was the day I got David Ginola on the phone for her.

I was co-presenting a sports chat show on BT Sport with Tim Lovejoy, and David Ginola was a guest panellist. Cool, charming, effortlessly French; it was peak Ginola. After the show, we were in the green room, and I asked if he'd send my mum, Jan, a little voice message. Without missing a beat, he looked at me with those smouldering eyes and purred, 'Call her up.' Oh God. So I did. Thankfully, Mum answered, and before I could even speak, David *took the phone out of my hand* and strolled off across the room like he was starring in a L'Oréal advert. From across the room, I heard David say, 'Hello … is this Janice? It is David Ginola here. Oui, this is really him.'

The scream down the phone that followed nearly cracked the screen. They chatted for a solid two, maybe three, minutes, David being his casually charming self; Mum, clearly ascending into the heavens. Eventually, he sauntered back, still holding my phone to his ear, and said, 'It has been lovely talking to you, Janice. I will now give you back to your daughter, Gail.' Except ... she was done with me. Hung up. Just like that. Didn't even say goodbye.

She then went radio silent for two hours, because she was calling literally *everyone* she knew to say *David Ginola* and her had been on the phone together. Eventually, she called me back. Beaming. Triumphant. Ready to speak to her daughter again, now that I'd become, however briefly, the golden child.

Thanks, David. You absolute legend.

Dancing on Ice ... Goes Gold, Glam and Off-Balance

To celebrate London 2012, ITV decided to combine the spirit of the Olympics with sequins, spray tan and high-stakes triple salchows (well, mild gliding). Enter: *Dancing on Ice Goes Gold*, a one-off special featuring actual Olympians attempting not to faceplant on national television.

The line-up was top tier: Tessa Sanderson (javelin queen), Pippa Wilson (gold medal sailor), Olga Korbut (actual gymnastics legend), Jamie Baulch (speedy 400m dude), Colin Jackson (hurdles maestro), Steve Williams (rower with terrifyingly strong arms) ... and me. I was paired with the lovely Łukasz, a pro skater who very quickly realised I was more 'game' than 'graceful'. Learning the skating was surprisingly okay; however, learning the dancing was a complete shambles. Łukasz would look at me, panic in his eyes, and mutter things like, 'Can you just ... try to be elegant?' 'What are your hands doing?' 'Smile? Can you smile?'

Bless him. He soon clocked that sporty girls are sporty girls for a reason: lots of coordination, yes, but graceful jazz hands, not so much. The last time I learned a dance routine was with my sister in the living room to 'I Will Survive' circa 1990. And now here I was, upside down, being spun around to Rihanna's 'Only Girl in the World', fake-tanned to within an inch of my life and wearing a leotard that looked like it belonged to a Year 8 gymnast. And yet, somehow, I got through it. No falls. No flashing. No cracked ribs. The lifts landed. The moves worked. I even cracked a smile.

I came fourth. Steve Williams and his steely rowing biceps took the win, which was fair enough.

It's the only time I've dipped my toe into the reality TV world. I've been asked about doing other shows before (no, not *Love Island*, calm down), but this is the only one I ever said yes to and, even as a one-off, it took over eight weeks of my life. Eight weeks. For one glitter-drenched performance.

And here's the thing: in sport, you train, you turn up, you perform, and the result is based on what you do. In the ice dancing world, it's also about how you look, what music you've got and whether you can sell sass in a leotard. I struggled with that bit. Łukasz kept whispering, 'Smile, Gail! It's all about the smile!' But what if I didn't want to smile? What if I wanted my intense athlete focus face? Apparently, that doesn't fly on ice.

Still, huge thanks to Łukasz and the whole team. It was chaotic, exhausting, hilarious and, yes, I can now skate backwards. No gold medal, but a newfound respect for anyone in Lycra doing the cha-cha on ice.

London 2012: Not Competing, but Cashing In

I'm not going to lie, there was a part of me that was absolutely gutted not to be competing at the London 2012 Olympics. A home Games! The buzz! The kit! *The kit*! Watching all the athletes talk about how excited they were made me feel a very specific kind of Olympic-level envy. I was sat there trying not to weep into my non-technical hoodie. But while they were locked in ice baths and strict training camps, I was doing something far more glamorous: rinsing the speaking circuit.

With current athletes unavailable (what with training and, you know, competing), there was suddenly a huge demand for Olympians to visit schools, companies and pretty much any group of humans willing to sit down and listen. Of course, the big guns like Denise Lewis, Sally Gunnell and Sharron Davies were out there smashing it, but if your budget couldn't stretch that far, guess what? You could book Emms.

And I said yes. To *everything*. Corporate events, school assemblies, sports days, you name it. I drove the length of the country with a suitcase full of medals and motivational chat and made more money that year than I ever had during my actual sporting career. Honestly, any lingering doubts I had about retiring were erased the moment I saw those day rates. 'Should I have stayed in sport?' Nope. Not when the post-sport hustle pays this well, thanks.

Now, there was a downside. Heather Small. Actually, these words: 'What have you done today to make you feel proud?' I heard that song approximately 673 times. I wasn't counting. I twitched every time it came on in a school assembly while 200 small children swayed earnestly in front of a PowerPoint with the words of that song displayed. I'd sit there thinking: 'Well, Heather, what *have* I done today to make myself feel proud?' Not a gold medal, that's for sure. Not even a podium finish in laundry. But I've managed to keep a toddler alive, juggle work, childcare, three bags of snacks and my own fragile mental health. And I've got matching socks on. So yes, Heather. Today, I am proud.

I was at the opening ceremony of London 2012 and got to go into the main part of the stadium as a previous medallist. To date, there have been 6,113 athletes who have represented Great Britain in the Olympic Games. And I am one of the 600 who have won a medal. When the stats are said like that, it makes the reality all the more special. Sitting amongst legends of other sports makes it incredibly humbling. Then, listening to the Spice Girls screech 'Wannabe', it all comes crashing back down to Earth. Dear God.

I was invited to work for the BBC to commentate on the badminton, which was being held in Wembley Arena. My lead commentator would be the late David Mercer, and we tackled the schedule the best we could. It was relentless. Even toilet breaks were hard to get in as we were in that arena from 8am until midnight. It was the first time that group stages were introduced, and it was the 'brilliant' idea of the BWF to get more badminton on TV when it was in the Olympics. I was a bit confused by this: there was really no need to change a competition structure that has worked very well in the past. And my suspicions about this new format were proven right, as I was suddenly caught up in one of the most scandalous chains of events in Olympic Games history.

It started because there was an upset in one of the group matches in the ladies' doubles. Danish girls Christinna Pedersen and Kamilla Rytter Juhl beat the Chinese seeded pair, which meant those two pairs qualified for the quarter-finals, but with the Chinese pair as the second-ranked pair in the group. This all happened in the morning session. As the result came in, I turned to David and said, 'Uh-oh, that result is going to affect the afternoon matches.' No one in the afternoon matches wanted to win their group, as they would go into the same half of the draw as the Chinese girls who had lost earlier. Whoever came second in the group would go into the top half of the draw with the Danish girls, and that's what the Chinese, Korean and Indonesian girls all wanted.

So, we ended up with two ladies' doubles pairs on a badminton court, *both trying to lose the match*!

The thing is, the coaches, the managers, even I had all warned the tournament referee and the BWF, but we were told, 'Don't be silly, this is the Olympic Games, that won't happen.' Yes, it is the Olympic Games, and the players are going to do everything they can to get the gold medal. Which means trying to get the best draw possible.

The players went on court. The crowd, who had paid good money to see the top players in the world, was then subjected to the chaos that ensued. In the first match between China and South Korea, errors began occurring during routine shots, including purposely hitting serves into the net or returns long. The crowd reacted angrily, and the first game in the match featured no rallies of more than four shots. I was fuming. The crowd was shouting and the players were deliberately missing the shuttle. The umpire was telling the players to play properly, but they were doing what was best for them.

It happened again in the next match with Indonesia versus South Korea. *Exactly the same.*

There were arguments going on everywhere. David, a stalwart in commentary, was getting visibly upset; this was not sport and the fair play of the Olympic Games spirit. The umpires then issued black cards to the players and they were all disqualified, with a review from the BWF finding them guilty of 'not using best efforts' and 'conducting oneself in a manner that is clearly abusive or detrimental to the sport'.

The four ladies' doubles pairs, one from China, two from South Korea and one from Indonesia, were all replaced by pairs previously knocked out. It was the right decision, yet I feel for the players who were involved; it wasn't their fault that the BWF had screwed up the format and had allowed for that to happen. You *cannot* have a match in the Olympic Games where *both* teams are trying to lose. What was more annoying was the fact that the pairs promoted to the next rounds were girls whom Donna and I used to beat regularly. I messaged Kellogg. She agreed. Bollocks.

You'll be pleased to know that to avoid a recurrence of these events, the competition format for the next Olympics was revised: trying to keep face, the BWF kept the groups, but all second-place pairs from the group stage would enter a separate draw to determine their quarter-final opponents, while each group's top pair would be assigned a fixed position aligned with their designated seed in the knockout stage. Just bring back the knockout format. Keep it simple.

After the badminton had finished, and I had been all over the press talking about the scandal of badminton, I worked as a roving reporter for local radio stations. I got to the Olympic Park and was sent out with a microphone to interview people and get some vox pops (short interviews that all stations can share and use) and I set out to work.

I saw a family coming over the bridge: dad, mum, son and daughter. They were walking with purpose; the dad was clutching a handful of tickets. I went over, 'Hello, I'm working for BBC radio, just wanted to interview people here at Olympic Park. May I ask what you are going to see please?' The dad, the leader of this family, said, 'Basketball! We are off to the basketball!' 'Oh, amazing! What match?' I asked. 'Senegal vs South Korea!' Or something like that – I can't remember the exact countries, but I know for a fact that when that dad applied for tickets for London 2012, he was tasked with getting the 'good sports' like athletics and swimming maybe. Perhaps a cheeky beach volleyball ticket, eh dad? I am sure he wasn't targeting the Senegal vs South Korea basketball match, but here they were, the family, all extremely excited to be in amongst the crowds, lapping up the Olympic atmosphere, squeezing the tickets so hard as not to lose them, and delighted that they can say they watched the Senegalese basketball team.

Say what you like about London 2012, but that's what I will remember. The sheer delight of people watching random sports, who moaned and complained when they didn't get the tickets they wanted in the ballot, and were allocated random ones, yet it didn't matter. For three weeks, and then two weeks for the Paralympics afterwards, London was a joy, a celebration of sport, and again I felt wanted and respected. People had a newfound love for sport, felt inspired and wanted to hear my journey. Life was good again. It masked the pain that I wasn't competing, and the 'fear of missing out' I felt watching the first Olympic Games since I had retired.

I got to see some other sports: hockey, swimming and athletics. As I turned up at the Olympic Stadium, I saw my university mate Lucy. She was driving the golf buggies that gave lifts from the warm-up track to the stadium, and she told me she had driven Usain Bolt the day before!

I had a media pass, and I got a bit confused as I was so used to being an athlete. I made a couple of wrong turns, opened this door, and found myself in the holding room of the men's decathletes. They were about to be announced into the stadium and were in various states of stretching and warm-up as I walked in. Trying to be cool and look somewhat official, I counted them, in my panic (what the hell, why did I do this?), nodded, and said, 'Good luck, everybody!' and walked back out.

From 'Very Average' to 'Very Sparkly' – My Champions UK Story

Post-London 2012, I was flying. Work was busy, life was full and I was still riding the Olympic wave (without the pressure of actually having to do any sport). But then, my management company went under, and I found myself unrepresented and pregnant with Ollie. Not ideal timing.

Enter: Champions UK. I'd heard they were a growing family-run agency doing great things, so I waddled into their office to see what they were all about.

Now, the founder, John Hayes, has a *very* John Hayes way of introducing me whenever I host one of their events. He tells a room full of businesspeople, 'When Gail first came into my office, I thought ... she's very average.' Gasps. But I *love* this introduction, because that has been the story of my career – being underestimated. Told I was average. Told I'd never be excellent. Then quietly (or loudly, depending on the situation), proving people wrong. To John's credit, he gave me a shot. He offered me options, let me fail a bit, learn a lot, ask questions, ask for feedback and improve. And I did. I've been working with Champions ever since, and they've been brilliant. I owe a huge thank you to John, his family and the entire team for backing me when others might not have bothered.

I still remember my first hosting gig. Leicester Business Awards. Full glam. Hair sprayed into position. First time using autocue – you know those clear Oscar-style panels? That.

I walked on, thinking I was smashing it. Walked off, proud as punch. John's feedback? 'A bit wooden.' Right. Cheers, John. Noted.

Since then, I've hosted hundreds of events, some with autocue, some with cue cards, some where I'm completely winging it and hoping no one notices. I've had co-hosts I adore and a few who've tested my patience, but I've learned how to read a room, keep a show moving, and I like to think I'm a joy to work with: punctual, professional and always 100 per cent in.

There are perks, too. Lumbers Jewellers in Leicester is owned by a friend and client of Champions, and sometimes they loan me jewellery for the events. Once I wore £500,000 worth of diamonds. If there was ever a moment for someone to stage a kidnapping of me, that was it. But no one did. (I'm not sure whether to be relieved or offended.) Dominic, if you're reading this: you're brave. Because if *anyone* is going to drop a diamond necklace down a toilet, it's me.

Now, I'd love to say I've always been a shining example of professionalism … except this one time, and I blame John's son, Jack. He booked me on a celebrity fishing TV show, the day after my birthday. I arrived, post-Brighton-beach-rave (yes, a two-dayer), still technically drunk, telling myself, 'Just go to bed early.' Jack had other plans. Champagne. More champagne. Brandy. Maybe tequila? I've blocked it out.

Cut to 8am the next morning, and my hangover level was *biblical*. I had to sit down in the shower. I walked to the fishery, immediately threw up behind a bush, then tried to look vaguely alive while the smell of fish bait and maggots made me dry heave every ten minutes. At one point, I collapsed mid-walk to the loo. My legs gave out. My vision blurred. I rang my mate Jamie, whispering, 'I think I need to go to the hospital.' He thought I was being dramatic. But, honestly, I might have needed a drip. I vowed never again. And the following year, I kept that promise, I came back sober, brought Harry and Ollie with me, they helped run the show, met David Seaman, Luke Littler and Ellis Genge, so they were absolutely buzzing.

I didn't win the fishing, but I *did* catch my first carp. Now there's a sentence I never thought I'd write.

From Olympic stadiums to dodgy fishing chairs, from hosting award nights in diamonds to vomiting behind bushes, it's been quite the ride with Champions. And I wouldn't change a thing.

Sport Relief: Top Dog

For my 30th birthday, in July 2007, Ed decided to buy me a puppy, a gorgeous West Highland Terrier we named Alfie. He was absolutely adorable. But just three days later, he died from parvovirus. He'd caught it from the breeder before we could get him vaccinated. It was utterly devastating. It's still a sore spot, especially when I'm joking with Ed about some of his more questionable gift choices over the years.

After Alfie, we found another Westie breeder, and along came Rafa. Named after Rafa Nadal, because we were tennis fans at the time. Truthfully, we preferred Federer, but 'Roger the dog' didn't feel quite right ... a bit on the naughty side.

One day, while out walking Rafa, I got a call from a TV agent asking if I had a dog. I said yes, and ten minutes later a panicked researcher rang me up, practically bursting with excitement. 'Fantastic! And just to check ... it's not a black Labrador?' 'Nope. He's a Westie called Rafa.' '*Thank God*! Every celeb seems to have a black Labrador!' Then came the dreaded question, 'What tricks can he do? Is he obedient?'

Now, anyone who's owned a terrier knows ... *obedient* is not a word that applies. They have selective hearing, a nose that overrides any sense of loyalty and an ability to disappear into bushes for hours chasing squirrels or ghost smells. I've lost Rafa in the wilds of suburban Milton Keynes more times than I can count, only for him to casually stroll back and scratch at the front door like nothing happened. So, I hesitated. 'Well ... sometimes he sits when I say "sit".' There was a long pause. 'Okay ... does he fetch? Swim? Respond to commands?' 'Erm ... depends on his mood?' The researcher sounded deflated and eventually hung up. I kicked myself for not fibbing a bit more. But hey, I didn't know what the show *was*. I wasn't about to claim he could solve a Rubik's Cube.

An hour later, clearly having exhausted the celebrity dog pool, I got a call back.

Rafa and I were in. We were going to be on *Sport Relief: Top Dog*. We turned up at the studio and met our team-mates: Ian and his dog Maysie, Jeff and his dog Buzz; both fire rescue dogs. These dogs were smarter than half the people I know. Ian and Jeff clocked Rafa, looked at me, and realised instantly: Maysie and Buzz were carrying this team.

The show had obstacle courses, relay races, that sort of thing. Our first round was against comedian Debra Stephenson and her chocolate lab, Biscuit. Somehow, God knows how, Rafa managed to behave, and we made it through to the semis. Then we beat Jenni Falconer and her dog Alfie. It was tense, it was scrappy, but we clawed our way to the final.

And who was waiting for us in that final, but none other than Sally Gunnell, my childhood hero. The woman who made me want to be an Olympian. It was Olympic gold vs Olympic silver. Me and Rafa vs Sally and her black lab, Diggy. Now, Diggy was good. Like, very good. But he had one fatal flaw: food. Sally had done her research, though. She knew Rafa's weakness: squeaky toys. So, there we were, battling it out, Sally squeaking furiously to distract my dog, and me trying to channel every bit of tactical genius I had left. I sellotaped chicken to my legs under my trousers. Rafa, driven entirely by his nose, locked in on that chicken scent and followed me like he'd suddenly discovered loyalty. The obedience looked miraculous. The audience gasped. The judges nodded. And we won.

Rafa – Top Dog 2014, surprising absolutely everyone, including me, Ian, Jeff and that poor, flustered researcher.

Rafa lived a brilliant life until the ripe old age of 15 and a half. He was with me through the best and worst of times, the ultimate companion and the boys' best mate. Losing him was heartbreaking, as every dog owner understands, but I'm endlessly grateful he was ours. He was stubborn, cheeky, disobedient … and a winner. Just like his namesake.

2017

I USED to call 2017 'My Year of Hell'. But maybe that's not fair. Maybe I need to see it through a different lens; not as a year of torment but a year of impossible choices and aching love. My dad was dying. There's no softer way to put it. The asbestos he'd spent decades working around had finally caught up with him. His lungs, once so strong and steady, were now drowning him; slowly, cruelly filling with fluid, leaving him tethered to oxygen just to breathe. He used to tell me stories, those 'good old days' when he was just an apprentice, sitting on asbestos-covered floors, eating his sandwich, dust thick in the air, not a mask in sight. Nobody warned them back then. Nobody protected them. And now, it was his body paying the price.

Watching someone you love fade away, and knowing there's nothing, absolutely nothing, you can do to stop it … it chips away at you. Piece by piece. It's brutal. It's silent. It leaves you hollow. The care home wasn't a choice I *wanted* to make. It was a choice I *had* to make. And still, it felt like surrender. Like I was handing him over. Like I was failing him. Failing as a daughter. Failing as someone who promised they'd always be there.

Because the truth no one tells you is that putting someone you love in a home, even a good one, can feel like betrayal. There's this deep, unbearable guilt. The kind that sticks in your throat and weighs on your chest at 3am. The kind that makes you wonder if you're selfish or just surviving.

The day I moved him in, something in me cracked. I can remember the exact moment, standing outside the building, keys in hand, while he looked at me with tired eyes. It felt like my soul was being eaten from the inside out. All I could think was: 'I should have done more.' I wanted to build him a space of his own, to convert the garage, to keep him with us. But we couldn't afford it. We had two small boys, jobs to hold down, a life that was already balancing on the edge. Ed was right. Practically. Logically.

But logic doesn't dull the ache. He was 'my dad.' But love doesn't always win against reality. Not when the house isn't big enough, the bank account isn't full enough and the days aren't long enough. We live in a world where homes are not built for multigenerational care, and support systems are fragile, if they exist at all.

So, I did what I could. What I *had* to do. And still, the guilt kept coming. Like waves. Crushing and relentless. I try not to dwell. I try not to live in that pain. But the truth is that year changed me. Not just because I watched my dad slip away, but because I learned just how hard it is to love someone fiercely while also letting them go. My wheels fell off.

Goodbye Dad

Dad died on 9 October 2017.

Mum and I were holding his hand when he took his final breath. His lungs were drowning in fluid, and there was simply no space left for air. Each breath was a battle, each moment a fight he didn't want to lose, even though his body was so clearly done. It was unbearable. The nurse was there too, and still … it felt like we were utterly alone, watching the light leave someone we loved. Watching death come for someone, someone who used to have so much life in his eyes, even as his body gave out.

There are no words for the sound a soul makes when it leaves a room. But I heard it. I felt it. Afterwards, Mum and I walked out to the nursing home garden. We sat under a grey October sky and made the calls. One by one. The words came out of my mouth, but they didn't feel real. 'Dad is gone.' How can the world still turn when someone dies? I wanted it to stop. Just *pause*, if only for a second, and honour the man who has just passed away. But it didn't. Cars passed, phones buzzed and people laughed. The world carried on, utterly indifferent. Inside me, something shattered. It felt like someone had scraped out half my being; my DNA, my wiring felt ripped and severed. Something vital in my soul had died with him.

And then came the funeral. I'd never organised one before. And now I was planning *his*. Seeing Dad's handwriting on the notes he'd left behind was a punch to the chest. Seeing his music choices, his request for a burial, the flowers and the type of coffin. It helped, yes, but it also broke me. I couldn't even look at the eulogy until the night before. I just … couldn't. I wasn't ready to speak about him in the past tense.

But then came the moment. My turn. I stood, my heart hammering in my ribs, and spoke about the man who raised me, about his love for Norwich City, how football pulsed through his veins. I told the story of when he was really ill, and I got us Club Wembley tickets to the 2015 Championship play-off final, Norwich vs Middlesbrough. We sat together and I could see the pure joy pour through him as Norwich scored, not once, but twice. He fumbled with his phone, desperate to take photos, heart probably racing more than it should've been. And then he turned to me, glowing, alive, and said, 'This has been the best day of my life.' I remember laughing and saying, 'Thanks, Dad – not the day I was born, then?'

At the end of the funeral, we said goodbye with yellow roses, Johnny Cash's voice filling the chapel and a Norwich City scarf draped lovingly across his coffin. Adam, Lisa, Mum and I stood there together.

Losing a parent changes you. The world doesn't tell you that. It doesn't prepare you. You carry on because life demands it, but something inside is never the same. I would get in my car, driving to jobs, and suddenly grief would blindside me like a wave crashing through my chest. I would sob, hysterical, alone behind the wheel, trying to pull myself together before stepping into meetings and pretending I was okay.

But I wasn't okay. Grief doesn't pass. It just moves inwards. And you learn, somehow, to live around the hollow space it leaves behind.

Steph: Did you manage to keep going through the grief? There was obviously a lot to process.

Gail: Sometimes I have the ability to completely shut down. I will go into that dark, numb place, and just feel hopeless, but I know I can switch back. I just have to ride it out. Then I have too much time to think and I start to catastrophise.

Steph: I note you have switched to the present tense. Do you still feel like this now?

Gail: Yeah, it still happens. Especially when I've got too much time to think. But I am more aware of it, and I can feel it coming. When I'm busy, I'm alright.

Steph: So, when you have got too much time to think, what is it that's stressing you out?

Gail: Still money, life, love, myself. Everything.

The Double Whammy

As if Dad's death wasn't enough, it coincided with a crisis of confidence. There was a time I thought I had it all figured out. The house, the two beautiful boys, the career that once soared; I was doing everything, being everything. I was superwoman. Or so I told myself. But underneath that polished surface, I was crumbling. Slowly, quietly, invisibly. I was sinking.

Work had dried up completely. After the high of London 2012, which had been a golden moment for me, financially and personally, I had assumed Rio 2016 would bring the same opportunities. But it didn't. No one cared. Britain had had its Olympics. We'd danced, we'd celebrated, and now … it was over. I was yesterday's news.

From the outside, I looked like I was gliding, a serene swan on calm waters. But underneath, I was paddling like hell. I was desperately trying to keep myself afloat, dipping further and further into the savings I once thought would last for a long time. I can admit it now: I should have acted sooner. I should've seen the spiral for what it was. Instead, I waited, and waited some more for the phone to ring. Waited for the next opportunity to magically land in my inbox. I was paralysed by pride and disbelief. I had built a life on hard work and ambition; how could it just *stop*?

By early 2017, I was sending my CV anywhere and everywhere. At first, I was hopeful. Then I got no replies. Not even a 'thanks but no thanks'. I widened my search. I applied for roles I didn't even want, roles I barely understood, roles I was overqualified for, or underqualified, depending on how you looked at it. I was 40 years old, with the CV of a 22-year-old. One company offered me an unpaid internship. *Unpaid*. With two young children and a train fare I could barely afford.

Then came a sliver of hope – a meeting with a sports marketing agency. I pinned everything on it. I did my research, prepared my pitch and convinced myself this could be it. The train to London cost me £45.70 – a punch to the stomach when I saw my dwindling bank balance, but I paid it. Because I *had* to believe this would be worth it.

I arrived early, heart racing, and told the receptionist I had a 10am meeting. She blinked at me. 'It's not in the diary, but I'll call him.' My chest tightened. Fifteen minutes later, he strolled in, bleary-eyed, clearly hungover, clearly uninterested. 'Shall we grab a coffee?' he muttered.

I wanted to cry right there, but something inside me snapped. I wasn't going to let this moment fall apart. I gave him everything: my passion, my ideas, my plans. I showed him I had done the work. That I *cared.* And when I finished, chest tight with hope, all he said was: 'Have you thought about being an agent?' That was it. Dismissed. Just like that.

He left without paying for our coffees. I stood at the till, shaking, praying my card wouldn't be declined. I had 22p left in my account. That was it.

I got on the train back to Milton Keynes and burst into tears. Uncontrollable, streaming tears. People asked if I was okay. I couldn't even answer. I wasn't okay. I was empty.

I went into victim mode. I felt that no one gave a s**t about an old Olympian who was one cycle out of date. In that moment I resented everything and everyone. What was the point? What was the point of my medal? I actually said those words. What was the point in playing badminton?

When I got home, I sat down at the kitchen table, opened my laptop and poured everything out. I wrote with no filter. No ego. Just the truth. I wrote about being lost. About feeling forgotten by the sport I gave everything to. About the loneliness. About the money. The silence. The shame. And then I sent it to Sue Mott, my friend and a brilliant journalist behind *The Mixed Zone* online magazine. She called me immediately. I told her I was just … tired. Done. She asked if she could publish it. We agreed she'd wait a few weeks. I tried to forget about it. Tried to push the pain back down and carry on.

Then, one morning, I woke up and saw a message from Matt Pinsent. *Matt Pinsent?* My phone was pinging, over and over, messages flooding in. It was terrifying. His message said, 'I'm so sorry you're feeling this way, Gail. Let me know if there's anything I can do to help.' That was the moment I knew. The article had gone live.

Hundreds of messages suddenly came in from people I knew, people I didn't know. Support from strangers, athletes, media. It exploded. The piece had gone viral and *The Sun*, *The Mirror*, *The Express* all picked it up. My inbox overflowed. Someone even sent me £20 with a note that simply said, 'You're not alone.'

I was seen. Finally. But in a way that left me feeling raw, exposed, grateful and ashamed all at once. What started as a desperate plea turned into a lifeline. But I'll never forget that moment in the coffee shop. That crushing silence. The humiliation. The sense of worthlessness. It was rock bottom, but from rock bottom, you can see clearly, you stop pretending. And that's where the rebuilding begins.

Steph: This sounds like the first time you had allowed yourself to be vulnerable and admit how you really felt?

Gail: Yes. This was nine years after my retirement, and I finally got to say how bad it was. I just wish I had done it sooner.

Steph: But even though the reaction caught you out, writing everything down must have been a big turning point? You were finally coming to terms with the enormity of losing the only thing that had defined you.

Gail: I was honest and real, but I wasn't ready for the reaction I got. I didn't really think about the consequences of it.

Steph: I hope the outpouring of support validated your feelings. What I mean is knowing others understood or were going through similar things; that's healing.

Gail: That's true, but I still struggle with people being nice to me.

Steph: Perhaps you can reflect on that? What is it about people being nice to you that you can't tolerate?

Gail: (Sobbing) It makes me feel like I've failed again.

THE GLITTER AND GRIND OF HOSTING LIFE

A Doctor in the House?

There are moments in life that burn into your memory, not because they're planned or polished, but because they shake you to your core. It was the Leicester Business Awards, held at the Leicester Tigers rugby stadium. The room was buzzing, full of energy, clinking glasses, and the usual mix of celebration and expectation. I was on stage, mid-script, presenting to a crowd of around 800 people. We were just about to announce the nominees when I turned to introduce the Leicester City football legend Alan Birchenall.

I was in the zone, following the autocue, smiling at the crowd. The words rolled out of my mouth, 'And now, let's look at the nominees …' and all eyes shifted to the big screens. That's when Alan leaned in, so close I could feel the unease in his breath, and he whispered, 'I don't feel well, Gail.' I instinctively covered my mic and whispered back, 'It won't be long up here,' trying to calm him, reassure him. Just hang in there a minute longer, I thought.

But it wasn't going to be just a minute. It wasn't going to be okay.

He turned to step off stage, and then everything stopped. He didn't make it. He collapsed, just 2ft from where I stood. In that instant, time warped. The crowd hadn't yet registered what had happened, but I had. My heart was thudding, my mouth was dry. I picked up the mic and said the words no one ever wants to have to say. 'Is there a doctor in the room?' And then chaos. Quiet, urgent chaos.

People rushed forward. Three doctors were in the crowd. There was a defibrillator machine from the rugby stadium. Someone threw up a makeshift screen around him. And on that stage, in front of 800 people dressed in tuxedos and gowns, Alan's heart stopped. Once. Twice. Three times. And three times, the doctors brought him back.

He was taken by ambulance, had emergency surgery … and somehow, against all odds, survived. He's fine now, a miracle, walking around as if death didn't try to drag him away that night.

I was shaken to the bone. It haunted me to think if Alan had stayed home that night, if he'd decided he felt 'a bit off' and cancelled … he wouldn't be here now. It was sheer luck – or fate – that he had his heart attack in a room with doctors and the right equipment. It was horrifying and awe-inspiring all at once.

So now, when people say they're not sure about going to something because they're not feeling great, I half joke but mean it with all my heart: if you're going to have a heart attack … do it at a business awards event. You never know who might be in the room to save your life.

Hands Off the Host, Please

I was hosting a charity dinner at The Brewery, a swanky venue on Chiswell Street in London. Gorgeous spot, buzzing crowd, top-tier vibe. The event was run by two brothers, total legends, and once the formalities were over, the party kicked off. Scouting for Girls hit the stage, DJ Luck and MC Neat were spinning, basically it was a certified banger of a night.

So, there I am, heading to the bar for a drink, soaking it all in, when I clock this guy in his mid-50s, grey suit, full stare mode, and not subtle about it. He walks up, oozing that creepy confidence, and says, 'I know who you are. You're that badminton girl. Why didn't you say that onstage?' I smiled, all poised and professional, 'Well, it's not about me tonight, I'm just here to host.' But inside, I was thinking alarm bells. Something wasn't right. I tried to make a polite exit, but he wasn't having it. For the next hour, he shadowed me like some Poundland Bond villain, always hovering three or four metres away, just sipping his drink and lurking. I'd go left, he'd go left. I'd go to the loo, guess who's suddenly hanging outside like a toilet troll?

Then he tried handing me a drink – big red-flag energy. I said no, obviously, but it didn't stop there. I had finally had enough and went over to the brothers and said, 'Look, I've done hundreds of these gigs and this has never happened, but do you know who this guy is?' They didn't, which was odd, because they knew pretty much every guest. It was their party. They confronted him, and asked who he was, who he was with and, let me tell you, he did not like that. He pushed one of the brothers and as I was right there, I got shoved too. I went flying, and it was not exactly the kind of mic-drop moment I was aiming for.

And then it kicked off. Full-on punches thrown, security swooping in like Avengers, and this guy was physically removed from the venue. Like, launched. Apparently, he'd been drinking since sunrise and was a plus-one for someone who'd already left. Classy.

Now, normally, if someone's drunk and too flirty, I can handle it. I've got banter. But I've also got boundaries. There was one time, and I swear this still makes my blood boil, where I was taking photos post-event, and this guy in a group decided to grab my arse. I turned, took his hand off, and said, 'Not the arse, thank you.' He laughed, slurred an apology … and put it *right* back on my bum again. This time, I didn't just move his hand. I stared him down and said, 'Oi. I said not the arse. Do that again and I'll punch you.' His charming response? 'Fine. Your tit instead,' and then grabbed me there.

That was it. I yanked his hand off and went full swing, right hook incoming, but his mates dragged him off before I could land it. They were mortified, apologising all over the place while I was standing there, absolutely seething. 'Get him the f**k away from me!' I snapped.

Here's the thing: when alcohol's flowing, people are dressed up and the music's loud, it brings out the absolute worst in some. I've been doing this long enough to know the drill, and you need skin thicker than steel. It's not for the fainthearted or, frankly, the overly 'woke'. There's always innuendo. There's always that guy. Sometimes they're guests. Sometimes even celebs. And yes, I've smiled through moments that made me want to vomit in my mouth. But the show … oh, the show always goes on.

The Conservative Party Gig

It all started with a last-minute message from Champions agency: 'Hey, Gail, are you free tonight? Last-minute motivational talk in Surrey – someone's dropped out.' I looked at the fee (very decent), the location (not a million miles away), and said yes without even checking who the client was. Rookie mistake. Huge.

Fast-forward to that evening, I pull up to a very posh golf club, the kind of place where trousers are pressed to within an inch of their life. I clock a sign by the door: 'Conservative Party Agenda Dinner.' And thought, 'Oh wow, that's going on here too?'

Sweet summer child. It was the event.

Cue the internal scream. I am not political. I steer so far clear of politics, I don't even like group WhatsApps – as we all know, I get chucked out within minutes. But alas, there I was, about to address the blue-rinsed, blue-blooded, Surrey Conservative Party faithful.

I took a deep breath and approached a very stately older gentleman (the type who looks like he owns three Labradors and a hereditary title). I introduced myself, 'Hi, I'm Gail. I'm your speaker this evening!' He blinked. Slowly. Looked me up and down and said, and I swear this on my Olympic medal, 'But … you're a woman? Why on earth would we be listening to a woman talk?' I smiled through every feminist impulse in my body and replied, 'Well, I've been to the Olympics, won a silver medal and was a world badminton champion.' More blinking. More bafflement. And then came the gold medal in patronisation, 'Well … well done you. Isn't that bloody splendid? Women doing sport, eh? Who'd have thought!' And off he tottered, probably to tell his pals what a surprise they had in store, as there was a woman going to talk to them all at dinner.

Now, I've never walked out of a job before, but this … this came very close.

As I composed myself (and desperately wished I had a secret flask of gin), Michael Gove wandered in, gave a speech to the pensioner-heavy room, and dinner was served. I was announced as 'the speaker', but they conveniently left out the part where I'd replaced a well-known male TV presenter, presumably to prevent a mass exodus to the car park. I kid you not, for the entire evening I heard: 'Such a shame xxxx couldn't make it!' 'Would've loved to have heard him speak!' Meanwhile, I'm standing there like a polite grenade in a cocktail dress.

But it was showtime. I stood up, looked around at a room that was 80 per cent male, 100 per cent uninterested and radiating!! 'don't-you-have-a-husband-to-go-and-make-dinner-for?' energy. But I gritted my teeth and smashed it. To their surprise, and my satisfaction, they actually started listening. I even got a round of applause. The cherry on the cake was that same old-school gentleman shuffled over and said, 'Well, that was actually … okay. Jolly good, in fact.' High praise from the patriarchy. Others followed, giving me 'tips' on public speaking (because clearly it was my first ever talk) and complimenting how 'brave' it was that women are 'getting out there these days'. I smiled, nodded and mentally transported myself into another dimension.

The second I was done, I bolted. Gone like the last roast potato at Christmas. And let me tell you, that invoice was sent before I even got to the car. Lesson learned: always check who the client is. But also, there's something delicious about shaking up a room full of men who weren't expecting to be confronted by Gail-freaking-Emms that evening.

Mic drop.

Monaco Baby – Racing Cars, Helicopters and Maseratis

Look, I'll be honest, Formula 1 isn't exactly my thing. I get it: fast cars, screechy turns, testosterone-fuelled pit stops … vroom vroom, etc. But if you ask me, let's ditch the Ferraris and give those boys banana skins and red shells and make it more Mario Kart style. Now *that's* a race I'd watch with popcorn.

Anyway, cut to me, not knowing much about F1, but still getting invited to host at the Monaco Grand Prix. Naturally, I said yes, because, hello, Monaco, even if I was dragging myself there on EasyJet from Luton after a night of raving to The Chemical Brothers. Yep, I was glamour in a hoodie and slightly vibrating with last night's vodka.

I landed in Nice on Saturday morning, bleary-eyed and blinking, only to be told to head to a certain desk at the airport and give them my name. Done. Then I was casually informed that my transfer to Monaco would be … by helicopter. Cue my jaw hitting the polished floor.

So, there I was, flying along the French Riviera like some kind of Bond girl on her day off, landing next to yachts the size of small countries, only to step out of the chopper in full view of photographers expecting Zendaya, and instead getting 'hungover badminton girl in sweats'. The audacity.

Let me tell you, Monaco knows how to party. It was champagne, canapés and more billionaires than a tech IPO. At one particularly lavish soirée, I was introduced to an Indian billionaire. The man practically oozed rupees. And clinging to his arm like a very shiny handbag was a very stunning, much younger, Russian 'model', a term I'm using loosely but respectfully. She was introduced as his girlfriend. Of course she was.

We chatted, she was charming, in that 'I-know-what-I-want-in-life-and-I-am-going-to-get-it' sort of way, and then, like something out of a fever dream, he turned to her and purred in his thick Indian accent, 'Right, darling, I will buy you that Maserati now.'

He got his phone out, made one call: 'The car is being delivered tomorrow, my darling.' Her response was a high-pitched squeal of: 'Oh my gosh, thank you, darling!!' Meanwhile, I'm standing there with two other guys, watching this spectacle unfold, and we all shared *that* look. That collective, unspoken moment of clarity: 'Yeah. I'd probably sleep with this man for a Maserati too.' None of us got the offer to, though.

So yeah, not much of an F1 fan, but Monaco, definitely '*chef's kiss*'. Helicopters, hangovers and high-end transactional relationships. Who needs a podium finish when you've got stories like these?!

Who's that Girl?

So, picture this … I'd been invited to Twickenham for the Autumn Internationals. Don't ask me which match – but I know it was pre-digital ticketing, aka ye olden days, when they posted the ticket to you like it was a handwritten invitation to Hogwarts. Rugby isn't really my specialist subject, and this was my first ever time at Twickenham, but I knew the ticket was posh – posh-hospitality-level posh. Fancy.

I turn up, solo, rocking my Olympic silver medal energy (internally, of course) and head towards what looks like the main hospitality entrance. The moment I stepped in, a woman from the Twickenham staff sprinted towards me like she was about to hug a long-lost relative at an airport reunion. 'Oh my *goodness*! Thank God you're here! I've been looking everywhere for you!'

Now, let's pause, because I'm thinking, 'Wow, Twickenham really knows how to treat an Olympic medallist!' I mean, sure, I don't expect a red carpet everywhere I go … but if they insist, who am I to argue? I gave her a humble little smile and said, 'Oh, no worries, I'm here now!' Like the icon I clearly thought I was.

Off we trot, my new BFF and I, up the plush Twickenham stairs. She keeps glancing at me like I'm carrying the Olympic torch and I'm absolutely loving the attention. My ego was now hugely inflated, with my head flying high in the clouds. My assumption was that, clearly, she's a diehard badminton fan. Obviously.

We reach one of the *bougiest* hospitality suites I've ever laid eyes on. She beams, throws open the doors like a palace butler and says, 'Here you go! Have a wonderful day!' Honestly, I felt like royalty. Champagne in one hand, lobster in the other, I was living my best posh Twickenham life. Then I noticed her again, across the room, pointing at me and whispering to some staff, beaming with pride. Except… the staff weren't smiling back. They looked … confused. Two of them shook their heads. Oh dear.

Within seconds, the dream shattered like a dropped prosecco flute.

Two men in suits came over. 'Excuse me, madam,' one said, 'I'm afraid you're in the wrong place. You'll need to leave.' With my mouth full of lobster and a plate piled like a buffet Olympian, I attempted charm: 'Mmm-hmm. Can I just … finish this plate?' Cue the biggest Bambi eyes I've ever done. 'No. Please put the plate down and leave.'

Savage.

Turns out, the overexcited staff member had mistaken me for none other than Zara Phillips, now Zara Tindall. As in the Royal Family Zara. And I, ladies and gentlemen, was in the royal suite. Champagne in one hand, exquisite seafood in the other.

I was gently escorted out (still chewing), and as I passed the poor lady who started it all, I considered offering her an autograph, you know, to ease her embarrassment, but she hid behind one of the other staff members. She was hiding from me! Eventually, I found my *actual* hospitality suite, where I enjoyed the rugby with a pie and a pint, which was far more my vibe anyway.

That wasn't even the last time I got mistaken for Zara. Red carpets, sports awards … photographers shouting, '*Zara*! *Zara*! This way, please!' And then someone always pipes up, '… wait, Gail who?'

And yes, I did eventually meet Zara at the Cheltenham Festival. I was introduced with a casual, 'This is Gail, she does badminton.' To which Zara replied, 'Oh, how lovely! I love Badminton – such a beautiful event.' No, hun. *The sport.* Not the horsey village. But I nodded politely and committed to the lie. So now, apparently, I'm an equestrian athlete too. Hey, if I'm going to be mistaken for a royal, I might as well ride it (pun fully intended).

Men's Euros, Wembley, England

The Euros Final. England vs Italy. Wembley Stadium. The Big One. And yes … I was there. Thanks to years of networking, sportsperson charm and a mate who has football tickets on speed dial, I bagged one of the hottest seats in the country. I nearly had to sell an organ to afford it, but was it worth it? That's debatable.

Let me rewind. I'd been at the Denmark semi-final (humble brag), and, after that magical win, getting to the final became a national obsession. Enter Dan Smith – football whisperer, ticket magician and mate of mine since he ran toddler footy classes called Let's Kick It. My eldest, Harry, was in them at 18 months, already a ball-kicking prodigy (and, more importantly, better behaved than 95 per cent of the others). Dan and I bonded over sport, kids and trying to stay vertical through Saturday 9am hangovers. Dan usually won the 'hangover competition', but I made a strong comeback when kid number two arrived.

Dan managed to source two golden tickets. My bank account cried, but my football-loving soul screamed 'YESSSSS!' and off we went.

Now ... Wembley. It was *feral.* As soon as we got off the train, I knew something was off. The air was thick with tension, testosterone and the unmistakable scent of lager, sweat, cocaine and regrettable life choices. Grown men looked like they'd been on a three-day bender and snorted the entire contents of Glastonbury. And it wasn't just rowdy, there was *aggro.* Packs of fans roaming, shouting, waiting for any excuse to fight a bin.

We pushed our way in and there was beer absolutely *everywhere,* floors slicker than an ice rink. Then came the smash. I looked over and saw the disabled entrance of Wembley Stadium being stormed. Hundreds forced their way in while security looked like underpaid extras in a zombie film. Suddenly, all hell broke loose. People pushing through turnstiles, using one ticket to let entire football teams in. It was bedlam. Terrifying bedlam.

Dan and I finally made it to our seats ... except someone was already in mine. I politely said, 'Excuse me, I think that's my seat?' and miracle of miracles, the man actually moved. I'm pretty sure it was only because I'm a woman. If I'd had a beard and beer gut, I'd have been eating nachos on the stairs.

Inside, it was like musical chairs from hell. Fans who'd barged in were grabbing any spare seat, arguments were sparking everywhere, kids were crying and security was doing *absolutely nothing.* I sat there pretending to be zen while low-key praying I didn't get punched in the face before half-time. Then it was kick-off, and a couple of minutes later I looked at Dan and said, 'Right, I'm off to get a pint.' Priorities. The queues had been biblical before the game. I grabbed my beer and just as I took that first sip of overpriced liquid gold … *Luke Shaw scored, in the final, at Wembley*! I was *in* the damn stadium and *still* missed it. I've never been good at downing lager before, but that night, it took ten seconds, and I ran back to my seat, arms waving '*Woooo*!' trying to join the celebration while screaming internally: '*Why did I go for a pint*?!'

The rest, we all know. Southgate parked the bus, Italy brought the shithousery and it went to penalties. I turned to Dan and said, 'If we miss, I'm running out of here as fast as I can.' We missed. I was out. Dan stayed to meet his mates. I activated 'Olympic sprint mode' and bolted through Wembley like a woman possessed. Dodged beer puddles, drunken bodies, crying children; it was like the *Ninja Warrior* finals, but emotional and slightly tipsy. Honestly, I moved like a gazelle. I just wanted to get home before the inevitable riot kicked off.

Strangely … it didn't. The mood post-match was eerily sombre. Not violent, just heartbroken. We were so close. And here's the thing: I'm *so* glad I went. It was a once-in-a-lifetime experience. But let's be real, Wembley was a mess, an absolute shambles. Fans were terrified, security was non-existent and the organisers need to take responsibility for how badly it was handled. I got lucky. Many others didn't.

But, dear FA, if you ever need a good luck charm at big matches, feel free to invite me. I'll graciously attend … and then nip to the bar or toilet. Because, clearly, that's when England decide to score. You're welcome.

BBC Sports Personality

I remember my first ever invitation to *BBC Sports Personality of the Year*. The excitement was off the scale. I'd made it – I was going to BBC SPOTY! The glitz! The glam! The free wine! It was a time before they let the general public in, aka the golden era, when athletes could drink, dance and disgrace themselves with only a small risk of it ending up on Instagram.

There I was at the pre-show drinks, chatting to some fellow athletes, feeling very A-list, when suddenly – *whack*! Something smacked my hand. I gave the person I was talking to a full-on death stare and said, 'Did you just hit me?' They looked horrified and swore it wasn't them. Seconds later – *whack* again. I spun around and there he was: Chris Eubank, in all his monocle-wearing, cane-carrying glory. Apparently, I had committed the unforgivable sin of standing in his path. So naturally, rather than say, 'Excuse me,' he whacked me with his actual cane to move me out of his 'Direct Eubank Line'.

Now, I didn't realise 'personal space' meant nothing when you're Eubank; the man walks like he's Moses parting the Red Sea. I turned back to my mates, stunned, probably leaking a bit of Pinot Grigio, when his bodyguard (because, of course, a professional boxer needs a bodyguard?!) literally picked me up like a misbehaving toddler and moved me to the side, all just to clear the path for The Eubank. Iconic, honestly.

Another year, I found myself sitting right behind the one and only José Mourinho, during his Chelsea days. And let me tell you … the man is divine. Sue Barker told me in the toilets that he smelled amazing, so, naturally, I went back to my seat, pretended to rummage in my handbag and sniffed him. Yep. José Mourinho: smells like leather-bound books, sexiness and winning.

The great thing about the pre-public SPOTY years was the freedom. No fans asking for selfies every two minutes. Just athletes, slightly tipsy, letting loose. I danced for an entire night with Sir Bobby Charlton. That man had better rhythm and energy than most of Team GB. Try doing that with 300 screaming people filming it on their phones.

Of course, alcohol and confidence are best friends. One night, after a few glasses of wine, I spotted Paula Radcliffe. Now, Paula and I go way back, and, by that, I mean I'm from Bedford too and lost the Bedford Sports Personality of the Year title to her for five years straight. So, naturally, I staggered up to her and launched into a monologue.

'Hi, Paula! I'm from Bedford too! You went to Sharnbrook, I went to Dame Alice, I play badminton, I've got an Olympic silver medal, same Olympics as you! Cool, right?'

She smiled politely, probably praying for a fire alarm. Did I stop there? Oh no. I saw this as my moment to address a long-standing injustice. I proceeded to rant about how I had lost Bedford Sports Personality of the Year to her *every single year* from 2000–2005. I gave the full stats. '2004 Olympic medallist! STILL lost!' She just nodded like I was a mad woman on a bus. I even refused to attend the 2006 awards because I was convinced it was another Radcliffe stitch-up. I phoned the organiser in a full diva strop, saying, 'I'm not coming. I've had enough. Stupid awards!' Then they hinted I might actually win that year. And lo and behold, I did. It took a European, Commonwealth and World title to finally win Bedford Sports Personality of the Year. Redemption! For one year, anyway. Paula won again the next.

To her credit, Paula didn't call security or throw a water bottle at me. A true professional. Although she does have a road named after her in Bedford. I do not. Watch this space, Mayor. I will be organising a petition, but I don't want my road to be called Emms Passage like in Kingston-upon-Thames.

And then there was the time tennis player Johanna Konta mistook me for the hair and make-up team. I was backstage, loitering in the glam zone, when she sat down and demanded I fix her hair. No one else was around. Any normal person would have mentioned that they were not 'hair and make-up', but my brain went: 'Never done hair before? Cool. Let's give it a go.' What could possibly go wrong? Armed with about 76 hairpins and a can of Elnett hairspray bigger than my face, I went full Vidal Sassoon. Was I stabbing her scalp? Probably. Did I know what I was doing? Absolutely not. Did it look good? Weirdly, yes. She thanked me like I'd just saved her from a follicular breakdown.

Just as she left, Clare Balding walked past and clocked me. 'Why were you doing Johanna Konta's hair?' I told her the truth: 'She thought I worked here, and I thought, f**k it, why not?' Clare spent the rest of the night looking at me like I was unhinged. Fair enough.

My crowning SPOTY moment, though? That would be when I was offered a dwarf threesome. Yep. That happened. I was dancing away, as you do, when one of the para-athletes with dwarfism asked me for a dance. Inclusive queen that I am, I said of course! I was expecting a respectful boogie. What I got was breast-height grinding. He was very into it. I was trying to be polite while inching away, when his mate joined in – from behind. One at the front, one at the back. I was officially a dwarf badminton sandwich. It was less *Strictly*, more 'Carry On Paralympics'. I tried to wriggle away, citing 'drink break', and as I left the floor, they asked if I wanted to come back to their hotel room for a … *ménage à trois*. I declined. Politely.

There have also been random celeb collisions. I walked straight into Tyson Fury, who was mid-photo op, and bounced off his chest like a cartoon character. Somewhere out there is a priceless image of me rebounding off 'The Gypsy King'. The only other celeb I've done that to was Hugh Grant, at The Oval. I was walking and talking, and bang, crashed right into him. It was like the scene in *Notting Hill*, but minus the orange juice and post-coital scenes. Ed was there, so that would have been awkward.

So yes, BBC SPOTY: it's glamour, chaos, inappropriate dancing, accidental hairdressing and being literally moved by Chris Eubank's cane. A night where sporting legends collide with athletes like me … and occasionally offer a threesome. Bring on the next one. I'll bring the bobby pins.

Fore! Four?

Like many retired athletes who can't quite let go of competition, I thought, 'Golf! Yes! That's what I'll do!' A perfect retirement hobby. Golf has open spaces, fresh air, polo shirts, and absolutely no shuttlecocks. I had this vision of myself gliding across lush green fairways, nailing every shot with my famously reliable hand–eye coordination. Honestly, I was picturing myself waltzing through celebrity pro-ams, charming the pants off Lee Westwood and maybe even being known as 'that badminton legend who's also a golf goddess'. Turns out, I am absolutely terrible at golf. Like, *shockingly* bad. Offensively bad. 'We've called in insurance on the show car' bad.

Despite being good at pretty much every other sport I've ever touched – no, really, I'm annoyingly competent at everything – golf continues to humble me in ways I never knew were possible.

Let me take you on a tour of my personal 'Golfing Hall of Shame'.

Exhibit A: The Reverse Shot at The Grove: I took my tee shot with confidence, it connected beautifully … with a wooden post directly in front of me. The ball ricocheted *over my own head* and landed at the feet of pro golfer Hannah Burke and her coach, Daniel Field. They looked at me the way you'd look at someone licking batteries. To this day, Hannah still says, 'I've never seen anything like it.' Not in a good way.

Exhibit B: Tree 1 Gail 0: Same course, but this time, I was stuck in the trees. I lined up a heroic shot through a small gap. The ball hit a tree and came straight back at me like a boomerang of shame. Mid-air, I baseball-swung at it like I was in the Yankee Stadium. I connected perfectly and the shot went on to the fairway. I was thrilled. '*Did you see that*?!' I shouted with the unearned pride of a toddler showing off a finger painting. The course manager, who unnoticed, was behind me, replied, completely deadpan, 'Yes. That's a foul shot.' He rolled his eyes and drove off in the buggy. But I remain spiritually proud of that shot.

Exhibit C: Duckgate at Celtic Manor: I drove a beauty … until it veered toward a pond and struck a duck square on the head. He was just waddling along with his duck mates, having a nice day, when *boom*, Gail Emms, international avian threat. The duck went down. I waited for him to shake it off and flap away like a hardened golf course resident. But he didn't … he *stayed down*. I still don't know if I stunned him or sent him to the great pond in the sky. I couldn't check. I panicked and I fled. That duck visits me in my dreams. I don't know duck CPR. I just … left.

Exhibit D: La Manga, La Meltdown: I was paired with a lovely French professional who was initially delighted to hear he'd be playing with an Olympic medallist. Ah, how naive. After my first three holes, he looked like he'd seen a ghost drive into a lake. He spent the round muttering and pointing angrily, as if I was a rogue goat who had somehow been allowed on to the course. He may have retired immediately after.

Exhibit E: The Picnic Incident at Nailcote Hall: Farmfoods British Par 3 – first tee, I hit my ball into a steep bunker. 'You'll need to whack that out!' said one of the other players. Echoing those words in my head, I *whacked* it. And it *flew*. Not 10ft. Not 20ft. Try 90ft, and straight into the 'Safe Zone' where a sweet pensioner couple were celebrating an anniversary. The ball landed in their picnic, sending them flying in panic. I had ruined their beautiful moment and possibly their egg mayo sandwiches. A moment of silence … followed by absolute hysterics from my fourball. We didn't recover. Emotionally or physically.

Word got around. I became a sort of sideshow. People started following me just to see what chaos I'd cause next. Players started shouting, 'It's safer behind Gail!' which was ironic given the reverse shot incident.

Oh, and the show cars on the course, you know the shiny new Bentleys and Jaguars they park on the course at these events to make it all look slick, as those car companies are sponsors? They moved those. *Because of me.* After I nearly took out a Bentley windscreen with a rogue nine-iron slice. They've since 'Gail-proofed' the entire Farmfoods event.

But don't get me wrong, I still love it. I do. I've been lucky to play at some incredible courses. But if you ever get paired with me at a golf day, here's one simple rule: *Do. Not. Coach. Me.* If you lean in and say, 'Maybe just open your clubface slightly on that chip ...' I will smile, nod and internally rage.

These days, I prefer hosting the after-dinner bit, where I'm unlikely to kill birds or pensioners. I even hosted a golf day at Trevose (a stunning course near Padstow), but ... let's just say getting there was an event in itself. I'd been at Ascot the day before (drinking my body weight in champagne, as is the law), and the thought of a six-hour drive made me want to fake a leg injury. I moaned to my mate James, 'I need a bloody helicopter.' He said, 'I know someone with a helicopter.' And just like that, 'Nigel with a helicopter' entered my life.

The next morning, still slightly fizzing with Veuve Clicquot, I was airlifted out of Bedford in a chopper like some Bond villain with a hangover. We even flew over my house and the boys' school, probably scaring the Year 5s. As we descended on to Trevose Golf Club, sand whipped up from the bunkers, golfers scattered like pigeons and I landed, dazed, dusty and very ready to tell jokes, and *not* swing anything remotely club-shaped.

And that, dear reader, is how Gail Emms plays golf. Badly. But enthusiastically. Sometimes airborne. Sometimes legally questionable. But all with good intentions.

Strongmen ... Ready!

In 2004, I was unexpectedly asked by Channel 5 if I'd be interested in being the TV interviewer for the first ever live broadcast of *UK's Strongest Man*. At first, I was surprised, it wasn't the kind of event I thought I'd be considered for. But they weren't just looking for a presenter, they wanted someone who understood the heartbeat of live sport, someone who could connect deeply with the athletes and bring their world to life for viewers. I said yes immediately. It sounded like an incredible opportunity.

And then the reality hit: I was stepping into an arena I knew absolutely nothing about. I was a complete newbie, except for one thing: I knew how to perform under pressure. But that wasn't enough. I had to earn the right to be there.

So, I picked up the phone and called Kelly Proctor, a strongwoman competitor and, by coincidence, someone I had trekked to Everest Base Camp with. She was brilliant. Patient, passionate and generous with her knowledge. She walked me through the events, the athletes' training, what this world meant to them, and I was hooked. I hadn't even stepped into the arena yet, but I was already captivated.

Then came show day. I stood among the Atlas Stones and Fireman's Carry tanks, the roaring crowds, the sheer force of human will in motion, and I felt something I still struggle to define: a mix of wonder, intrigue and pure adrenaline. And then I met the athletes. Towering men of power and presence. I looked like a hamster beside them, but they welcomed me in like one of their own.

That weekend, I got to tell their stories, interview them in moments of triumph and exhaustion, and showcase their grit to the world. And I loved every second of it. When they asked me back in 2005, I didn't hesitate. This time it was even bigger. More athletes. More events. A larger stage.

And I brought my boys, Harry and Ollie, with me.

I wanted them to see me doing my job, yes, but also to witness something deeper. To see men in their raw, honest, unfiltered strength. To understand the beauty of power with humility. In a world where boys are growing up bombarded by distorted ideas of masculinity, I wanted mine to witness men who push their limits, not for fame, but for the love of challenge.

Especially Ollie. Built for strength, he was instantly drawn to 23-year-old rising star Alex Feri. Watching Alex pull a 7.5-tonne truck lit something up in him. That moment, the photo they took together, became more than a memory. It became a blueprint of what's possible.

These athletes, often overlooked, are the beating heart of what sport should be about. They train outside of the spotlight, often holding down full-time jobs. One competitor, William Jones, is an antique clock repairer by day. They do this with little funding, little recognition, and yet the camaraderie and respect they show one another is immense.

And the lesson? Strength comes in many forms. These men aren't just muscle, they are discipline, fire and humility wrapped into one. They reminded me to be proud of my own frame – my 5ft 3in powerhouse body, and for the first time in a long time, I appreciated it fully.

So, thank you, Strongman Community, for letting me be part of something so powerful, so human, so real. People often ask if I had a favourite competitor. I always said no … but I had a soft spot for the older athletes; those who had weathered the years, the setbacks, and kept going anyway. They reminded me that behind every great body is an even greater story.

Never judge a book by its cover. It's not what you look like. It's how you show up. It's your attitude, your effort and the legacy you choose to leave behind.

COVID TIMES

IN EARLY 2020, just before the world came to a standstill, I was already starting to fall apart. Quietly and invisibly. I'd been mentoring a former athlete, not for money, not for a pat on the back, just because I cared. Maybe too much. At first, I thought I was helping them. But over time, it became something else. They drained me. Every call, every message, every unspoken expectation that I would drop everything and run to fix their world. And the most frustrating part was that I *did*. I ran to them, helping every time. It took me a while to realise that in helping them, I was running from something in myself. Pushing down my own hurt, my exhaustion, my sadness, because if I focused on them, I wouldn't have to deal with *me*. But eventually, I broke.

I went to the doctor one day, and I didn't even make it to the chair. I just walked in and cried. Head on the desk. Twenty straight minutes. No words. Just tears. I felt so empty. So mentally fried. And completely alone. I refused antidepressants as I wasn't ready for that. The doctor referred me to a mental health team, and I thought maybe, just maybe, I'd finally get some support. But the questions they asked were cold, checkbox style. 'Do you self-harm?' 'Have you had suicidal thoughts?' No, I hadn't, so they concluded that I didn't qualify for help. I was left to figure it out on my own.

I couldn't afford therapy. I was trying to build the events side of my business, so all my money was going into that. And I was too embarrassed to ask anyone for help. The shame was suffocating. I made the only decision I could: cut contact with the person draining me and throw myself into work. I wasn't healthy, not mentally nor emotionally, but at least I had a plan.

Then … the Cheltenham Festival. I went there for a bit of hosting work and a change of scenery. But that's when the whispers started … the *C-word* was spreading through the crowds. Covid. No one really knew what it meant yet. Yet, two days later, back home, I couldn't stop sleeping. Not sick exactly, just … completely wiped out. Deep down, I knew I'd caught it. The tiredness was bone-deep.

The following weeks were a blur of denial. I told myself Covid wouldn't be that bad and that it would pass. That events would still happen, people would still need speakers, hosts and energy. But the messages started rolling in. 'We're going to postpone.' 'We have to cancel.' 'We can't take the risk.' And then the prime minister stood in front of the nation and said the word I feared most: lockdown.

I crumbled. I went to my room and just sobbed. Not in front of the boys. Quietly. In the dark. Ugly, heaving sobs that I couldn't stop. Every job, every plan, every ounce of security I'd clung to was gone in an instant. I do know I was one of many thousands of freelancers and entrepreneurs, all in the same boat, all screwed, but my walls started closing in. And the thing is, we were living in a big house at the time, but it didn't matter. It felt like a prison. And I had no idea how to survive it.

At least Ed was still working. As a policeman, he had no choice. The boys were climbing the walls: they are active, social and full of energy, just like me. We tried our best; we had the dog, we went on walks, I escaped for the odd run along the river just to breathe, to think, to *not* lose it completely. But inside, I was breaking all over again.

And then there were the people. The judgement. The nastiness.

I remember having a socially distanced catch-up with my friend Kelly as she'd been stuck in lockdown alone with three young boys and a full-time job. We hadn't seen anyone in *eight weeks*. We sat on my drive, socially distanced, drinking prosecco, two women trying to feel human again, and a neighbour shouted out across the road, 'You're killing nurses!' Like we were criminals for trying to cope.

That same neighbour later left me a note, a *threat*, because I'd driven to Bedford for a family emergency during lockdown. She had seen me leave. I came back to that message and felt like I'd been punched. The compassion was gone. It was Covid or nothing. Humanity was replaced with fear and finger-pointing. I never spoke to her again, and I never will.

I've moved since, thank God, but I'll never forget how the world felt then, how *I* felt. I was completely untethered, overwhelmed and unseen. Everyone was shouting about the virus, but no one seemed to notice the quiet grief in people like me. I wasn't just losing work. I was losing pieces of myself.

Finding Purpose in a Pandemic

At one point during the pandemic, I knew I had to get out of the house. Not just for a walk, not just to the supermarket, I needed to *do* something. The walls were closing in, and I was going stir-crazy with the uncertainty of everything. I saw an ad asking for volunteers to work as Covid-19 testers in Milton Keynes. All the paid jobs – the supermarkets, the delivery routes – had already been snapped up. So, I put my hand up. I'd had Covid already, as mentioned earlier. It knocked me out with exhaustion, but nothing worse than that, and I felt fit, healthy and capable. I wasn't scared. What I *was* craving was purpose and direction. Something that made me feel useful again.

And, honestly, it was the best decision I could have made. No, it wasn't glamorous. It wasn't paid. And wearing layers of PPE in the heat of a car park wasn't exactly how I envisioned my midlife career detour. But it grounded me, and I had a reason to get up in the morning. I was part of something that mattered.

I'd stand at the drive-through site, swabbing throats and noses, a process that still makes people gag, wince, or both, and I'd try to be kind, efficient and maybe even a bit reassuring. People would pull up, anxious and unwell, coughing through their windows, scared for their loved ones, desperate for answers. And there I was, sticking a long swab into their sinuses with as much empathy as I could muster. It was messy. It was hot. It was intense, but it gave me a sense of control in a world that felt utterly out of it.

Three months in, though, I realised something: I was the only one not being paid. I asked if that could change, and they said 'no'. I did what I had to do, and I said 'no' back, and I walked away. By then, fewer people were coming through. The urgency had faded. What hadn't faded, though, was the sense of waste I saw everywhere. Wasted resources, wasted money, wasted decisions. Some people were making a fortune out of the crisis, but I wasn't one of them.

Just as I felt the rug pulling out from under me again, something else appeared. A local bar, the Blossom Room, in The Hub, Milton Keynes, reached out to me. They needed someone to help navigate the new rules of hospitality: social distancing, groups of six, test and trace, and table service. The world had changed, and they needed someone adaptable to help them survive it – and that someone turned out to be me.

Blossom Room was exactly what I needed at that point in time. It was beautiful, full of soft pink lighting and cherry blossom branches overhead. And more than that, it was alive, and I needed that energy. I threw myself into it. I built the booking system, redesigned the table layout and created menus that worked in a world of QR codes and sanitiser. On Friday and Saturday nights, I was 'front of house', greeting guests, guiding them to their tables, remembering their names and making the VIPs feel special. I cleaned tables, served drinks and made people laugh. It filled me up in the way only human connection can.

And then came another lockdown.

I'll never forget that moment. I was alone in one of the VIP booths when the announcement came through. The lights were off. The heating was off. The place was silent. I sat there, still in my jacket, and just cried. It was a grief I didn't know how to name.

Eventually, I had to step away. The reality of parenting two young boys and a full-time bar management role was too much. I didn't want to walk away, but I had no choice. I hoped there might be a space for me in some other form, but a new manager came in who didn't like me and, just like that, I was out. I was gutted. Completely. I'd poured so much into that place; my time, my energy, my heart. Blossom Room had become my safe place when the world felt uncertain and I felt lost. I had worked hard. I was good at it. And for a while, it gave me hope.

The cherry blossom decor reminded me of Japan, where I'd competed all those years ago – a place of calm amidst chaos. Seeing people laughing again, enjoying a cocktail with friends felt like healing. It reminded me that joy was still possible. Maybe one day I'll open my own little bar. Something intimate, beautiful, full of warmth. A place where people feel looked after, where stories are shared and where I can pour someone a drink and know, just for a moment, that they feel seen.

If the pandemic taught me anything, it's that even in chaos!! we find new paths. Sometimes out of necessity. Sometimes out of desperation. But often, because in reality we're stronger than we realise.

The Jab and the Jolt

I didn't want the vaccine. There … I've said it. Not because I was waving placards or diving into conspiracy theories, but because, deep down, something in me hesitated. But the world was shifting fast in May 2021, and a different kind of pressure had arrived. It wasn't spoken outright, but it certainly felt that way. If I didn't get it, would I be able to work again or travel? Be allowed to live the life I was trying to rebuild? So, I did what many of us did. I resigned myself to it.

That morning, the AstraZeneca vaccine was what they were offering at the Milton Keynes centre. No real choice, just roll up your sleeve and take it. The nurse told me to sit down for ten minutes afterwards, just in case. 'Tingling fingers? Call 111,' he said, with a reassuring half smile.

I felt fine at first. I drove home feeling okay, but as I walked through my front door, something felt … off. Not dramatic, just a weird weakness, a sudden drop in energy. I did what any seasoned Brit would do in a moment of vague unease: I made a cup of tea with two sugars. The age-old cure-all.

It was Ollie's, my youngest son's, eighth birthday party that afternoon – there were balloons, cake and chaos in the living room, so I took my cup of tea upstairs to rest. I sat in the corner of my room, trying to shake off the heavy feeling. Then it started: the tingling in my left hand, the side I'd had the jab, and not the kind of tingling you ignore.

I called Ed. I felt too weak to move and when he arrived, he didn't like what he saw. I was white as a sheet, and now there were sharp, shooting pains climbing up my left arm. He called 111. The questions came quickly: 'Can she speak? Can she respond?' At that point, yes, I could.

But the pain was rising into my neck, and then into my jaw. My arm was spasming. And then … I couldn't speak. My jaw had locked tight. The 111 co-ordinator called an ambulance to my house immediately. All I remember at this point is trying to tell the paramedics about my naturally low blood pressure, but I couldn't speak. I was writing notes on the bed with my right hand, as my left side wasn't working. I could hear the two of them moving around my bedroom, a woman and a man with a Northern Irish accent, but my eyes were shut as I couldn't open them. My limbs were heavy, cramping, curling. I couldn't move.

I vaguely remember being stretchered down the stairs, while my boys were told to stay in the living room and not to open the door. I was slumped, but inside my body, I was still listening. In the ambulance, I counted the Milton Keynes roundabouts like some kind of mental tether. One … two … three … trying to place myself in a world I could no longer see.

At A&E, I was hooked up to machines and an ECG. Voices blurred in and out. Then, three hours later, I began to come back to myself, but I was groggy, foggy and exhausted. The doctor came in and said I was … 'stressed'.

Stressed.

I laughed. A weird, hollow laugh. No mention of the vaccine. Nothing but a patronising diagnosis. I crawled, quite literally, out of the hospital that evening. I couldn't walk straight. I was clinging to the walls like I'd done ten tequila shots, legs jelly, head spinning. Me, someone who'd never been in a hospital outside of giving birth. No allergies. One of the fittest 43-year-olds I knew. And suddenly, I was slurring my speech and spasming limbs and holding on to plasterboard for balance. Stressed? Really?

A few weeks later, I saw my GP. Quietly, he said what the hospital hadn't: it had been 'mini' or 'borderline' stroke-like symptoms. He looked me in the eye and told me not to get another dose. As if I needed telling. But the world was still shouting over him.

I took six months to recover. My energy trickled back slowly, inconsistently. Even now, some strange health issues linger, ones that only began after that jab. And yet, we are not really allowed to talk about it. Not properly.

I tried once. I posted on Twitter, just a question, really, but I just said what happened. 'Amazing that I live in a world where my doctor says to me not to get the vaccine, but the government says I have to.'

It went viral with over six million views. I received abuse from all over the world. Then, a few weeks later, my account, with 40,000 followers strong, was hacked. Every tweet. Gone. Deleted. Coincidence? Maybe. Strange? Definitely.

I'm not here to campaign or convince. I'm just sharing what happened and leaving it there, floating between the lines. Because maybe the real story isn't just about vaccines or viruses. Maybe it's about how easy it is to silence someone, how quickly a narrative takes hold and how quiet the questions become when the answers make people uncomfortable.

Steph: Superwoman Gail was always busy running around with her superwoman cape on. When you took it off, you felt exposed. Subconsciously, you were so desperately trying to cling to the elite athlete part of you because, without it, you were having to face the fact that you didn't have a vision of what your future might look like, and that's scary.

Gail: But I would still quite like to rule the world. It's just that it is a scary one.

Steph: Fear is normal. It's a natural reaction to feeling threatened, and you're feeling threatened because you still don't know what's going to happen in your future. I want to tell you that that's normal too. And I want you to give yourself permission to feel scared because it's fine. But hundreds of athletes have been where you are now, and they've gotten through it and to the other side. So, this unknowingness that you've got, you don't need to let it suffocate you. I heard a little something which stuck with me which I want to share ... FEAR doesn't have to mean 'face everything and run'. It could also mean 'face everything and rise'.

In sport, we often use the phrase 'control the controllables', a simple yet powerful reminder that athletes can only truly influence two things: their thoughts and the actions that follow. Everything else, the opponent, the officials and the playing conditions, is outside of their control. Yet ironically, the more pressure we feel, the more we crave control over everything, trying to pre-empt every possible outcome to reduce uncertainty. But this mindset is exhausting. It drains mental energy, clouds decision-making and ultimately pulls us away from performing at our best. Letting go of the need to control everything isn't weakness, it's wisdom. It's a vital part of the healing process, allowing us to shift from anxiety to presence, from fear to focus. Releasing control opens the door to resilience, adaptability and peace, both on and off the field.

THE LOST LIONESSES

IT'S FUNNY how much I've spoken about my mum over the years, in interviews, on stage, to anyone who's ever asked me where my love of sport came from. She was the reason I picked up a badminton racket in the first place – the woman who thrashed me again and again in that tin hut in Bedford, like a military coach. But as much as I talked about her badminton influence on me, there was the other part of her story I'd casually mention, the part of her story where she had once played football for England.

The story of the 1971 Women's World Cup in Mexico, the 'unofficial one', was one I included in motivational talks here and there. People would politely nod, maybe mutter, 'Oh, that's interesting,' and then move on. It wasn't the right time. Women's football hadn't yet caught the public imagination in the way it has now.

That changed in 2022 when the England women's football team, the Lionesses, won the Euros and, in 2023, I was commissioned to write a book about 'The Lost Lionesses'.

My mum, as mentioned earlier, was playing for Chiltern Valley Ladies, and they were making headlines in the local Bedfordshire newspapers. The team even started playing internationally with tournaments in Italy and Sicily, which were the qualifiers to the Mexico 'Copa 71' World Cup. Mum, aged just 19, along with 13 other girls, represented England in this tournament against the wishes of FIFA and the FA.

When my mum returned to the UK, the FA banned the girls for three to six months for defying them. Harry and June Batt, who ran the team, were banned for life. An interesting fact for you from the book, to tease you into purchasing it: there have only been six English people who have scored in the iconic Azteca Stadium, which is situated in the capital, Mexico City. Gary Lineker is top of that list with three goals; my mum is next with two. I'm so proud of that stat.

All of the 14 teenage girls who, against all odds, travelled to Mexico in 1971 to represent England in a women's World Cup are still unrecognised to this day by the FA. And suddenly, I found myself telling their story, writing it, and weaving it into the tapestry of all the women who had been silenced or forgotten for far too long.

I interviewed every single one of them – all 14 of the original squad. I also spoke to Keith Batt, son of Harry and June Batt, the brave and brilliant couple who had the guts to defy the authorities and get these girls on a plane. It was one of the most rewarding and emotional things I've ever done.

I'd never written a book before (and now you are reading my second), and it was the first time I had sat down with my mum and really *listened*. I felt guilty at first, realising how little I'd known about her childhood. She opened up in ways she never had before. And with each woman I interviewed, I felt an invisible thread connect us, across time, across sport, across experience. They spoke of football in the same way I spoke of badminton, about the freedom it gave, the escape and the identity. For girls constantly told how to dress, how to act, how to *be*, sport was rebellion and sanctuary rolled into one. On the pitch, they were wild, strong, fast, messy, brilliant. And when they came home from Mexico, no one believed them. No one cared. Their story was buried in disbelief and misogyny. That made me furious, and it still does.

So, 18 months later, *The Lost Lionesses* by Gail Emms was published. It exists. I can hold it in my hands, and it still feels a bit surreal. It was hard to write, a lot harder than I imagined, but it was also cathartic. A way to honour my mum and her team-mates. A way to say, 'You mattered. You changed things.'

In November 2024, we lost Lillian – affectionately known as 'Chopper Harris' – the 5ft goalie with the leap of a cat and the energy of a firecracker. Fierce, hilarious, unstoppable. Her loss reminded me why this story matters – before more of it disappears.

The book has been noticed. It was nominated for the 2025 *Charles Tyrwhitt Sports Book of the Year* Award in the Women's Sports Writing category. I didn't win, but to be nominated was an honour I'll never forget. Especially knowing I wrote it all myself. No ghostwriter. Just me, my laptop and a determination to tell the truth.

Now, people are finally listening. They're understanding what these girls, and Harry and June Batt went through. The barriers they smashed down. The quiet revolution they led. And, as Serina Wiegman so beautifully put it, 'Women in sport are standing on the shoulders of giants.' I believe that with all my heart.

The Lost Lionesses is their legacy. I hope it's the start of many more stories like it. And if you haven't read it yet … well, I think it's not bad. But don't take my word for it, go and find out for yourself.

Steph: Wow! You have a true entrepreneurial spirit – deciding to write a book with no training or guidance. It's inspirational and it's brave. What I am enjoying seeing is how alive you are telling me about this. What a contrast to how broken and emotional you have been describing your past.

Gail: I enjoyed writing it. I've learned loads about these incredible women. I can feel the heat of Mexico, and I can hear the music of the mariachi bands. These women are my heroes.

Lisa and I at a Scissor Sisters gig in London.

On the set of Superstars 2004 *with host Johnny Vaughan.*

On the podium after winning the All England 2005 with Nathan. Nathan taking up a lot of space.

The winning feeling. World champions. I can't do what Nathan is doing with my knees.

World Champions 2005 – number one in the world. This was a good day.

Winning the Commonwealth Games mixed doubles with Nathan in Melbourne, 2006.

Celebrating beating gold medal favourites, Gao Ling and Zheng Bo in the first round of Beijing 2008.

Receiving my MBE from Princess Anne. I was only six months pregnant in this photo. You can see why they all were panicking thinking I was due any day as I am the size of a whale.

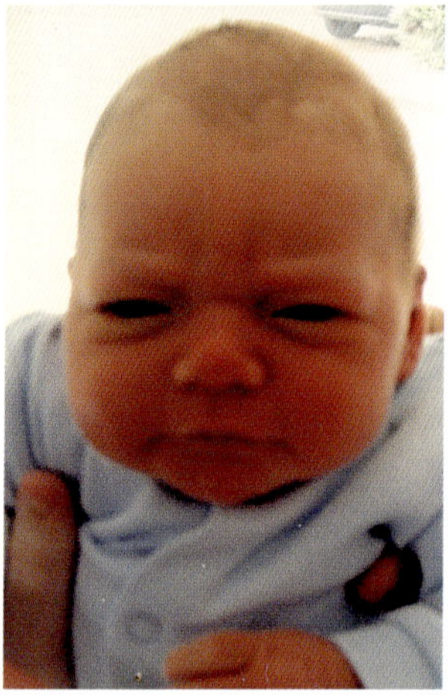

World's grumpiest baby if you woke him up – Harry. Aged three days.

My sons Harry and Ollie on a trampoline in our garden.

Dancing on Ice *with Lucasz. Please note the very straight leg. Thank you.*

Me on a bike at Ride London for SKODA. I don't look happy.

Finishing Ride London (100 miles) for SKODA.

Promo for SKODA cycling with the legend that is Dame Sarah Storey.

Results of me showering and washing my hair. I can brush up ok. Red carpet for Sport Industry Awards 2017.

Pre start of 2 mile Swim Serpentine to get my Big 3 medal with Olympic diver Leon Taylor. He swam very well. I finished eventually and got hyperthermia I took so long. I look good in a wetsuit though.

Another red carpet.
Another glam shot.

TV presenting – this time on a golf course. I don't know why the cameraman is pretending to be a flamingo.

Uni bestie Lucy and me – now.

HEARTBREAK

ED AND I split in the summer of 2020 after 15 and a half years together. Ed is one of the best people and the *best* dad to Harry and Ollie. We remain friends, and I am so happy he is happier now. That is what I wanted for him. Every split is painful and, most importantly, private.

Single and Forty

When Ed and I split up, I expected the grief, the tears, the awkward conversations with mutual friends. But what did surprise me, with singleness came an avalanche of judgment: on my clothes, on my Instagram, the way I raise my boys, my social life, the lot. I overheard two women gossiping about my break-up once, one whispering to the other, 'Well … have you seen her? I'm not surprised.' I wanted to laugh. Or maybe scream. Yes, I look after myself. I'm proud of my body and how strong it is. I go to gigs, I host black tie events, I dress up, but I guess people just want to see what they *want* to see.

I still love a walk in the hills, travel adventures, live music, a cheeky cocktail. And yes, I want to share that with someone. I was ready to date again. But wow … what a minefield.

I miss the good old days. Remember when flirting meant catching someone's eye across a room? When you'd throw on a skirt, maybe heels, and head out with your mates to a bar on the high street. No phones. Just music, vibe and maybe a brave guy wandering over to say something deeply romantic like, 'Alright, you're fit. Fancy a snog?' Then came the dancing, the snogging and if things were really going well, some wildly uncoordinated dry humping on a sticky dance floor under a broken strobe light. If you were *really* lucky, maybe a bit of light 'exploration', discreetly shielded by a circle of loyal mates forming a human wall. Ah, the romance.

Fast-forward to now, and dating is a digital disaster. I downloaded the apps. I swiped. I cringed. I tried to flirt, but somewhere between *real life* and *texting a stranger*, my flirting now resembles Jim Carrey in *Dumb and Dumber*. It's not sexy. It's not even coherent. Just me making wildly inappropriate jokes and wondering why I've been unmatched.

Dating in your 40s is like being stuck between two worlds: the one where you remember how it used to work, and the one you're told you now have to adapt to; full of filters, instant rejection and 'vibes' based on emojis.

And while I'm all for female empowerment, this new wave of dating culture feels … off. I've seen it first-hand, especially working in hospitality. I once watched a kind, slightly nervous man approach a woman to offer her a drink, and she looked him up and down and sneered, 'As if I'm going to have a drink with *you*?' No thanks, no smile, no grace. Just dismissal based on status and looks. It made me sad – for him, for her, for *all of us* trying to navigate this weird, disconnected dating jungle. I don't want designer champagne and status symbols. I want someone kind. Someone interesting. Someone who laughs at my dumb jokes. And doesn't run when I sing obscure 90s house music lyrics, or talk about sports metaphors for life.

I still believe in love. I'm romantic like that. I believe there's someone out there who'll love the full package of me, even the slightly chaotic, oversharing, fiercely loyal, Eric Prydz-obsessed part of me. And when that someone shows up, I'll be ready. Lip gloss on. Playlist queued. Until then, I'll keep being me: strong, flawed and fun.

Yet the more I date, the more I realise that my soulmate person died at birth or something.

Steph: Here's what I have read about women with dopamine addiction. They often become obsessed with narcissistic relationships. They crave constant validation and approval to feel worthy; they prioritise the narcissist's opinion over their own wellbeing. And they easily mistake emotional abuse for connection. It's all about trying to fill their own emotional void. This reliance on external validation can lead to unhealthy behaviours such as people-pleasing and perfectionism.

Gail: Wow. Well, that explains some of my dating choices! Relationships are difficult for me. And trusting others. Not sure on the perfectionism bit. My bedroom is a mess.

Steph: You seem to have a fear of abandonment. And yet also feel suffocated in your relationships.

Gail: Suffocated, yes. I get claustrophobic.

Steph: Your story has had some common themes. Struggling with expressing emotions and setting boundaries. Feelings of anger, resentment and sadness. Persistent feelings of emptiness and loneliness despite outward success.

Gail: The loneliness thing. I feel like sometimes no one else thinks like me. Is there another me? I know lots of people. I've got good friends. There are times I'm like, does anyone really get me? And that's the loneliness thing. I just want to be myself.

Steph: It sounds like you are frustrated about that?

Gail: Yeah ... it's that 'conforming' part which frustrates me. Why can't I just be me? Maybe I am the problem. I love who I am. But does anyone else love who I am?

Steph: What is it about you that you love?

Gail: I love the fact that I am unique. I love that I am feisty and passionate. I love that I'm a bit nuts. I love the fact that I'm funny and make people laugh. I love that I am active, want to do stuff, and am spontaneous. I love my energy.

Steph: I'm not going to ask you to change who you are Gail, but maybe consider this ... women who show up in the world as being so strong and brave, which you do, show the red side of their personality, you know, fearless, feisty, accomplished; but this is not the full story. There is a softer and gentler Gail in there, too. Maybe you need to reconnect with that part of you because this Gail may have lost her way. She's a bit more vulnerable, but she needs to be heard.

Gail: The masculine side, that red side, comes out so much that it's like a default.

Steph: You're living as if you're still competing, and you need to reconnect to some feminine, more vulnerable energy because your life isn't sport now. It's as if you haven't updated your wardrobe since you finished when you were 31. You're still wearing the same clothes, and you're still thinking the same way. This may help explain why men get put off dating you. You scare them away!

Where's the man's purpose in a relationship dynamic with you? What role do they have? Being in your masculine energy will make them feel inferior. No man likes to feel inferior – a man likes to feel strong. You're presenting yourself as this superstar achiever, and they can't compete.

Gail: So, no arm wrestling on the first date, then?

DATING APPS

DEAR GOD, someone tell these guys how to do a dating profile. For those of you who are unaware of what guys on dating profiles are like, let me give you some examples … but it all boils down to 'Swipe Right for Disappointment'.

It all starts with the first photo.

First up: ***Fish Guy***. Always a man proudly clutching a trout like it's the baby he's never emotionally prepared to raise. What's the logic here? 'Here's me … with something dead and slimy. Date me.' Hard pass, Captain Cod.

Next: ***Baby Guy***. Holding a child with the caption 'Not my baby'. Thanks for the clarification, Kevin. Because nothing screams emotional maturity like borrowing a baby to trick women into thinking you're wholesome.

Then there's ***Mystery Man***. Sunglasses and a hat – why not take the photo in the dark, mate? He could be handsome. He could be Shrek. *Who knows*?!

And the ***Ski Bro***! Helmet, goggles, full Michelin Man attire – no face, just vibes. Is this dating or 'Guess Who: Extreme Sports Edition'?

Then there's the classic ***Group Photo***. Five or six lads, all clumped together like it's a boy band reunion. I squint … I zoom … I think, 'Hmm, maybe the one on the left is kinda cute …' Scroll down … nope! That's his mate Dave. I've matched with the one holding the camera and emotional baggage.

Oh, and ***Fish Guy*** is back! Still gripping that pike like it's his personality. Because, obviously, I want to date a man who smells faintly of salmon.

And who could forget ***See Up My Nostrils Guy*** … Low-angle selfie so far up his nose, I've practically been introduced to his sinus cavity. There are hairs.

Next: ***Sports Action-Shot Guy***. Mid-rugby tackle, mid-marathon, mid-air and mid-face. I don't need to see your athleticism; I just want to know if you have a chin.

Then we meet ***Dr Dolittle***. He's with a dog, a cat, a goat, and maybe a horse? Are you trying to date me or start a farm?

Now entering: ***Car Guy***. Four photos. Same car. Different lighting. Honestly, I'm not sure if he's in love with me or his rented supercar.

And then … the ***Obvious Catfish***. The guy is so *hot* he looks AI-generated. He's 35, lives 'in your area', and has never, not once, replied to a message. Probably because he's also modelling in Milan … or, you know, *does not exist*.

Gym Bro makes an appearance – mid-bicep curl pose, veins popping like he's about to fight the Hulk. Arms the size of tree trunks, but the legs are questionable. Wearing a vest so tight it's technically a cry for help. Every photo, he's posing in the gym. Do you have a life?

Then … the captions. Ah yes, here is where the magic begins to shine through.

'Looking for my partner in crime' – what is this, a romcom or a heist?

'Controversial opinion: pineapple belongs on pizza.' Wow. So bold. So brave.

'Here for a fun time, not a long time.' Translation: I have zero emotional availability and no clean sheets.

And just when you're about to give up and move to a remote island with no Wi-Fi …

There he is. A man. A normal, reasonable-looking man. He's smiling like he's been to therapy. He has a hobby that isn't just 'the gym'. You message. You vibe. You get excited. And then … you read it:

'In an open relationship. Poly. Ethically non-monogamous.'

Of course he is.

Because dating in 2025 is just one long episode of *Black Mirror.*

Of course, the apps are all a bit different, but I have done my best to round them up for you. A 'Gail's Guide' if you like.

1. Hinge
The app '*designed to be deleted*' – probably because if you read one more profile about 'Sunday walks and roast dinners', you'll delete yourself. Every man's dream apparently is 'a golden retriever, a country pub, and *honesty, God damn it, that's all I ask*!'

2. Tinder
The digital equivalent of a nightclub at 2am. No one knows your name, no one *cares* what your name is, just answer one question: *'U up?'* It's less dating, more human speed dial for questionable decisions.

3. Bumble
Ah, Bumble. Where women make the first move … and men still manage to ruin it. From crypto bros to spiritual healers and everyone in between, it's like speeddating in a very weird Sainsbury's.

4. Raya
The A-list dating app for influencers, models and DJs you've never heard of. Everyone's too busy posing on cliffs in Tulum or filming a soft-filter reel to *actually reply*! Messaging here is like sending a pigeon into the Met Gala.

5. Feeld
Welcome to the wild, wild west of kinks. You joined out of curiosity; now you're fielding (pun intended) 47 daily messages asking if you'd like to join a unicorn-themed cuddle cult. You thought you were spicy … but Feeld said, 'Hold my leather.'

You can understand my pain and frustration. I give up over and over again. But then I believe … and then I date. Here is a selection of my 'interesting' dates so far.

The One with a Limp

It all started, as these things often do, with optimism. I'd agreed to meet this guy at Euston station, convenient for me, since that's where the Milton Keynes train dumps me, and I'm nothing if not efficient. The sun was out, I had good hair, and I thought, 'You know what? Let's keep this casual, cool, European-chic. A little walk over to Granary Square near Kings Cross, perfect for al fresco date vibes.'

So we met. He looked normal enough, there were no visible red flags, no football team tattooed across his face, not chewing gum with his mouth open. All promising. The small talk was pleasant; weather, weekend plans, that vague thing people call 'work' without actually saying what it is. All the usual date foreplay.

Now, in theory, the walk from Euston to Granary Square should take around 13 minutes. I know this because I once made it in 11 when I was late for a meeting, so when we were still crawling along Euston Road 20 minutes in and hadn't even passed The Standard hotel yet, I started to wonder. My first thought was, 'Aww, bless him. He likes me so much, he's walking slowly to extend the date.' Cute. But I hate walking slowly. I'm not a speed-walker, but if I can feel moss forming on my shoes, we have a problem.

I tried to subtly speed up. You know, the gentle power stride, just enough to say, 'Hey, I'm fit and dynamic and don't have all day.' He didn't budge. In fact, he was walking even *more slowly*. I started to wonder if he was trying to reverse time. That's when I noticed … the limp. Ah. Right. There it was. Subtle, but definitely a limp.

My brain instantly filled with jokes, because of course it did, but I smiled politely and limped on in solidarity. It took us nearly 35 minutes to get there. *Thirty-five*. I aged during that walk. I almost rang for an Uber halfway through, but I didn't want to be *that* girl. Anyway, we finally sat down, well, I sat. He kind of … lowered. With effort. I was concerned now, and I asked, 'Are you okay? Are you injured?' He looked sheepish and slowly pulled up his jeans to reveal ... a prosthetic leg. Right. That would've been useful information *before* the sponsored trudge across central London.

Now listen. I'm not someone who discriminates, not at all. I can deal with uniqueness. But what I *cannot* deal with is *deliberate omission*. You don't have to lead with, 'Hello, I have a bionic limb,' but maybe *some* warning that a leisurely walk might turn into an endurance test ... just a casual, 'Hey, by the way, I'm slightly slower on my feet,' would've done it. Anyway, I was trying to move past it. We sat in the sunshine, had a drink, and he was growing on me. Maybe we'd laugh about this someday.

And then ... he brought out the tissue.

No warning. No gentle segue. Just *produced* a tissue, dabbed his ear and, with zero shame, examined it, turned it *towards me* and said something along the lines of 'bit of an ear infection', before slapping it down *on the table* like it was his business card.

There it was. A soggy tissue, oozing bodily fluid, basking in the daylight between us.

That was my cue. I got up. Smiled. Nodded. Walked off *very* quickly – funny how my legs worked just fine when I needed an exit. Probably did the 13-minute walk back to Euston in 11. So yes. The one with the limp ... and the pus. A modern romance.

The 'Liar Liar'

After the episode with 'Captain Prosthetic', I thought, surely lightning doesn't strike twice. But oh, how the dating gods love to mess with me. There's a special place in online dating hell reserved for *height liars*. You know the ones, the men who proudly declare '5ft 11' in their profile when in reality they'd need a step ladder to reach 5ft 8 in stilettos. Now, I'm not fussy. I'm a solid 5ft 3 and a half (yes, the half matters, I've worked hard for that), and I genuinely don't care about height ... *unless* I've worn the wrong shoes.

That's the deal. If he says 5ft 10 or under, I go flats. If he says over 5ft 10, I break out the heels. I'm not asking for the moon here, just accurate measurements so I don't accidentally turn up looking like Gandalf escorting a hobbit.

This particular gentleman had been vague about his height. Classic red flag. So I played it safe and wore a low-heeled boot. Cute, practical, date-night safe. I got to the pub first – outside seating, crisp pint, ready for the inevitable awkward, 'Are you my date?' moment. And then … it happened. A *beast* of a Range Rover rolled into the car park. Brand new. Jet black. Fully loaded. Screamed midlife crisis. Or overcompensation. Or both. The door opened. And out slid … a man. Kind of. Sort of. He emerged like a kid tumbling out of a ball pit, with his limbs not quite in control. I swear I heard the sound of his shoes scraping the step like he was disembarking a tractor. And that's when I knew. This was *him*.

He strutted over in what I can only describe as an outfit curated by Marty McFly and accessorised by his mum's jewellery box. Silver chains galore. Oversized rings. Possibly a toe ring … I didn't ask. I stood up to greet him, and with my modest boot heel … I was taller. Taller. Now, I've dated men my height before. No issue. What I *do* take issue with is lying about it, and then showing up like a miniature rock star with an ego the size of his car. The man was pure attitude in a child-size portion. He oozed cockiness. Tried to inch closer to me on the bench like we were in some kind of romcom. I wasn't feeling it at all. My spidey senses were tingling, and not in the good way. More 'possible sex pest' than 'ooh, butterflies!'

So, I did what any woman with self-respect (and a full bladder) would do: downed my drink and made an elegant excuse involving an early morning and needing to walk my dog. He insisted on walking me back to the car park, which felt less romantic and more like a scene from Austin Powers. Me towering over him, like Dr Evil, and him, Mini-Me.

Let's be clear. I'm not ranting because the man was short. I'm ranting because he *lied*, turned up with the attitude of Conor McGregor in a travel-sized bottle, and acted like we were on a date from *Love Island: Inappropriate Edition*. So no, fellas, your height doesn't disqualify you. Your dishonesty, bad outfit choices and creepy bench tactics do.

The Gangster

I was still swiping right with the hope of meeting someone normal. Now I was looking at factors like 'owns a toothbrush', 'knows how to use cutlery', 'doesn't live with his mum'. The bar was low.

Enter: Mr South London Smooth. He had a cheeky smile, a sexy accent and the kind of charisma that made you forget to ask the important questions like 'Are you in a gang?'

Our first date was great. He was charming, funny and had that kind of street smart that made him sound like he'd done a TED Talk titled 'Survival Tactics from Croydon to Cannes'. I asked him what he did for work, and he muttered something about 'a bit of this, bit of that.' I assumed tradesman. You know, one of those jack of all jobs. He always paid in cash … always. Which I just thought was a 'working man' thing.

Anyway, fast-forward a few dates, and one evening he was changing into a shirt before we went out, and that's when I saw them: scars – all over his body. It looked like he'd tried to wrestle a tiger and lost. Naturally, I blurted out, 'Have you had, like, 47 operations or something?' He gave me the vaguest answer in the history of vague answers: 'Yeah, something like that.' Then carried on buttoning up his shirt like we were just popping to Wagamama, and not skipping past a major red flag.

A few weeks in, I decided I needed some clarity. He was cute and funny, but I still didn't know if he was a plumber, a painter or just between organised crimes. So I asked. We were in a pub, classic, and he gave me that look. That slow, dangerous grin, like a character reveal in a Guy Ritchie film. Then he said, 'Why don't we have a little fun?' and casually pulled out a bag of coke. I laughed awkwardly and said, 'Not my style, thank you.'

He stared at me, his blue-grey eyes boring into my soul like he was both flirting and deciding whether to bury me in the woods. He winked and said, 'Course, darling,' and tucked it away like it was no big deal. And then came the backstory dump. Oh, the backstory. Buckle up.

He told me he had been expelled from school at 14. He'd grown up in Croydon (fair enough), had been stabbed 23 times (23!), done prison time, and, here's the kicker, once shot someone with a crossbow. A crossbow. Who even has a crossbow? Was this man dating me or preparing for the *Hunger Games*? Then, as if that dramatic monologue wasn't enough, he finished with:

'So let's get this party started!' And whipped out the same bag of coke again, chopping it up on his phone with his gym membership card. (Apparently, he had time for quads and crime.) He then rolled up a note and hoovered the entire bag like he was Dyson-ing the countertop. Gone in 45 minutes. I sat there, stunned, blinking like I was in an episode of *Gangland.*

So, I did what any woman with self-preservation instincts and a fully functioning nervous system would do: I grabbed my bag, made an exit and ghosted him faster than he ghosted the education system. I never saw him again. Never want to. But shoutout to him for teaching me an important life lesson: ask more questions before seeing someone's torso.

The 'Going to Prison'

I matched with this ridiculously good-looking man from Hertfordshire, the kind of man who looked like he moisturised daily and probably owned a really expensive watch he never actually used to tell the time. We had a great first date – just a cheeky cocktail in Milton Keynes, nothing too fancy. He was charming, flirty, and had that twinkle in his eye that said, 'I've probably made some questionable life choices, but I look good doing it.'

Then he upped the ante. He invited me for a night out in London. Said he'd booked a restaurant and even offered to sort hotel rooms (separate ones, very gentlemanly). I asked if there was a dress code. He gave a little laugh and said, 'Well, it's not Pizza Express.'

Right. Fancy it is, then. So, I pulled out the big guns: heels, a dress that meant business (and also meant I couldn't eat bread for 48 hours beforehand), full glam. I arrived at the restaurant, which I'd never heard of, but as soon as I clocked the lobster tanks and saw meat being treated like Fabergé eggs, I knew I was in a different tax bracket.

We were seated, and the menus were handed over. He ordered champagne like he was the Duke of Belgravia and followed up with red wine and enough starters to feed a mid-sized hen party. I glanced at the menu, saw the cheapest starter was £75, and immediately started sweating behind my lashes. The food was *unreal.* Like, genuinely mind-blowing. I was in heaven.

We were midway through the mains when, in between bites of some outrageously tender wagyu, he casually dropped this line. 'I've got a £500-a-day coke habit … and I'm due to be sentenced on Monday.'

'I'm sorry, what?' I laughed, assuming he was joking. You know, weird banter. But, oh no … no laughter in those eyes. Just deadpan honesty and a slight shrug. Apparently, this wasn't just dinner, this was a *last supper.* I was eating soufflé with Tony Montana.

The bill arrived. I made the mistake of looking. It was close to £1,000. I almost had a cardiac arrest right there. I nervously offered to pay half, fully praying my credit card limit hadn't been torched by groceries and petrol that week. He just smiled and said, 'Nah, don't worry,' and paid. In cash. Of course he did. We parted ways shortly after. Shocking, I know, and I didn't hear from him again. Presumably because mobile phones are frowned upon in prison, but he did book me into a suite at the Hilton on Park Lane, so I can't say it was a total loss.

Honestly, it was one of the best meals of my life, but also one of the weirdest. A huge shoutout to the man who made me feel like a Bond girl for a night … just before heading off to court. You were wildly problematic, but you had excellent taste in restaurants.

The Vegan

So, the plan was a date in London. Food, and then a show. Sounds nice, right? Until I'm halfway to Euston on the train from Milton

Keynes, and I google the restaurant he sent me the location for, some place tucked away near Leicester Square, and *bam*. It's vegan.

Vegan.

Now, let me set the scene. I'm not just a meat eater, I am the poster child for 'Team Carnivore'. I eat meat, fish and occasionally something green if it happens to be stuck to a steak. My skincare is beef tallow and I drink bone broth. I'm not anti-vegans unless they try to tell me soy milk is saving the planet while their avocados are clocking up more air miles than a pilot. I support local farmers and local produce and animals that lived good lives ... no processed or GM food for me, thank you.

So, naturally, I panic-message the guy: 'Are you vegan?' His reply? 'Yes, and proud.' Ah. Excellent. This'll go well. Now, I'm not rude, but I *am* a gobshite with strong views and a wicked sense of humour. So, I couldn't resist poking the lentil bear. 'Just so you know, I'm carrying a leather handbag, and I'm moisturised in beef fat. I may as well rock up mooing.' He said, 'The staff are human, they'll cope. It's the cows you should be worried about.' I replied: 'Had one for breakfast, mate. Can't ask.'

Anyway, I arrived, looking fabulous and carnivorous, and we sat down in this dimly lit vegan den that smelled faintly of fungus. He ordered for us, naturally, and what landed on our table looked like something a rabbit would push away. Courgettes, mushrooms, sweet potato mash; all mushed up like a baby-weaning menu curated by Gwyneth Paltrow. I looked down at my plate and genuinely had a flashback to when I was blending vegetables for my toddlers ... except now I was paying for the trauma.

The place was also eerily empty. It was a Thursday night in central London, and this place had all the atmosphere of a dentist's waiting room. I thought, 'Fine, I'll order wine, get a bit buzzed, make it through.' But no. No wine. Just water. He ordered for the table and made it *very clear* that it was our only drink option. I hadn't eaten a single animal product in hours, and now I couldn't even numb the pain. Send help.

After the meal (if we're calling it that), we headed to the show. Once it ended, I spotted Charing Cross and said, 'Perfect! I'll jump on the Tube and catch the 11pm train with my mate Terri.' But Vegan Usain Bolt wasn't having that. 'No need for the underground! Let's walk!'

Walk. Walk?? For 50 minutes. Through London. At 6ft 3, he was taking Big Friendly Giant-sized strides while I, a modest 5ft 3 and a half, had to jog to keep up, like I was trying to keep pace with a giraffe doing power yoga. We finally got to Euston, I waved goodbye and collapsed on to the train seat next to Terri, who'd been at a gig in Camden. We were just about to debrief our nights when … it happened.

The vegan food struck back.

My stomach went into *mutiny*. Silent but violent wasn't even on the menu. It was full orchestral gas warfare. Terri, bless her, took it like a champ. She even thanked the random couple across from us for bringing their spicy biryani on board, as that was a saviour in masking what I was releasing into that carriage.

It was like my body was shouting, '*What have you done to me*?!'

When I got home, I flung open the fridge, grabbed leftover chicken straight from the Tupperware, and ate it like a victorious cavewoman flipping two fingers at that smug little quinoa pile.

Never again. Let the vegans live their best avocado lives, but next time someone tries to lure me into a restaurant with no actual food, I'm bringing a steak in my handbag.

The One with No Boundaries … or No Self-Awareness

I'm a woman who believes in boundaries. Big, bold, neon-lit ones. So, when I start messaging someone new, I lay down the ground rules early. No smutty nonsense, no oversharing, no unsolicited anatomy updates. Keep it classy, or I'm gone.

Enter this guy … who seemed okay at first. Polite, chatty, slightly flirtier than I'd like, but, hey, nothing terrifying … yet. I clarified, straight off: 'I'm looking to date. Not sext. Private life, not private parts, please.' His reply? 'Of course! Same here!' Spoiler: he lied.

We had a date planned, and the afternoon before we were casually chatting. Out of nowhere, he drops, 'I lied about my age. I'm not 49. I'm actually 52.' Mate. Really? I don't care if you're 52, 82 or Gandalf, but lying to sneak into the 41-49 search bracket is as grimy as a fake Rolex. It's the dating equivalent of using cling film as a condom – technically it covers something, but no one's impressed.

Still, I gave him the benefit of the doubt. A shaky benefit, on a wobbly chair. Then came the height question. He asked mine, 'I am 5ft 3 and a half thank you very much'. I asked his. The app didn't list it. He said, '5ft 10.' Immediately followed by, 'I'm tall when lying down.'

Oh God, no. We're not even on a date yet, and this guy's already horizontal in his mind. Then it snowballed faster than a lad's group chat on a stag do. 'Send me a pic of your boobs,' he said. 'They're my favourite part of a woman's body.' I said no. 'Okay, bum then?' Still no. Then came an hour-long barrage of sexual nonsense:

What I don't like in bed.

How horny he was.

Critiquing my hypothetical hand jobs.

Informing me his penis was his 'favourite body part'.

And the final showstopper: 'Do you swallow?'

What. In. The. Actual. Hell.

I reminded him, *again*, that I had boundaries. His reply? 'I don't see these as personal questions.'

I don't see you as dateable, but here we are.

To my eternal credit (and possibly a little too polite for my own good), I said I wouldn't be meeting him and wished him well. In hindsight, I should've sent him a link to therapy and blocked him with the force of a thousand suns. To be fair, he did apologise the next morning. But the damage was done. Respect had left the chat. What is worse is that he had two teenage daughters … how would he feel if someone was messaging them like he was messaging me?!

Although … I *am* still low-key convinced he lied about his height, too.

The One with Daddy Issues for his Dog

Looking back, I probably should've known this one was going to be a car crash. Not because he lived in Cornwall – lovely place, great pasties – but because the man was in his *40s* and still managed to say, completely seriously, 'You go to London for work? That's really scary!'

Scary? Mate, it's not a horror film, it's the capital city. I explained, calmly, that I've been to London *thousands* of times. I've eaten at its restaurants, walked its streets, been to its museums and navigated more Tube strikes than I care to count. My biggest fear is 'delays on Avanti West Coast', not 'phone thieves on bikes'.

But, bless him, he seemed convinced I was dicing with death every time I stepped off at Euston. 'There are drug deals happening everywhere in London.' Yes, just like there are drugs in your posh village in Cornwall, probably being bought by someone called Jeremy with a Barbour jacket and a cocaine habit. Still, for reasons unknown, I carried on messaging. I must have been bored.

Things were civil, even mildly entertaining, until one Monday evening when I was off being supermum at David Lloyd, supervising my boys playing badminton and pickleball. Mid-sprint between courts, I got a WhatsApp from 'Surfer Dude'. Nothing major, just more waffle about sea air and his dog. Not wanting to be rude, I hit him with the thumbs-up emoji. Simple. Efficient. Friendly.

Big mistake.

Two hours later, yes, *two hours*, I get this unhinged rant, 'Don't you know the thumbs-up emoji is the worst response you can *ever* send??!!' Two hours. He stewed over that emoji like it personally insulted his ancestors. Mate, we haven't even met. If a pixelated thumb is enough to send you spiralling, how would you cope with me saying the random stuff that comes out of my mouth?

I told him, politely-ish, to jog on. But, of course, there was more. He lived alone (no surprise), except for his dog, who he referred to as his '*fur baby*' and called himself its '*dog daddy*'. Repeatedly.

Look, I love dogs. Dogs are excellent. But when a grown man refers to himself as 'daddy' in every other message in relation to his pet dog, it stops being cute and starts giving me the ick. Full-blown *puke emoji*. And that, ladies and gentlemen, is how I dodged a Cornish disaster who thinks emojis are emotional warfare and being a dog's parent is a personality.

The Head F**k

When I first started writing this book, I was still carrying the weight of a relationship that had left me shattered. It had lasted six months, and he was meant to be the one flying out to join me in St Lucia. The split was traumatic. I won't go into the full story here, but I will say this: as painful as it was, I'm glad it ended. Because in the wreckage of that ending, something began.

That relationship cracked something open in me. It led me to my conversations with Steph, where I finally started asking the bigger questions. Why was I drawn to him in the first place? Why did his behaviour feel so familiar? That's when it hit me … his personality echoed others I had once loved and lost myself to.

And so, the real work began. The uncomfortable, confronting, painful work of looking inward. I had to face something I didn't want to admit: I was repeating patterns. I was tolerating control disguised as love. I was silencing myself to avoid conflict. I was blaming myself when their moods turned, when their affection disappeared, when they snapped and ended things as though I were disposable.

There were moments I genuinely believed them. All of them. They were masters at making me doubt myself. I started to think maybe I was 'too much'. Maybe if I'd just been quieter, less questioning, less 'difficult', they wouldn't have shut me out. I saw their new smiling photos online with their new partners, and wondered if I was the problem, just like they told me I was.

But that's what emotional manipulation does … it distorts the truth.

And the truth is I'm not perfect. God knows, I can be a pain in the arse – I say what I think, I laugh too loud, I feel things deeply. But I show up. I love hard. I give everything.

And for too long, I offered that to people who didn't value it, who didn't value *me*.

It took that last toxic relationship to finally see the pattern for what it was. I needed my friends to remind me I wasn't crazy. That my gut was right. That the way they spoke to me wasn't okay, no matter how many good moments we had, no matter how many plans we'd made. Because I have standards now. And I won't lower them just to keep someone from leaving.

I still feel sad sometimes. Sad for the girl who thought she had to bend herself into something smaller to be loved. But I also feel lucky, because I'm no longer that girl. I've grown into a woman who knows her worth, who knows that love isn't meant to hurt, confuse or diminish you.

This isn't just about men. This is about people – all of us – learning to choose respect, kindness and honesty. And, most importantly, learning to choose *ourselves*.

Steph: So, why were you in this relationship with this guy?

Gail: Because when we were together and he was relaxed and he was being normal, he was, and it was, just brilliant. We had such a good laugh, and it was great.

Steph: Didn't you think you deserved more than that?

Gail: Well, I do now. But also, there was no one else. It's not like I have a long queue of people. The guys I like don't like me. They go for these 'Instagram girls'. You know the type. I look a bit different. So, I don't have much choice.

Steph: Really? It sounds a bit like you are writing yourself off. I hope you might start to hear that the language you're using to describe yourself is feeding your insecurities and is very self-deprecating.

Gail: I guess I am just used to hearing one thing from a guy, then they do the exact opposite. They tell me what I want to hear, then do the opposite, so what do I do? I just wanted someone to appreciate who I am. And he did that – and he knew what to say to me. But then he used my personality and outlook on life against me.

Steph: Until you are more confident in who you are and honest about what you really want and need, you'll just go and repeat the patterns of previous relationships. I know it's hard for you to hear, but you will never be able to really love someone else until you love yourself.

Gail: Mmmmmmm, I think I'm bloody amazing, Steph, but that's not the kind of love you are talking about.

I've come to realise that the version of me who wore the 'strong, independent woman' armour, the one who carried everything, trusted no one and stayed in control wasn't just powerful, she was also tired. That role, though necessary at times, was hard on my nervous system. It kept me in a state of survival.

My true strength doesn't lie in always doing, fixing or leading. It lives in softness. In presence. In allowing myself to rest and surrender, knowing I am safe enough to do so.

For me, love isn't about dominance or equality in the way society sometimes pushes, like we're all supposed to be identical. I believe we're equal in worth, but beautifully different in how we're built to give and receive. That's what makes partnership so powerful; when a man and a woman (or whatever combination you prefer in a relationship) bring their complementary strengths together, it creates something whole.

I've learned that a woman will often stay in her masculine energy – hyper-independent, guarded, driven – not because she wants to, but because life has taught her to. It's a defence mechanism born from pain. From betrayal. From being let down by people she trusted. From having to pick herself up over and over again, because no one else would. That kind of strength is real, but it's also lonely. She's done it alone for so long. And she's not interested in opening her heart just to be let down again.

So, when she meets a man, she doesn't need him to rescue her, she needs to feel safe with him. Safe to soften. Safe to feel. Safe to let go of the armour. That's when her feminine energy returns … naturally and effortlessly. Until then, don't expect her to change just because you showed up. She's watching. Listening. Feeling. Waiting to see if this time, it's different. If this time, she can finally rest.

Because when a woman trusts a man to be her rock, emotionally, energetically, spiritually, she doesn't lose her power. She rises in it.

Steph: You do know that if you are going to have a healthy relationship, you need to learn to accept a compliment without making fun of it.

Gail: (Squirming)

Steph: When you're complimented, it's really destabilising for you because, in essence, praise is evaluation, right? And that's what you're scared of ... even when it's positive. It takes you out of the moment. It makes you more concerned about what other people think of you, and you have such a massive fear of being evaluated negatively.

Gail: Oh, my God. A massive fear of being rejected. If I've done something wrong in a test, I can cope with that. But someone's subjective opinion on me, something personal, it's horrendous.

If you're not happy on your own, you won't magically become happy just because someone else shows up. Love doesn't fill a void; it should meet you when you're already full. So first, find your joy. Dance at raves. Laugh until your ribs hurt. Chase sunrises. Let life be messy and wild and yours. There's so much more to life than waiting to be wanted. So much more than mourning people who didn't choose you. Your time here is too precious to spend it shrinking yourself or holding your breath, hoping someone will see your worth.

Discover yourself without waiting for anyone else to fall in love with you along the way. And when love does arrive, if it arrives, let it be a bonus, not a necessity. It doesn't have to be hard, or heavy, or leave you hollow. Fill yourself with your own love first. Learn what makes you feel alive. Become whole on your own, not half of something, waiting to be completed.

Take adventures. Sleep under the stars. Wander cities alone. Write poetry on bathroom walls. Leave secret notes in library books. Sit in coffee shops just because it feels good to be there. Do everything with love, but know that your life is already romantic, already worthy, just as it is.

You don't need to be in love to live a beautiful life. And living for yourself isn't selfish, it's sacred. I promise, being alone can be just as magical. Maybe even more.

Don't make yourself small for anyone. Be the awkward, funny, intelligent little weirdo that you are. Don't hold back. Weird it out. Be the glitch.

Steph: You know, you were never going to win in that relationship. Sorry to use the analogy of winning again. He didn't deserve you.

Gail: He's a charmer, and I got sucked into it.

Steph: So, can we put that one to bed?

Gail: Well, not literally, God, no. But yeah, metaphorically, please, I need to.

Steph: What did you do next?

Gail: I just went raving.

RAVING

I STILL remember my very first rave. It was the early '90s, and I was about 15. The days of pagers, phone boxes and whispered coordinates. It was like something out of MI5. You'd ring a number from a payphone, get the grid reference and suddenly you were part of something secret, something electric. We'd pile into cars with crumpled maps and hearts racing, driving into the unknown until, somewhere in the distance, you'd hear it … the thump of bass. That's when you knew: you'd arrived.

House music has always made me feel alive. That 120bpm rhythm, the melodies, the lights, the lasers, the drop … it just *gets* me. I grew up listening to Pete Tong, Judge Jules, Seb Fontaine. Ibiza anthems were the soundtrack to my youth, with tracks like 'Yeke Yeke' by Mory Kanté and 'Silence' by Chicane still pulsing through my playlists today.

Then life shifted. Sport became my world, and I didn't really have space to be a cheesy quaver anymore. But the music never left me. Just before Covid, I went to see Fatboy Slim at Wembley Arena, and something inside me reignited. As the bass shook the floor and the lights danced above us, I remember thinking, 'I'm home.' I've often reflected on why that moment hit so deeply. And I think it's this:

- After leaving elite sport, I missed the adrenaline. Raving gave it back to me.
- It's a space with zero judgement, just pure connection.

- The pace of the music mirrors the rhythm of a match – fast, intense, alive.
- It's freedom. For those few hours, I could let go and fly.

Raving soon became my happy place. The joy I once found on the court, I now find in front of the decks. The lights, the beats, the strangers who feel like friends. I dance my little socks off and feel like the most authentic version of myself, no pressure, just presence.

Yes, people have their opinions. The word 'rave' still carries stigma. But here's what I've seen: I've worked in bars and clubs, I've been out in town and, honestly, I've felt *safer* and more respected in a rave crowd than anywhere else. No drunk lads shouting. No unwanted attention. Just people from all walks of life, united by one thing: the music.

Rave-Husband Jamie

Jamie Unwin and I first crossed paths at a charity event where he was working. Something clicked, and we became mates. I know that Jamie is someone who *gets it.* A little while later, I messaged him, casually throwing out, 'Fancy a rave?' His reply? 'Yeah, why not?' And just like that, a shared love for music, madness and the dance floor was born.

Our raving partnership kicked off with a bang, Fatboy Slim (again, obviously), and we chased beats and basslines across the country from that point on. Then came Printworks. That cavernous, iconic venue in Bermondsey, an old printing press turned temple of sound. We'd heard it was closing soon, so we knew we had to make it happen. I had a friend, Joe, who worked there and somehow, with a few favours and some luck, we got tickets.

The moment we walked through the doors, I could feel it, that bass reverberating in my chest, the towering steel structures, the shadows of machinery long retired. It felt like walking into the heartbeat of underground London. We grabbed a drink, buzzing already, and Joe offered to show us around. But, honestly, Jamie and I just wanted to dance.

Instead, Joe took us through the backstage corridors and, to our surprise, right into the Green Room. Now, I know my house music. I can rattle off names of DJs like a playlist – but could I recognise them in person? Not a chance. So, I awkwardly stood there, face-to-face with some huge names, muttered 'Have a good set!' and promptly cringed my way back out.

That's when Joe dropped the bombshell: 'Let's see if I can get you two backstage.' Moments later, we were walking up the steps to the stage where the legendary Benji B was mid-set. It was surreal.

Up there, we instantly stood out. Not just because we were older than most of the crowd, not just because we didn't exactly scream 'cool', but because Benji's entourage was, quite frankly, hip as hell. Think sleek, stylish, young, sipping Laurent-Perrier Rosé like they were filming a music video. Meanwhile, Jamie and I were grinning like kids at a school disco, fully aware we didn't fit the vibe … but also not caring in the slightest.

So we did what we do best: we danced. Only … we danced like absolute maniacs. Full-body, joyful, chaotic dancing. Think two toddlers who've had too much orange squash. It was *not* subtle. Benji B turned around mid-set, took one look at us flailing in the background and raised an eyebrow. I panicked, gave him a thumbs up, which, in hindsight, definitely didn't help, and he went back to his decks.

We carried on, oblivious and loving every second. Took some selfies, soaked in the moment. But it was clear we were slowly overstaying our welcome. A few minutes later, Benji turned around again, clocked that we were *still* there and gave the bouncer a look that said everything: 'Get those two the f**k out of here. Now.'

Ouch.

We sulked off the stage, slightly mortified, slightly howling with laughter. But here's the thing: in those ten magical minutes, I got one of my all-time favourite photos. A perfect snapshot of pure joy, framed and proudly hung in my house to this day.

So, thank you, Benji B. You may have booted us off your stage, but you gave us a memory that still makes me smile. And Jamie's still my rave partner. No matter the venue, no matter the DJ, we'll always dance like no one's watching (even if everyone definitely *is*).

Keep Calm, Keep Raving

When Printworks finally closed its doors, it felt like the end of an era. But out of the ashes came Drumsheds, a new beginning for the London rave scene. Housed in what used to be an IKEA in Edmonton, it transformed into one of Europe's largest club venues, with space for 15,000 ravers and a vibe that hit different. The industrial openness, the vast expanse of bodies moving as one; it was made for nights that leave their mark on your soul.

I saw CamelPhat there and thought that experience would be hard to top. It was iconic with the sound, the crowd and the pulse of the music shaking the walls. But then came James Hype. That night was pure electricity. He absolutely blew the roof off. The energy in that space was untouchable, with the lasers slicing through the smoke, the lights syncing to every drop, every pause, every build – it wasn't just a DJ set, it was a full show.

That, for me, is what real DJing is about now. Too many just press play. Too many ravers are watching through their phones instead of living in the moment. Honestly, I wish every venue would ban phones on the dance floor. Raving is about connection with the music, with the people around you, and *not* filming for strangers online.

There's something about that vibration, the frequency, the way it hits your chest and recalibrates something inside you. You walk out dazed, smiling, drenched in sweat, filled with something bigger than yourself. If I had to name one of the greatest sets I've ever experienced, it would be Eric Prydz at Creamfields, the Liverpool site. Camping for three days with Conway, Claudia, David, Aaron and Becky, in a sweaty, hot tent, but magical all the same. Eric headlined Friday at the legendary Steel Yard with his HOLO set. David and I managed to squeeze into the perfect spot, and what unfolded was unreal.

Visuals danced from the screens and into the crowd – whales, astronauts, deep-sea divers, galaxies exploding into light, it was a full-body, all-senses trip. It was more than music. It was a journey.

And his track 'Every Day' will forever take me back to that night. That's what Eric Prydz does; he doesn't just play songs, he creates moments that live in your skin long after.

I've seen him since on Brighton Beach, on my birthday. The day before was Carl Cox, and even though his set had to be cut short thanks to 50mph winds and sheets of rain, it didn't stop us. David, Jamie and I turned up, soaked to the bone, battered by the storm but dancing with the diehard, hardcore ravers. I met a guy called Oliver that day. I fell in love with him just a little bit. Tried to find him after, but no luck. I guess it was one of those magic, fleeting moments that weren't meant to last. A beautiful, wild blip in time.

Raving has brought so many unforgettable souls into my life. Like Rachel, Hayley and Leah, three sisters who welcomed me into their world like I was one of their own. I'm now the unofficial fourth Powell sister. Rave Mum. Or, as they call me after one particularly hilarious fashion choice, 'Bay-bey', thanks to a green towelling romper that made me look like a giant toddler. No regrets, other than a video of me trying to get on to a changing table in a disabled toilet.

Forbidden Forest

If there was ever a lesson in not believing everything you see on Instagram, Forbidden Forest Festival 2024 was it. The social media sold a dream: fairy lights strung between trees, people dancing barefoot in the woods like glittery forest sprites, all wrapped in a kind of magical, earth-loving glow. The Powell sisters and I were in. It looked like the kind of escapism we live for – a nature rave, but make it ethereal. We booked our glamping spot, secured VIP parking and packed our rave outfits (and bikinis) with wild optimism, despite the ominous three weeks of non-stop rain and flood warnings leading up to it.

We should've known.

The moment we arrived, it was clear: this wasn't a woodland wonderland, it was 'Forbidden Mud Fest'. A full-on swamp. The organisers were completely unprepared. Cars were getting stuck, trolleys sinking, tents tipping over. People were literally being pulled out of 2ft-deep mud pits. Thank God for my wellies – the bikinis, less so. For a June festival, it felt closer to a survival exercise in the Arctic.

Somehow, we dumped our bags in the glamping tents (blissfully mud-free) and tried to salvage the experience. But between closed stages, freezing cold and wading through sludge just to get a glimpse of a DJ, the forest magic was lost. And somewhere between battling frostbite and slipping on a patch of grass that was probably alive, I had another realisation:

I was *old*.

Not 'a bit older'. Not 'seasoned raver'. Properly old. I scanned the crowd and didn't see a single face over the age of 25. Within ten minutes, a wide-eyed teenage girl tapped me on the shoulder and asked sweetly, 'Excuse me … how old are you?' I laughed, 'I'm 46.' Her jaw dropped. 'Oh my *God, I soooo* want to be you when I'm old!' and she hugged me like I was a living legend. This happened again. And again. And again. If I had a pound for every girl who told me I was older than their mum *but still cool*, I could've chartered a helicopter and flown straight out of there. I was basically the forest's honorary rave grandma.

Luckily, we had Ross with us, a music industry insider, who managed to get us backstage wristbands. Finally, a break from the age questions and the mud. We caught sets from Jamie Jones and, later, PAWSA. Now here's the thing: I had no idea who PAWSA was but, apparently, everyone else did. The moment his name was mentioned, people reacted like it was a sacred word. '*PAWSA*! Sooooo hot right now!' Think Zoolander levels of obsession.

So, there I was, on stage, next to Pawsa, all dreadlocks, bucket hat, hoodie and too-cool-to-care energy. The crowd screamed as he walked on. Phones were out. Photos were taken. Somewhere out there, there's footage of a 46-year-old woman raving next to PAWSA like she owns the stage. And honestly, I kind of did.

So no, it wasn't the magical forest rave we imagined. It was chaotic, cold and a muddy disaster. But it was also hilarious, unforgettable and unique. I might not blend in with the glittery 20-somethings anymore, but I sure as hell still belong on that dance floor.

My dancing, however, is more like a workout (I throw in a few tuck jumps and lunges just to add a bit of something different), and it wasn't really working to the sound of PAWSA's set. I thought, 'Maybe I should get down off this stage.' I looked around to my left, I looked to my right, and suddenly I realised I was on stage with some of the cast of *Love Island* and some of *TOWIE*. Now I really stood out as the old person. I looked like one of their mums as well.

I decided my best bet was to find a friend, someone I could chat to. Make it look like I'm supposed to be there and not somebody's mum. I couldn't see anyone – I was surrounded by children who were born after dial-up internet. Anyone would do, just someone who made it look like I belonged there and not like I'd wandered in after dropping my kids off at soft play. I scanned the crowd. Nothing but bucket hats, mesh tops and exposed nipples.

As I was looking around, there was this young man, bare-chested, just wearing shorts. He looked about 19 (you know they are about that age because the upper body is so ripped, and also hairless). Abs like Peter Andre from his 'Mysterious Girl' days. He had his sunglasses on and a man bag slung across his body like he'd just come from Urban Outfitters with a spiritual awakening.

He spotted me, lifted up his glasses and suddenly I recognised that look in his eyes. I could tell the 'MILF goggles' had just gone on. I was in trouble. He started moving towards me. 'Hey, how's it going?' he flirted, eyelashes fluttering away, puppy eyes, his hands out wanting to pull me into him. 'Yep, all going fine. Fantastic. Great. How are you?' I replied, thinking, 'I don't know what to do here.'

'Yeah, yeah, man, I am loving life! PAWSA's the best!' I agreed, nodding and smiling, and just carried on dancing, hoping that was the end of it. It wasn't. He carried on. And I nodded, like I'd been a lifelong fan and not just googled 'Who is PAWSA?' 30 minutes ago.

I started dancing again. Politely. Casually. Like a woman trying not to pull a hamstring.

'Man, you are so FIT! You are so sexy!' He came in a little bit closer. Oh, dear God. The abs were there in front of me, shimmering in the strobes like a sentient pack of Surf laundry pods. I could almost feel them. 'What's your name, gorgeous?' he asked. 'It's Gail. What's your name then?' 'Cody. My name is Cody.' He said it with pride, like he invented it. Like it's not the name of a boy who eats crayons in Year 4.

You know it's time to go when a 19-year-old called Cody starts trying to grind and get off with you. 'You're actually sexy as.' Oh, sweet baby Jesus. Not really a sentence that, Cody, but I'll let you off. Not an English lesson here.

He'd moved even closer. I could feel the abs. They were right there. Just hovering. Like they were about to give me a facial with their sheer firmness.

What happened next was a weird game of hide and seek, in which I was really trying to hide; yet, if Cody hadn't found his special talent by now, hide and seek was it. He found me every time, loving 'our little game'. If anyone can invent a 'Down Boy' spray for hot-headed 19-year-olds, please let me know; I will be your first customer.

It was time to leave. It's your sign from the universe: you've still got it, but you don't want it.

FROM COCKS TO BALLS

IN TRUE Alan Partridge, *Knowing Me, Knowing You* style, please imagine this in his unmistakable voice: 'From cocks to balls! Ah-haaa! Yes, our next guest has gone from smashing cocks to whacking balls … ooo-er! It's Gail Emms!'

Yes, it's official. I've gone full geek. And the reason is pickleball.

If you've never heard of it, think short tennis meets ping-pong meets American obsession. It's fast, fun and I've completely fallen for it. So much so, that after just ten months of playing, and with no singles training, I entered the National Championships 2025 in the 4.0 category (a solid, mid-tier, competitive bracket, for those not in the know about pickleball) and finished fourth. Not bad for a newbie, but I do have an Olympic-sized competitive streak.

What I love most about pickleball is that it's given me a new kind of joy. A fresh challenge. A whole new community. The court's the same size as a badminton one (bonus!), so I still move well. My overhead smash is a weapon to be afraid of and I'm loving every moment of learning, competing and connecting with people again.

More than anything, 16 years on, this sport has reminded me how important it is to *find your people*. Badminton shaped me, gave me drive, discipline and identity. But after stepping away, I needed something to keep that energy alive. Pickleball and the brilliant humans I've met through it have done just that. I may not have all the answers about what's next, but one thing's certain: I've still got fire. And yes, I'll still be *ultra*-competitive on the court.

Pickleball world … this is just the beginning.

AND NOW …

'Midlife, according to Jung, marks the emergence of a second self or what he calls the "non-ego". Up until this point, our lives have been dominated by the ego, the part of us that's focused on external goals – careers, relationships and societal roles. The ego thrives on control and stability, but midlife brings a wake-up call; there's more to us than the ego. This second self, often buried beneath the surface, begins to make itself known. It's like a self-division – Nietzsche, the German philosopher, captured this beautifully when he said, "One becomes two." It's a poetic way of describing a moment when the person we thought we were begins to shift, and we are confronted with a deeper, often unfamiliar part of ourselves. This isn't just a psychological process; it is a spiritual one. The non-ego demands our attention, challenging the ego's dominance and inviting us to explore questions about meaning, purpose and connection.'

I read that quote on Instagram, and it comes from a book called *Gods and Diseases*, by David Tacey. It struck a chord with me when I read it.

I don't know what the future holds, but I am excited. I used to be so fearful, but I am going to embrace every moment. I have my boys, I have my mates, I have my work. And without sounding too much like Natasha Bedingfield singing her song 'Unwritten', I have more to achieve.

'The more I heal, the less ambitious I feel' is a quote I read recently, and it hit me hard. Every day, I say it to myself, to give myself kindness and appreciation of who I am and who I want to be. Thanks to Steph, I am able to reflect on a fantastic life.

Steph: The end of something is traumatic. You should have been going through a natural grieving process, but you suppressed it. It has taken you all this time to realise that you needed to go back and face the pain and the hurt, so you could understand and accept how it impacted your life post-sport.

If you can get your story straight in your head and piece all the bits of the jigsaw puzzle together in terms of what happened, how that made you feel and behave, then you can get some closure, which means you can create some space for some new ways of thinking.

I know you can do this because you know how to be resilient, because if you weren't resilient, you would never have achieved what you've achieved or pushed through this far. You have such a competitive attitude, discipline and commitment to what you believe in. You're tougher than you think. You are just using your skills in a different way. I believe in you, Gail.

For the first time in my life, I truly believe it too.

I'm learning to shift away from the red, masculine energy that once served me so well in elite sport – that drive, that intensity, but which doesn't always serve life beyond competition, or in relationships. Now, I'm allowing other parts of myself to emerge – softer, more vulnerable, more open. It's unfamiliar territory, but I'm ready to embrace it.

I'm changing the narrative.

I'm stepping out of a 'victim mindset' and into a space where I can honour the more feminine, intuitive energy within me. I'm giving myself permission to slow down, to journal, to practise gratitude, to create and to enjoy the process of piecing my life together in a new way. This isn't a finish line. It's a beginning.

Steph: You're at a massive crossroads, and you can make a decision. Either, 'I am going to let the past keep pulling me back and deplete my energy and create all this negative self-talk' or 'Do you know what? I understand my story and what my story has gifted me in learnings.

I am going to use it to face the future in a completely positive way.' That's my challenge to you, Gail. There comes a point when you understand ... when you can go, 'Right. Enough of that. My past is not dictating my future.'

Gail: That would be quite nice.

Steph: I can't force you to heal, you'll heal when you are ready and when you decide to put the work in.

I'm choosing to heal … and to let go. I still dream about being on a badminton court. Sometimes I'm mid-match. Sometimes I'm late and panicking. Sometimes, bizarrely, I'm playing in my underwear. But the feelings in those dreams, all the adrenaline, the pressure, even the yearning, are always real. I wake up carrying the emotional weight of an elite athlete, long after stepping away from that world.

Those dreams remind me that I hadn't fully processed that chapter of my life. I buried the emotions and, in doing so, they found their way out in unhealthy, exhausting ways. Suppression doesn't work; it depletes you.

I've come to understand just how powerful mindset is … that perception and perspective shape everything. I've learned to steer my thoughts toward what's meaningful and nourishing, and to stay alert to the distractions and habits that pull me into dark, familiar spirals. Now, I'm approaching life with more curiosity and energy. I'm ready to take ownership of my choices, of my direction and of my healing. Sometimes we all need a reset, and mine was long overdue.

This is my time to reflect, to understand, to accept … and to release. Like a bird. And the truth is that I feel good now. It's taken time – a *lot* of time. If I had written this book ten years ago, or even five, or even a year ago, it would have been a very different story. I wasn't ready then. But I am ready now, as I'm in a better place, emotionally, mentally and spiritually, and from here I can look back with honesty, humour and a bit more kindness to myself.

My emotional rollercoaster has been wild, and I know I'm not alone in that. If you've been on your own version of the ride, I hope my story helps you feel seen. We all have good days and bad days, but every single one of them has shaped who I am today.

And now, I say bring it on. I'm writing a new soundtrack to my life.

THE END.

LETTER OF LOVE

WHILE PUTTING the finishing touches to this book, I decided to write a letter to my younger self, something I found incredibly emotional to do … here we go:

Dear Ten-Year-Old Gail,

You're just starting out on this badminton journey … nervous, excited, full of energy and dreams. I see you, pink C&A tracksuit and all, playing for hours at Bradgate Road. That little girl is bursting with something special, even if she doesn't quite know it yet.

Let me tell you something that may not make sense now, but it will: your competitiveness and fiery determination won't always make you friends. And that's okay. You're not unkind, you just haven't yet learned how to understand that fire inside you. One day, you'll learn when to turn it up and when to soften it. But don't ever be ashamed of that spark. It's part of what makes you … you.

You might feel like you don't 'fit in'. Other girls might talk about things that don't interest you, or act in ways you're told girls should act. Don't force yourself to follow. You *will* find your place, your tribe, your rhythm. Because sport … sport will be your joy. Your peace. Your saviour.

You have a body built for power, for speed, for pushing limits. Your athleticism is your superpower. But so is your mind. Your strength won't just be physical; it will be mental too, and it will carry you through things you can't even imagine right now.

Just ... be kind to yourself, okay? Especially when you don't win. Especially when it hurts. You are so much more than medals, trophies and results. Beneath it all, there's a creative, colourful, people-loving soul. She matters too. Don't forget her.

Please don't apologise for being yourself. But do try to *think* before you speak. Not everyone will get your humour (and, let's be honest, not all the jokes land). But keep laughing. Keep dancing! Dance in your bedroom, at training camps, in hotel rooms. Dance to feel *free*. It clears your mind. It connects you back to joy.

Hug more. I know it's awkward now, but you'll realise later how much it matters. You'll wish you'd hugged Mum and Dad more. They're doing their best. They love you deeply. And one day, when they're not here anymore, you'll understand just how much.

A hard truth is that you can't save everyone. I know you'll try. But the world can be brutal sometimes, and it's not your job to fix it all. Just do your bit, with love and integrity.

Oh, and stop believing *everything* boys tell you. Sometimes they say what they think you want to hear. Keep believing in people's potential, yes, but don't ignore reality. You need both.

Keep smiling. Even on the dark days. And when you need help, please ask. Your stubbornness is strong, but it can isolate you. You *need* your people.

Most importantly, never lose sight of why you started. Play for the love, the joy, the fire. That essence, that innocence is everything. Protect it. Hold on to it. Let no one dim it.

I wish I could protect you from all the hurt you'll face. But you need to go through it. It will shape you, build you and toughen you. Just don't lose that little girl. She matters just as much as the Olympian you'll become.

You've got this. I'm so proud of you already.

With love,

Gail (47 and still learning)

P.S. And sadly ... no cowboy boots for you. Your calves are incredible for sport, just not for fashion. But that's a trade-off I promise you'll be proud of ;)

FROM THE AUTHOR – THANK YOU

IT HAS been one hell of a therapeutic ride, writing this book. I have laughed, I have cried, but I have the book that I want to be out there. I hope you enjoyed reading more about me and my world.

I have to say thank you to the following people – I really wouldn't have got through it all without you.

Firstly, a huge thank you to **Nathan Robertson**.

Looking back now, with time, perspective, and the benefit of distance, I can say without hesitation: I would not have achieved what I did without Nathan. We needed each other. And not just in the tactical, training partner, on-court synergy kind of way. We needed each other in the deeper sense; two very different people who somehow unlocked something vital in one another. I've joked for years that he is 'my lobster' (*Friends* TV show reference), and I still remind him of that every chance I get. But the truth behind the joke has always been real.

Over the years, that bond has only grown. We're closer now, and he is one of my best friends. During the Covid lockdowns, when everything felt uncertain and the world was upside down, we'd go for long, socially distanced walks with our dogs. He was working as a coach for the national badminton team and was often on his own, navigating the stress of coaching, daily testing, sanitising rackets and shuttles, and preparing players for a Tokyo Olympics that looked like it might not happen. And I was trying to stay sane, trying to keep my head above water. Those walks kept both of us grounded. We didn't need to say much; just being in each other's company helped. The silence, the occasional rant, the confused attempts to make sense of everything – that's what real friendship looks like.

Our career together was full of extremes – momentum swings, glorious wins and gutting losses. Certain tournaments just seemed cursed for us. But we stuck together through it all. I often had people ask me, 'How do you put up with him?' They'd shake their heads, not quite able to get a handle on him. Still to this day, people make comments, trying to understand, trying to decode him. But I've come to see that as a sign of true greatness. The most special talents are often the ones that can't be explained. Nathan was never steady or predictable – he was electric. He could turn a match on its head with a moment of brilliance. Sure, it came with risk. But given the choice between being consistent and being unforgettable, I know which one I'd choose. And Nathan was unforgettable.

One of my favourite memories happened after I'd retired. I was speaking with a Korean coach, someone I deeply respected. He shook my hand and asked why I'd stepped away from the game. I told him it was time. He nodded and said, 'You and Nathan were the only pair we were afraid of. You … you were so fast at the net, so powerful. And Nathan … wow. We never knew what he would do. Some of the best shots we've ever seen came from him. You two together – excellent. The only Europeans we never wanted to play.' He smiled and added, 'Maybe we are happy you retired.'

That moment meant more to me than most medals ever could. Badminton is a sport dominated by Asia, and, as a European, you often feel like an outsider; respected, yes, but still … not quite *in*. So, to be acknowledged by someone from one of the sport's most revered nations, that was validation on a deeper level. It felt like acceptance. Like we belonged.

People have tried for years to figure Nathan out. Coaches, teammates, opponents. They analysed him, tried to change him, refine him, fit him into a mould. I never did. I never wanted to. And I think that's why we worked so well. I accepted him for all he was, and all he wasn't. His contradictions, his genius, his frustrations, his fire.

I let him be Nathan. Probably because I've never wanted anyone to fully figure *me* out either. And that mutual space, that quiet respect for each other's mystery, that's where the magic happened.

Yes, I moaned about him. Rolled my eyes. He did the same to me. That's part of any relationship under pressure. Elite sport demands more from a person than seems humanly possible sometimes. But underneath all that noise, there was always trust. And there was respect.

That's what matters in the end. Not if we liked the same music or shared the same routines. But we trusted one another. On and off the court. That's the foundation. And that's why we lasted.

We made each other better; for a moment in time, *the best*.

DVD Nostalgia and Closure

Not long ago, Nathan messaged me with a suggestion that was both bizarre and brilliant. He said, 'Come round. Let's get smashed on wine and watch old DVDs of our matches – and the old motivational clips too.' At first, I hesitated. The idea of watching our younger selves sprinting across courts in tight kit, emotionally charged and physically on edge, filled me with a weird mix of curiosity and dread. I'd spent years stepping away from badminton, creating space between who I was then and who I am now. So, the thought of diving back into that era … yeah, it felt loaded.

But Nathan was insistent and, frankly, annoyingly enthusiastic, as he is still immersed in the sport we once lived and breathed. I, on the other hand, am not. Still, part of me was intrigued. So, I relented, and I went. And you know what? It was bloody brilliant.

There we were, 15 years later, sitting in his living room like some retired married couple on *Gogglebox*, wine glasses in hand, hurling insults at our past selves on screen. 'What was *that* shot?' I'd shout. 'Why would you even try that?!' Nathan, glass half full, would shout back, 'Oh, come on, you missed that net kill by a mile!'

It was chaos. And it was hilarious. We laughed so hard I thought we might knock over the DVD stack (which, by the way, is enormous; who knew Nathan had archived practically every match we ever played?). It was also strangely healing. We found ourselves reliving not just the games, but the ridiculous little moments between points: the bum smacks with the racket, the exaggerated eyerolls, the silent fury. All of it came flooding back. Except now, with distance, it was funny rather than fraught.

What struck me most was how freely we spoke that evening. During the height of our playing careers, we didn't communicate properly. If we had something to say, it had to go through Andy, our coach, and, at times, our relationship referee. But that night, there were no filters. We asked each other the questions we had never dared to ask back then. And we answered them. Honestly. It was like we were finally finishing the conversations we had started years ago, in the warm-up areas, airport lounges, and tense post-match silences.

By 5am, we were both passed out on a sofa each, an open bottle of red still breathing on the table, the DVD menu screen looping quietly in the background. I joked with Nathan that if this is how he spends his Saturday nights, reliving his own mixed doubles glory, it might be time for an intervention. He just grinned and said, 'So what if I do?' And you know what? Fair play to him. That night reminded me that sometimes, in order to move forward, you have to look back, not with regret, but with curiosity. With affection. With a good glass of wine and someone who was in the trenches with you.

It was one of the best nights I've had in my retirement. A reminder that while the trophies gather dust and the routines fade, the connection, the journey, the sheer madness of it all, that still lives on. Even if it's on DVD.

Thank you, Mr Roberson.

More Thank Yous

My boys, Harry and Ollie – It can't have been easy having me typing away on a laptop a lot, while I wrote this book, but you really are the reason I live. Both of you make me laugh so much. I still believe I am the funniest out of the three of us, but I love how we giggle constantly between the battles of life, sport and card games. I love you so much.

Ed – You are the best dad to our boys and deserve a medal for putting up with me. Thank you.

Lisa and Adam – I am the golden child. Just accept it. I love you.

Mum – I am the golden child, right?! Always remember that David Ginola phone call. Love you.

Terri – Who would have thought that a chance meeting in The Swan MK Village with our dogs would lead you to being my carer? Thank you for being a mate and being there for me. Your phrases of 'my laptop is being a p***o', 'been such a slug today', 'J'aime giblet' will always make me cackle. You are a f**king kick-ass woman from The Bletch, and I am so proud of you.

Kelly – Whenever I want to rant and smash things, you have the ability to see the nice and help me see the other side when I really can't. There is no one in the world who is as lovely as you; you have a superpower that more people should have. You are a saint in disguise, and thank you for being there for me. I love being there for you, and we can't live more than 50m away again: 250m is *tooooo faaaaaarr.*

Chloe – Slimy fish, St Lucia was obviously a sign, and I am very happy you walked up to me on the pickleball court and asked if I was on my own at the resort. I was so hungover, and very nearly cancelled and ran away from you, but what happened next, I am sure Stolen Time regret putting us in the next room together. That place will never recover. It was meant to be. 'I want that one!' Love you, slimy xx

Jamie – The raves, the giggles, have been the best days of my life. Love ya.

Sunny – Bunny!!! I love you and I wish we could see each other more. I am so proud of you, and we need to get this comedy up and running soon!

Andy Wood – You are a star and deserve a medal of your own for putting up with what you did. I love it when people ask what our motto was, and I say, 'F**k it.' Crazy gang 4ever! Thank you.

Badminton Girls – Donna, Natalie, Jo, Jo D, Sarah, Ella, Hannah, thank you for putting up with my drama queen antics and having the best time in the most random places in the world. Nat – your obsession with finding lasagne or spaghetti bolognese in the Far East still haunts me.

Conway and David – Dogging every weekend with you two is my fave part of the weekend ;)

Lucy – 'Ah Pe Teh Pe Teh!!' Love you, ski guide map queen.

Suzanne – Raving and skin treatments, we have certainly put the world to rights and it has been great connecting with you post-badminton. Thank you.

Claire – We will get married in St Paul's … one day … it *will* happen. Love you.

Rachel, Hayley, Leah – My liver hates you, but I love you. I will always be your rave mum and Beh-Bey!

Everyone at Pitch Publishing – thank you for all the support you have given me in writing this book, for enabling me to tell my story and for all your expertise.

And finally, a heartfelt thank you to **Steph Burge**.

At the time I met you, I didn't believe I was carrying trauma, but I was, on two fronts. One from a recent break-up, and the other from never having truly processed the end of my badminton career. I was still dreaming of playing, still masking the pain with humour and my trusty 'Gail Fails' routine. But when I spoke to you, even while sitting on a beach in St Lucia, when I was utterly lost, I felt a connection and I wanted to say more.

I'd always been unsure about life coaching or therapy, whether it would really work for me. But after just three days with you, I felt like a different person. A weight I didn't even know I was carrying had been lifted, and suddenly my story made sense. I was in the right headspace to begin writing this book.

Thank you for the work you do, especially with athletes. I hope I've made you proud. I know I'm still a work in progress. (Aren't we all?) You reminded me that it's okay to change, to reflect, and to grow. And that it's never too late to reclaim your narrative.

I'm rewriting my script. And that's thanks to you.

STEPHANIE BURGE

Entrepreneur | Life Coach | Mentor | Sports Parent

Stephanie Burge is a businesswoman, entrepreneur and transformational life coach with a powerful story of resilience, reinvention and mindset mastery. As the sole survivor of a serious car accident, she has turned trauma into a driving force for personal growth, purpose and helping others navigate life's toughest transitions.

A mother to two daughters, one a successful entrepreneur with ADHD, and the other an ex-GB and England hockey player now thriving in a career in corporate finance, Stephanie understands the highs and lows of the neurodiverse brain and the player journey after elite sport. She is passionate about ensuring athletes, parents and professionals develop the right mindset to thrive beyond competition.

Now, Stephanie coaches injured, psychologically broken and de-selected athletes to process their loss, rediscover their identity and build fulfilling new careers. Many, like me, have finally realised they need to make peace with their past and reconnect with the joy of sport.

Stephanie brings raw honesty, practical insights and thought-provoking perspectives. Her message is clear: you are never too old, too broken, or too stuck to rewrite your future. The past is unchangeable, but how you think about it isn't.

Stephanie is a regular podcaster and writer and has created a body of work, much of which is available on her LinkedIn profile. Connect with her as a facilitator of powerful conversations and intuitive insights coupled with a good dose of humour and positive vibes.